The GARDEN through the YEAR

Graham Stuart Thomas

OBE, VMH, DHM, VMM, GARDENS CONSULTANT TO THE NATIONAL TRUST

FOREWORD BY FRED WHITSEY, VMH

PREFACE BY WAYNE WINTERROWD

PAINTINGS AND DRAWINGS

BY GRAHAM STUART THOMAS

First published in the United Kingdom in 2002
by Thames & Hudson Ltd,
181A High Holborn,
London WC1V 7QX

OPENING: My original pen-and-ink drawing
which has appeared as a logo in all my books
FRONTISPIECE: *Camellia* × *williamsii* 'Citation'

British Library Cataloguing-in-Publication Data
A catalogue record for this book is available from the British Library

ISBN 0-500-51110-1

Printed in Hong Kong

What was Paradise?
But a garden, full of pleasure
and nothing there but delight.

WILLIAM LAWSON,
A New Orchard & Garden, 1618

CONTENTS

FOREWORD

How could one man, in one lifetime, even so long as Graham Stuart Thomas's, have got on terms of such close intimacy with such a vast repertoire of plants as he reveals in this deeply erudite book? True, his long consultancy to the National Trust, not only England's but the world's richest custodian of gardens, gave him a unique overview of the greatest diversity of gardens for which anyone had ever been responsible. They range from courtyards to ducal acres. In character they embrace woodland and heathland. In the soil on which they have been created they are chalky and acidic, deep and rich, shallow and deficient in what nutrients they can offer plants. To Mr Thomas each site has been a wonderland of horticultural opportunity, offering scope for its individual landscape and community of plants.

But he could not have embroidered, developed or conserved plants as he has without sensitivity to their individual environment and character, profound knowledge of plants and of the history of garden making, experience of the techniques of garden practice—and his acutely observant eye for detail.

None of the Olympian plantsmen whom he quotes in his encyclopedic books—Gertrude Jekyll, William Robinson, A. T. Johnson, Mrs Earl, E. A. Bowles and Reginald Farrer—knew as many different kinds of plants—species and their cultivated varieties—as he does. His range runs from mighty trees to diminutive alpine plants, taking in the great rhododendron family, bulbous plants and even the formation, texture and colouring of stone as a garden component.

OPPOSITE: *Galanthus nivalis* 'Plenus', *Galanthus* 'Magnet', *Galanthus caucasicus*, *Galanthus nivalis* 'Straffan' and *Galanthus nivalis* 'Scharlokii' (LEFT TO RIGHT)

ix

He was a leading figure in the current preoccupation of influential gardeners with hardy herbaceous plants, and, no less importantly, in the technique of using ground-covering plants as a low maintenance element. Both fields have been enriched by his influence, revealing plants unknown to those luminaries of the last century.

All this is in addition to his most scholarly achievement—the study of roses. In his earlier days it was with the old-fashioned roses that he was most notably associated. But in further books he soon revealed a comprehensive knowledge of the roses of the twentieth century as well.

Mr Thomas's work has not simply been in plantsmanship, however. Throughout his many books he has been teaching us how to use plants with grace and artistry as gardens are made. His writings show that he has had direct personal experience of creating partnerships with plants in harmonious communities in which they support, enhance or flatter one another.

For in his sympathies he outsoars the twin worlds of plantsmen and designers; he is a botanical artist himself, whose paintings have been reproduced in an album which already, in his own lifetime, has become a collector's item.

Although he has received all the chief official honours of the world of horticulture, I unreservedly dub Graham Stuart Thomas the greatest gardener of all time. We who garden ourselves are blessed by the good fortune of being able to enrich and advance the craft we follow with the help, learning and wisdom he gives us in this beautiful book.

FRED WHITSEY, VMH
Surrey, England
October 2001

PREFACE

When Graham Stuart Thomas was a young man, he pedaled from Woking to Munstead Wood to take tea with Gertrude Jekyll. Then very old, nearly blind and quite infirm, she was no longer receiving visitors, a fact she had made gently clear in her preface to *Home and Garden* (Longmans Green, 1900), where she wrote:

> May I go one step further and say that, while it is always pleasant to hear from or to see old friends, and indeed all who work hard in their own gardens, yet, as a would-be quiet worker who is by no means over-strong, I venture to plead with my kind and numerous, though frequently unknown friends, that I may be allowed to retain a somewhat larger measure of peace and privacy.

The fact that Miss Jekyll, who was to die fifteen months later at the age of eighty-nine, made an exception of the young Graham Stuart Thomas must itself have indicated his great promise as a gardener, and presaged his eventual renown. Unable to walk about with him, she instructed him to pick a leaf of anything about which he was curious, and bring it back for discussion over refreshments. Though we know from Thomas's own notes what actually did interest him (*Aster divaricatus*, late-blooming *Lilium japonicum*, *Gentiana asclepiadea*, "little *Cornus canadensis* creeping through the mosses and ferns" and "Michaelmas Daisies showing early flowers"), and that he "was spellbound," we know little of that eventful tea, except that Miss Jekyll invited him to riffle and sniff the first stages of her famous potpourri, for which 11,000 rose blossoms had been picked. To the very end of her life, she was attentive to such details.

Clearly, however, a sort of mantle was passed that afternoon of September 6, 1931, at tea time. For Jekyll, who authored ten remarkable books that changed forever the act of gardening, and who numbered among her friends Canon Ellacombe, Dean Hole, William Robinson, the Reverend Charles Wolley-Dodd and Miss Wilmott, smiled graciously on the young Graham Stuart Thomas, who now, at ninety-three, has been granted every honor a British gardener may receive, and is the author of so many books that he himself confesses to have lost count. Though it could well be argued that GST, by which initials he is generally known (and which fit with so many that follow ... OBE, VMH, DHM, VMM), is the world's greatest living gardener, just as Gertrude Jekyll was in her day, he himself might demur, "Not yet."

For the most important fact about Graham Stuart Thomas is that he has been a great learner all his life, and is in no way prepared to stop. In this book, for example, he comments on the exciting new Chinese epimediums "that are becoming known and grown." One notes that in his mind, the second condition follows the first as the night the day. "But these," he remarks, "must wait for another chapter or book." Who is to say he will not write it? Not, certainly, Mr. Thomas, who is hardly about to quit a passion that has extended from the age of six, when, as he recorded, "My Godfather gave me a large-flowered Fuchsia ... which set me on my earthly career." And, as this book makes clear, that career is being pursued with as much seriousness and passion as it ever was.

The miracle of Graham Stuart Thomas's life is not actually that he has done so many things, written so many books, served in so many important capacities, or been honored, both publicly and privately, so richly for them all. It resides rather in the fact that over a period of active gardening now extending to more than eighty years, each morning he appears to wake up full of a sense of the wonder and glory of the natural world, of the gardener's world, waiting, just there, just outside the window, and in any season. The love of plants, the sheer, aching, tender love of them is on every page of this book. When it is in full flower, he finds *Davidia involucrata* var. *vilmoriniana*, the fabled Chinese Handkerchief Tree, "an experience worth a long journey." The Cuckoo Flowers, *Cardamine pentaphyllos* and *C. heptaphylla*, are "two more of the garden toys that gladden our eyes in the early year." About the double Morello cherry, *Prunus cerasus* 'Morello,' he comments, "I know of few plants of any kind that have flowers of such a cold pure white." He asks us to consider whether there is "any fragrance so appealing as a whiff of wallflowers on a warm, sunny day?" And he reminds us, lest we carelessly forget, that "to let a season go by without inhaling the heady scent of lilac is a sad omission." Though always aware of the new and the good (such as the Chinese epimediums that are so stylish at present), his memory embraces almost a century of plants, and so among tulips, he specially favors " 'Generaal de Wet,' a pure yellow with a sweet fragrance that reaches up to you."

So much in this book does reach up to you. Mostly, however, it is to be understood as an invitation for a stroll, a walkabout, to see what is good in the garden, just today, and whatever the season. So struggle into your Wellingtons, don your rain gear, take up an umbrella if positively necessary. For the weather may be cold and drizzly, but still there are things to see. Perhaps there are the best things to see in the whole gardening year. In any case, pick a leaf, and we'll discuss it, over tea. For this book, among all the other things it is, is a chat. Not to understand that is quite to misread it, and that would be a pity.

The book is called *The Garden through the Year*, and it is a gathering up of all the plants, rare and common, that one treasures—or might come to treasure—in any month and for any reason, whether for bloom, berry, bark, twig or leaf. It is not actually a compendium of good growing advice, though Mr. Thomas, a child, after all, of the Arts and Crafts Movement, firmly believes that "the art is be allied to the craft," and so will pause to tell you that a little winter shade, a damper spot, some extra lime, a warmer wall or timely snip, might work wonders with a difficult plant. Still less is it a book for specialists, for lovers of roses (Thomas is a great rosarian) or rock gardeners (though he began there, seventy years ago, with his schoolboy pennies and a lime outcrop in his father's garden), or for people who stupidly think— as has for so many years been fashionable—that the garden begins and ends with flowering perennials. For rosarians and perennial enthusiasts he has written definitive works on their passions, which may require nomenclatural revisions from time to time, but which will never be superseded, any more than the works of E. A. Bowles, Margery Fish or his contemporary and good friend, Beth Chatto. Rock plants he touches gently all along the way, remembering that he began there, with six plants purchased from Messers. Casburn and Welch on a Saturday market day for the very large sum of "an entire half crown."

But it is worth repeating that this book is not in the first instance a "how to" manual, or a thorough botanical description of whole classes of plants, or a series of suggestions about how the bit of land around the cottage might be laid out. It is, rather, a walk through the garden, during which this fine thing is noted and then that, with comments on what makes each plant special in its season and worth its place. Or, occasionally, not, for though *Sambucus canadensis* receives a kind word, "Other elders, coarse and overbearing shrubs, are hardly worthy of a note in these pages." Generally, however, Mr. Thomas judges all plants on their merits, and never because they are rare or common. For within his mind there exists no such distinction, and he reminds us that everything in the garden must be looked at closely, and evaluated in its moment for whatever beauty or subtle charm it possesses. Where else, for example, will you find praise of Colchicum species for their handsome, pleated foliage in late June, rather than for their mauve chalices of bloom in October? Rare and common conspire, for there is an affectionate defense of *Spiraea*, that sadly neglected genus, on the same page with *Staphylea*, among the most aristocratic of hardy, undiscovered shrubs.

So try to imagine, if you can, the privilege of walking through the world's greatest botanical garden with the world's greatest gardener, on any day of the year, or at least once a week, say, every Sunday at 2:00 P.M., rain or shine. Then you will have an idea of what this book contains. Thinking that way, you will perhaps also realize that the greatest value of your guide is primarily for the dark months of the year, when sight must be keen and knowledge extensive. Remember that any simple schoolchild can find things to love in the garden in July, but that it takes heaps of experience, years of knowledge and habits of the closest observation to understand the beauty of February.

If I were a new gardener—and, next to Graham Stuart Thomas, I am that, certainly—I would sit with this book on my lap, and a stack of specific references at my knee, through many a long winter evening, for gardeners realize what Browning meant when he wrote, "Well I know what I mean to do / When the long dark evenings come." I'd buy two copies, one to keep clean and one to annotate copiously, and I would make notes about plants—bulbs, perennials, ground covers, shrubs and small trees. I would also use this book to liberate myself from the tyranny of believing that the garden year begins in April and ends in November, with a sort of crescendo somewhere in July. For if one is a gardener, it is a poor thing to reduce one's life by ignoring half the months of the year. But mostly I would be grateful— terribly grateful—for so much knowledge, so many years of direct experience and observation, so many judiciously formed opinions, so much wise advice. "When we are young," Graham Stuart Thomas wrote in his somewhat premature autobiography, *Three Gardens* (Sagapress, 1983), "every obstacle is surmounted by the imagination." But it is so at any age. One gardens mostly in the mind. This book proves it to be so.

WAYNE WINTERROWD
North Hill, Vermont
September 2001

THE GARDEN
THROUGH THE YEAR

INTRODUCTION

It has always been my desire to have a garden where on any day of the year I can go and pick a flower, or just admire it. Now, after trial and error over some seventy years, I have come to the conclusion that my findings may interest other plant- and garden-lovers, so here they are.

Dean Hole, founder of the National Rose Society, wrote, "Every day brings to a gardener its special interests. There is always something worthy of his care and admiration, some new development of beauty, some fresh design to execute, some lesson to learn, some genial work to do" (*A Book about the Garden*, 1892). His words are equally true today.

There is one mighty adversary with which we all have to cope, and that is the weather. The climate is something apart which we have to understand before setting spade to the soil. But the weather may well be against us and may result in failure to find a blossom for picking, smelling or just admiring, because of a total freeze-up. This is beyond our jurisdiction unless we have frames and greenhouses—equipment with which this book is not concerned. It is solely concerned with what may be found in the open air of the garden.

It is my opinion that the ideal can only be achieved by the use of trees, shrubs, perennials and bulbs. (You may add annuals if you wish.) Only by so doing, by using the whole garden palette, and by interplanting and underplanting throughout

OPPOSITE: The author in his garden at Briar Cottage, Woking, Surrey

xvii

the borders and spaces, can we achieve our ideal. Here we come up against a fundamental—the size of the plot. It would take a garden of several acres to accommodate even half of the plants I have included in the following pages. But there would be no point in listing only a select few; that would imply that each garden should resemble its fellow. And so in my mind's eye I have tried to survey all the plants of whatever size that might be ranged before us, to select whatever most delights the intending planter—and there are many different types of intending planters. There is almost infinite variety in the styles of gardening that may be pursued. Some delight in a blaze of bedding in summer; some plant shrubs only, believing they create a minimum of work; some like to tend their gardens by the use of machinery; some want roses *ad infinitum*; others want a herbaceous border. Then there are others who will go in for fruit trees and bushes and those time-consuming things, the vegetables. But none of these ideals need concern us if we choose a mixture of trees, shrubs, plants and bulbs. I believe it is a very great art to combine all these disparate elements into one satisfactory whole; in fact, I would go so far as to say it is the most difficult of all arts when one takes into consideration the soil, the aspect, the rainfall, colours, heights and seasons. It is an art that has come very late in mankind's endeavours. There are times when I think that our lives are too short to achieve the ultimate in gardening; we never stop learning and seeing ways to improve our schemes.

Gardening is really a progression; it is a never-finished art allied the whole time to the craft. The observance of the rules of the craft is essential if success is to be made of the art, and the art and craft are needed together if the seasons are to be appreciated to the full. Spring comes with such ecstatic joy, summer with a wealth of colour, autumn with its sense of fruition and winter—what of winter? Is it not the note of finality and the anticipation of spring? I venture to think that in the following pages, those devoted to the winter months may command the greatest attention.

Shade is a very important asset and also a limiting factor in gardening. The passing of shadows over lawn or border is one of the delights of the day. Fortunately there are just as many beautiful plants that thrive in shade as there are for sunny positions. This is one of the "great thoughts" that underlie all gardening; we cannot afford to ignore the value of shade. It may not be of our own making: trees and buildings in neighbouring properties may be the perpetrators, but it is wise to make full

Flowers for August:

Crocosmia × *crocosmiiflora*

'Star of the East' (TOP),

'Vesuvius' (RIGHT)

and 'Queen of Spain'

use of such positions. On the other hand, as one's garden trees and shrubs grow, they also create shade, which can at times be disconcerting. Our trees and shrubs may get large enough after some twelve years or so to support a climbing plant. But to make such an addition from the art point of view means that the craft must also be invoked; no new climber (or other plant) will thrive without thorough and wide preparation of its position.

A garden is a growing thing; no two seasons bring precisely the same results, and a garden of the sort of mixture I have suggested needs a lot of care, weekly, sometimes even daily. Something always needs cutting or pruning, or just dead-heading or weeding. I was about to add "or staking" but thought better of it. Plants that need staking are not in my scheme of things: plenty of perennials are self-reliant. Then there is seasonal adjustment of bulbs and things like irises which wander; both need attention during the summer. Bulb-planting time may be autumn, summer or even spring according to the season of performance. The grand panorama is never still; it is always on the move.

To weld the numerous different plants into a harmonious whole needs great knowledge. This book does not seek to give all details of height and width throughout; rather, it should be looked upon as an appetiser, to lure you on to fresh delights.

The front garden at Briar Cottage in December 1998 shows how well shrubs, mostly evergreens, furnish the author's garden in winter. To the left are *Mahonia × media* 'Lionel Fortescue' (spikes of yellow flowers), *Elaeagnus × ebbingei* 'Gilt Edge', *Pinus sylvestris* 'Moseri' and *Hebe pinguifolia* 'Pagei' (grey in foreground). *Cornus sanguinea* 'Winter Flame' (bare red stems) proved, after several years of bright and gentle growth, to be a rampant spreader and has been removed.

The east lawn in the author's garden: *Iris pallida dalmatica* and *Alchemilla mollis* this side of the Jekyll pot, with hybrid *Philadelphus* at left and *Campanula latiloba* just beyond

Although throughout these pages I have often given details of cultivation, I am going to refer you to two of my earlier books, *Perennial Garden Plants* and *Ornamental Shrubs*, for the finer points of cultivation and siting. In them will be found answers to most questions regarding the craft of gardening. To rely too much on the information given on garden-centre labels is to court disaster. For instance, the ultimate size of forsythia is often given as about four to five feet (1.2–1.5 m), whereas seven to eight feet (2.1–2.4 m) is nearer the mark. But to give this as the ultimate size would limit sales. If it gets too large, a shrub cannot be reduced in size without spoiling its outline; furthermore, the growth resulting from the pruning will produce, usually, even greater growth.

Bulbous plants, if given the right position at planting time, seldom suffer from drought. Much the same may be said of perennials. There are some thirsty plants, such as phloxes, that benefit from a good soak in dry periods. In the southeast of Britain, we are suffering from several seasons of abnormal dryness. Even so, with my advancing years resulting in a disinclination to do more than is absolutely necessary during the summer months, I find that phloxes and rhododendrons are quick to show signs of distress and need succour. They must be watered —copiously—if the next season's crop of flowers is to be assured. It often amazes me that of the thousands of plants used to furnish our gardens, some from widely different countries, climates and conditions, so many are content to grow in each little plot. It is obvious that there must be failures from time to time.

I offer one last counsel to those about to acquire a new house and garden. Do inspect most carefully—in summer, if possible—the whole plot, and note the weeds that may be present. A most persistent weed (totally ineradicable by cultivation) is *Equisetum*, or Mare's Tail; Ground Elder can be coped with; and the small pink *Convolvulus* is a most troublesome inmate. In short, inspect thoroughly, and do not plant anything except in temporary quarters until a growing season has passed. The time lost will really be gained and the results will be assured.

So come with me and let me show you the riches, some of which may be yours if you plant thoughtfully and intelligently: there is more in gardening than just digging and hoeing. There is, it is true, much hard physical work, but also brain work if the art is to be allied to the craft. Study the lie of the land and the drainage, remembering that even moisture-loving plants need drainage, and that to be successful, the soil should be "opened" by the admixture of decaying matter to yield humus. There are other important details such as shade and encroaching roots from neighbouring trees. Last but by no means least, try to assess what difficulties have been conjured up by the builders of new houses by removing or burying topsoil, for example. On old properties unexpected foundations, pipes and other bogies may also be found.

About This Book

It is a survey of many good garden plants arranged month by month. Such are the vagaries of the weather, there may be as many as two or three weeks' difference in the times of flowering, especially in the early months, but there is a general progression towards autumn. Plants do not, of course, provide us the great convenience of flowering according to our calendar; they may begin in one month, continue in another and conclude in a third. I have tried to avoid repetition by discussing each plant once, usually in the month of its greatest prominence, unless another brief mention seemed justified. Some kinds of plants, such as rhododendrons, have representatives flowering both early and later in the year; these, of course, require several entries.

Helleborus lividus, a study in greens for February, for warm gardens

   Each month begins with trees, then shrubs and climbers, followed by perennials and bulbs, which are, after all, merely perennials with a swollen stem or root. In the depths of winter, flowers are scarce, and I have accordingly included sections on foliage and berry. For convenience, plant names are arranged alphabetically, although some are grouped under headings, such as Viburnums, and Coloured Leaves, to allow me looser rein in discussing them. The index gives easy access to individuals, while the arrangement of chapters in the main text by month guides their choice and deployment in the garden.

WINTER

JANUARY

With the shortest day past and Christmas over, as likely as not some mild days ensue that give an opportunity to start the pruning of roses. I can see no point in waiting until March for this work; such delay only results in cutting off the new, inch-long shoots. Pruning also gives an opportunity to peer about and see what is burgeoning. The early year, full of promise though it may be, is always hesitant in Surrey, where cold spells alternate with the mild. I sometimes think that after a hard frosty January, with or without snow, plants seem to respond to the sunshine and lengthening days most quickly. At all events, in my mind I have January 4 as a day when we can generally find the afternoon a little lighter, though this does not apply also to the morning, which remains dark.

In reasonably mild parts of the country we can usually see signs of awakening well before the end of January, and what a wonderful thing it is to watch the year unfolding. Some flowers have been with us for weeks, such as *Prunus subhirtella* 'Autumnalis' and *Viburnum farreri*, while the varieties of *Mahonia* × *media* are having their last fling, *Rhododendron nobleanum* 'Venustum' comes and goes with mild spells, and the Winter Jasmine likewise.

OPPOSITE: *Narcissus* 'Jana', one of the very earliest and most exquisite of daffodils

BELOW: *Stachyurus praecox*, a creamy flowering shrub for the early year

1

RIGHT: *Clematis cirrhosa balearica*
BELOW: *Chimonanthus praecox*
'Luteus', a fine form of
the Winter Sweet, deliciously
fragrant and frost-proof

Shrubs

Chimonanthus praecox, the Winter Sweet, is an early-waking shrub whose drab little flowers have an unforgettable and lovely fragrance. The variety 'Grandiflorus' has petals of clear yellow around its red brown centre. In the variety 'Luteus' the dark central colour is missing. Like the rhododendron and the jasmine, the flowers last well when cut.

Clematis cirrhosa balearica grows on a holly of some twenty feet at the bottom of my garden. It is an evergreen clematis that has swarmed up the holly to the top and is smothered with small bellflowers of cream. There is a form called 'Freckles' which is heavily spotted with warm brown. The species seems quite hardy, though it hails from the Mediterranean.

Corylus avellana, Cob Nut, or Hazel Nut, hung with its creamy yellow catkins is an appealing sight few shrubs can equal in the early year. They are reminders of my boyhood—before rhododendrons and winter-flowering clematises had reached my ken. To pluck a stem heavily hung with tight green catkins and watch them unfolding in the warmth of the room was a wonderful experience—despite the disappointing glance from my parents at the mess of pollen on the table. Cob nuts are too big for the average garden but seemingly will grow on any soil. The variety 'Contorta', whose twisted twigs are in striking contrast to the vertical catkins, is favoured by flower arrangers, but it is a dull shrub for the rest of the year when in leaf. It is a wild variation whose contorted branches were found in Gloucestershire in 1863, and all plants in cultivation are derived from this original.

C. maxima, the Filbert, is a similar big shrub most planted in its coppery purple form, *C. maxima* 'Purpurea'. The catkins are richly tinted and the leaves assume very dark colouring by midsummer.

HEATHS

There are so many varieties of heaths it is difficult to know where to start: I will call attention to a few that have especially pleased me and leave you to inspect a large garden or nursery collection to make your choice. Apart from the earlies which we shall see in November—*Erica carnea* 'King George' and 'Queen Mary'—there is the superlative 'Springwood White', at once the most prolific and the strongest grower, with clear white flowers offset by rusty brown anthers. 'Springwood Pink' takes a bit of beating for vigour and clear colouring. There are many pink varieties, but 'December Red', 'Myretoun Ruby' and 'Vivellii' are noted dark forms. The second is almost as vigorous as the 'Springwood' cultivars while the last is the darkest, with dark foliage; it is a compact grower. While all these carnea varieties are performing, *E. × darleyensis* will also be full of flower, but on rather taller plants. 'Arthur Johnson' in soft pink, with long spikes makes a good pair with the best white, 'White Perfection'. There are also several forms with cream-tipped young foliage, such as 'Ghost Hills' and 'Margaret Brummage'.

ABOVE: *Garrya elliptica*, soft yellow-green catkins backed by dark green leaves
BELOW: *Erica carnea* 'December Red'

LEFT TO RIGHT: *Hamamelis mollis*, *Hamamelis* 'Pallida' and *Hamamelis* 'Brevipetala'. All are sweetly scented and frost-proof.

And where should we place the true heathers, or callunas, which have brilliant red, orange and yellow foliage varieties? They are splendid colour-givers and blend happily with the sere flowers of the autumn bloomers, but war with the pink and crimson of the *Erica carnea* and *E.* × *darleyensis* flowers, though they are quite acceptable with 'Springwood White' and 'White Perfection'. There is no doubt that these foliage variants are some of the year's highlights.

WITCH HAZEL

Although the first alphabetically, *Hamamelis japonica* is a less popular Witch Hazel. It is tree-like, with attractive wayward growth but comparatively small flowers. The same may be said of the last to flower, *H. japonica* 'Zuccariniana', which has a more upright habit, flowers of pale greenish yellow, and a less pleasant scent.

H. mollis, one of the most famous of winter flowers, is surprisingly frost proof. The vernacular name Witch Hazel comes from a likeness in leaf to *Corylus* and the fact that it was similarly used for divining water by early settlers in North America. There is no doubt that *H. mollis* is the most popular of the Witch Hazels; it makes a good-sized, well-balanced shrub up to about eight feet high and wide, provided that the soil is well mixed with peat or leafmould and is devoid of lime or is at least neutral. The leaves are large, rounded, velvety and a good yellow in the autumn. The flowers, mere wisps of narrow petals, are of soft yellow with dark reddish centres. But all this would scarcely raise it to the height of popularity it has gained; its reputation is due to its delicious scent, long lasting in the open or when cut. Taking Witch Hazels all together, they form a desirable group with the spring-flowering *H. vernalis*, and fortunately they all excel in autumn colour. Many new forms and hybrids are on the market, with flowers from yellow to tones of red, some of which I mention here. Because they are usually propagated by grafting, they remain expensive.

H. 'Arnold Promise' is one of the most noted of hybrids with *H. japonica*. There is also the orange-coloured, larger-flowered 'Jelena', but in the dark days of January I find the darker coloured forms are less conspicuous than the yellows.

H. 'Pallida' surpasses its parent, being of brighter, clearer yellow than *H. mollis* and is its equal in all other respects. If it has a drawback, it is on account of its rather wide-spreading habit.

ABOVE: *Hamamelis* 'Arnold Promise'

LEFT: *Hamamelis* 'Jelena' has larger flowers than most Witch Hazels; those shown are slightly enlarged photographically as well.

Lonicera × purpusii often flowers before the end of December, but it will go on opening its intensely fragrant little creamy flowers for many weeks.

Mahonia japonica opens sprays of little lemon yellow bells, usually by the end of January (sometimes before). This is another shrub noted for its fragrance. Moreover, it is a shrub of magnificent foliage, pinnate but otherwise holly-like, which makes it a fine shrub for contrast.

Rhododendron dauricum provides the real awakening, when in the first week of January it opens its blooms from leafless twigs; they are small but of intense crimson-purple and look splendid with the yellow jasmine in a vase.

R. nobleanum during mild spells will produce its fine heads of flowers of traditional shape. Though there are red forms, I find that the pink form of *R. nobleanum* is the most appealing and reliable. My plant, some twenty-five years old, is about five feet high and wide, despite having had numerous flowering shoots picked when in bud to open in the warmth of the room.

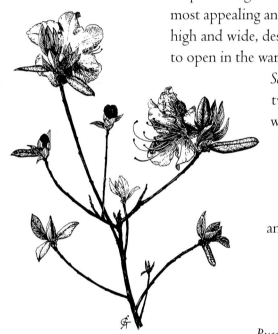

Sarcococca hookeriana seldom exceeds three feet and has prettily tinted twigs and flowers, but my choice of Sweet Box is *S. hookeriana digna*, which sometimes reaches that height, but is often shorter. All sarcococcas have small tassel-like flowers exhaling a honeyed perfume, and it is lovely getting a whiff of this in late January, growing perhaps by the garden door. They all increase slowly by underground stolons, growing, even excelling, on chalky and limy soils, and take kindly even to rooty, shady places.

S. hookeriana humilis, only a foot or two high, is suitable for the smallest gardens.

S. ruscifolia makes a spreading shrub to about three feet with shining dark evergreen leaves (like those of the Butchers' Broom, *Ruscus*).

Viburnum farreri (*V. fragrans*), a notable shrub, is easy to layer, producing heads of small blush flowers with a heady scent of Heliotrope in spring and autumn. *V. grandiflorum* I find rather more susceptible to frost but a better laster in water. *V. × bodnantense*, the hybrid of the two, makes a large erect shrub with good flowers and scent. All varieties, such as 'Dawn' and 'Deben', may be expected to produce flowers from autumn onwards.

V. foetens opens pure white flowers rather later than most other viburnums. The epithet "foetens" refers to the aroma of crushed leaves or bark, the flowers being

ABOVE: *Rhododendron dauricum*
OPPOSITE: Collection of young conifers at Talbot Manor, Norfolk, showing some of the wide variety of tints and shapes available

sweetly scented. It is a smaller shrub than any of the above and like them, is not particular about soil.

V. tinus, the old Laurustinus, keeps up its display of white flowers from evergreen bushes. I place 'Gwenllian' at the top of the many forms selected and named. This small selection of viburnums is from a very large group standing high for garden usage in almost any category of shrubs you like to choose: flower, foliage, autumn colour and berry.

Coloured Bark and Twigs

During the few weeks in the middle of winter in Surrey, when flowers are usually scarce in the open garden, we have to look around for other colours than berries and evergreens—plain or variegated. Some maples, plums and birches come to mind, but the Silver Birch is a large tree and not many small gardens today have room for it. Since these and most other trees grown especially for their bark are grafted onto ordinary seedlings, it is important in planting to see that the union is just below the soil; otherwise, the less attractive stock may show.

Acer davidii is one of the best of the so-called Snake Bark maples, most of which are from the Far East. The young bark is markedly striped with pale grey on a green background. As the trunk gets older and bigger, the striping tends to disappear, but is retained on young growth.

A. palmatum 'Sangokaku' ('Senkaki'), whose young twigs are bright red, is a brilliant spectacle in winter when placed to catch the afternoon sun.

A. pensylvanicum is another handsome Snake Bark best known for the superb variety called 'Erythrocladum', whose young bark is scarlet and pink streaked with white. It is native to the eastern United States.

A. rufinerve, similar to *A. pensylvanicum*, has bluish new shoots on which red new leaves hang from red leaf stalks.

Betula ermanii is a birch famous for the creamy buff colour of its bark, but it is another large grower.

Winter stems (LEFT TO RIGHT):
Cornus alba, *Perovskia atriplicifolia*,
Cornus alba 'Elegantissima', *Cornus alba* 'Sibirica', *Leycesteria formosa* and *Cornus stolonifera* 'Flaviramea'

B. papyrifera, the Paper Birch, makes a great smooth bole of white.

B. utilis jacquemontii is one of the many species and forms from the Far East noted for their creamy white bark and comparatively large leaves.

B. verrucosa 'Laciniata', a variant of the Silver Birch more suitable for small gardens, is slender and silvery white in the bark.

Cornus alba has white berries that decorate the bushes in early autumn before the leaves colour, then drop to reveal the many stems of dark crimson. The more brilliant form is *C. alba* 'Sibirica', whereas the variegated form 'Elegantissima' will, after repeated prunings to reduce its size, give us startling small twigs with scarlet bark and plain white leaves. All cornuses, also known as dogwoods, in this paragraph make large shrubs some seven to eight feet (2.1–2.4 m) high and wide. For the annual cutdown to stimulate young growth, I find it worthwhile to reduce only half the number of shoots to near ground level, leaving the remainder to give interest in early summer. For contrast, there is *C. alba* 'Kesselringii' with nearly black stems. *C. stolonifera* 'Flaviramea' is a complete contrast with greeny-yellow bark, and two new developments from it are 'Bud's Yellow' and 'White Gold' in paler tints. Together they make a fascinating set and though particularly suited to damp ground will also thrive mightily in ordinary good soil. They are not so successful on chalk or heavy

ABOVE LEFT: *Betula papyrifera* and white daffodils

ABOVE RIGHT: *Cornus sanguinea* 'Winter Flame'. Though this species will thrive on dry, limy soils, it has an unfortunate propensity to sucker, sometimes as much as eight feet (2.4 m) from its parent plant.

limy soil; for those, we must turn to *C. sanguinea* 'Winter Flame', but it spreads wildly at the root.

Kerria japonica has green bark bright enough to make some effect in the bleakest month. For this perhaps the well-known double-flowered 'Pleniflora' should be by-passed in favour of the single-flowered species, and the selection 'Golden Guinea'.

Salix alba 'Britzensis',
Elaeagnus × ebbingei
'Gilt Edge' and
Cornus alba 'Sibirica'
(BOTTOM RIGHT)

Leycesteria formosa, richer green in the stem than *Kerria*, and duller of flower, still contributes to the winter garden when placed to contrast with, say, *Cornus alba*. But perhaps we should leave the lawn-grass, and *Hebe rakaiensis*, to provide this colour. They will take care of fresh greenery until spring really starts.

Parrotia persica is one of those trees that, like the better known but gigantic Plane Tree, shed bark in patches. Exposed areas reveal the paler young bark, forming a fascinating patchwork of colour.

Pinus bungeana, the Lace Bark Pine, is most striking in maturity, when the bark becomes white and the contrast with its peeled patches is greatest.

Prunus maackii and *P. serrula* are two of the most attractive of trees for bark display. They both make medium-sized trees, the former with glossy orange-brown bark and the latter of shining coppery brown with a metallic lustre. The flowers of both are insignificant.

Salix irrorata and *S. acutifolia* are two willows with dark plum-coloured bark, so heavily coated with white wax that they appear to be pale grey in bright light. (The same applies to *Berberis dictyophylla* and *Rubus biflorus*, but the latter is a huge shrub not suitable for confined areas.) Two other good willows with telling bark colour are *S. alba* 'Britzensis' and *S. alba* 'Vitellina'. The former, large trees of which may be seen lighting the landscape, is coral red, and the second is mustard yellow. For the landscape garden they are best coppiced, that is, cut down to near ground level in late spring to get the maximum quantity of twigs with freshly coloured bark for the following winter. They make large clumps and are no use for confined spaces.

Sorbus aucuparia 'Beissneri', a Rowan, or Mountain Ash with coral-coloured bark, may be expected also to give an autumn show of berries, but I cannot remember seeing it in berry. Perhaps the birds, who quickly devour these fruits, were always ahead of me.

Stewartia pseudocamellia, the most colourful of trees with flaking and peeling bark, is named for the resemblance of the flowers to those of a single camellia. It has reached fifty feet (15.0 m) in its native Japan, but is a much smaller tree in Britain.

Snowdrops

Colour is scarce, and perhaps we should not be too choosy in regard to flower in the depth of winter. A few little things cheer us, such as the earliest snowdrops, among which I find *Galanthus nivalis* 'Atkinsii' a wonderfully reliable bulb that never fails to delight in about the second week of January. 'Atkinsii' has a rather narrow outline, but there are more opulent varieties: following it comes 'S. Arnott', which has all the good points that one looks for in a snowdrop—vigour, well-rounded large flowers and scent. All the *G. nivalis* varieties have pairs of flat greyish leaves through which push the flower stems. To see a bed, border or woodland glade thronged with even the Common Snowdrop, *G. nivalis*, makes winter worthwhile. *G. elwesii* is an early starter too, but its flowers lack beauty of outline. The group differs from the common variety in that the grey leaves enclasp the stems, like those of a tulip. And we must not forget their distinguishing green marks on the inner segments.

If snowdrops flowered at midsummer they would not attract much attention, but coming as they do in the darkest months they have numerous keen devotees. Some have rich green shining leaves, but these mostly belong to the later flowering sorts such as *G. latifolius*. There are some lovely variants: 'Straffan', 'Magnet', 'Beth Chatto', 'Mighty Atom', 'John Gray' and many more, the first and third of these having two flowers to the bulbs, thus prolonging the display.

Taking them as a whole, snowdrops seem to thrive best in a rather heavy limy soil and readily put up with shade. Dried bulbs from merchants are not usually very successful; the most satisfactory way of increase is to divide or purchase them soon after the flowers are over while the leaves are still green. On my dry and sandy soil they need a deal of care and attention to keep them going.

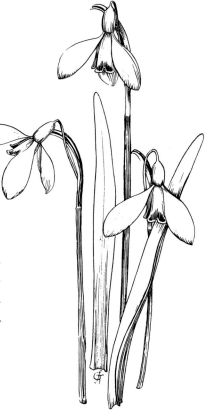

Galanthus nivalis
'S. Arnott', a splendid
large-flowered Snowdrop

FEBRUARY

There comes a time, usually by the middle of the month in southern England, when the first glimmer of greenery is noticeable in the hedgerows and thickets. It is from the willows and sallows whose catkins precede the young foliage—a greyish, silvery green that grows in strength as the days lengthen. The commonest is the Goat Willow, *Salix caprea*, but this and most others are too vigorous for the average garden. One of the most acceptable is 'Blue Streak', a form of *S. acutifolia* whose bark is dark plum enlivened by a waxy white covering. The catkins, like those of all I am about to mention, are silvery; *S. acutifolia* forms have first a rosy flush, opening into yellow stamens. A rather larger, stouter plant is *S. daphnoides* 'Aglaia', while *S. repens argentea* is a low sprawling shrub with silvery leaves later. Among larger trees we could hardly do better than *S. alba sericea*; apart from the early catkins, the silvery leaves are a delight through the summer.

OPPOSITE: *Helleborus argutifolius* (*H. corsicus*), a study in pale green for February and March
ABOVE: *Crocus fleischeri*

13

Trees

Prunus cerasifera, Myrobella or Myrobalan Plum, in its ordinary white form is not to be ignored, though it is usually used for hedging.

P. conradinae is a pleasing small tree whose pinky-white flowers have stamens tending to project in the bud. It is very good and a free-flowerer.

P. davidiana 'Alba', a stiff, upright, small grower with shapely single white flowers, is for me unequalled among early flowering trees. The pink form in cultivation is less upright, and the flowers have not the quality of the white, of which there is a drawing in my *Colour in the Winter Garden*.

P. incisa 'Praecox' is another of those earlies which foretell of later joys; it makes a comparatively large twiggy tree and is usually a veritable mass of flower, white, touched with pink.

P. mume, the Japanese Apricot, has been treasured and selected for centuries in China and Japan, with the result that there are numerous named forms from white to light crimson, single and double, and all ravishingly fragrant. Unfortunately flowering stems when cut do not appear to enjoy heated rooms. They make small trees, and in Japan their flowering often signals a holiday to enjoy their beauty and perfume. My acquaintance is mainly with 'Benishidori' in light crimson and 'Omoi-no-mama', white with an occasional pink petal.

Cornus mas

Shrubs

Abeliophyllum distichum will often be in flower before the end of the month. The small, four-petalled flowers are borne in profusion on all the young shoots. For this reason it is well to make it grow vigorously in a sunny spot to its full height of six to eight feet (1.8–2.4 m).

Camellia × *williamsii* 'November Pink', unusually precocious, will probably still be in flower this month, when it may be joined by *C. japonica* 'No bilissima', a good reliable double white, and 'Otome', a good single pink. *C.* 'Cornish Snow' and its blush counterpart 'Jermyns' usually appear in February. Camellias demand lime-free soil, as do rhododendrons, but several other shrubs in my list also have this preference, which I shall mention as we go. Camellias do not usually suffer in times of drought.

Cornus mas, Cornelian Cherry, displays numerous tiny bunches of yellow, sharply scented stars on bare branches. At first sight it may be taken for an early forsythia, but its assets are more numerous: it has red, cherry-like fruits in summer and usually good autumn colour. It eventually reaches twenty feet in height and then is especially handsome if trimmed early in life to a single-trunked tree.

Coronilla glauca, best tried in a warm sheltered corner, has the pleasing combination of neatly lobed, blue green, small leaves and bunches of bright yellow vetch-flowers. At about three feet it is easily placed near a door or window where, in maritime and other warm districts, it may flower throughout the winter.

Daphne bholua is frequently in flower in late February. In its excellent form 'Jacqueline Postill', it produces head after head of scented pink-and-white stars for many weeks. It is a vigorous upright shrub which seems to thrive in gardens where lime-free soil is available, but not in my own.

D. mezereum will slowly ascend to about six feet (1.8 m), its youngest twigs studded with starry flowers in shades of pink and purplish red and exhaling a sweet scent. They last long in flower. On the whole I think I prefer the white flowered forms, especially the one known as 'Bowles's Variety'. These are good two-season shrubs; by summertime the flowers are replaced by showy berries, red from the purplish forms, yellow from the white.

D. odora, a low evergreen, is tricky and sometimes short-lived, but for its wonderful sweet scent it is well worth any amount of trouble. The best known is 'Aureo-marginata', believed to be tougher than its plain-leafed version, and it does particularly well at Wisley. All daphnes have substantial, small flowers, often of a crystalline texture. Although I have grouped them with lime-hating shrubs they will put up with some limy soils so long as they are cool and deep.

Erica 'Irish Dusk', a strong, upright growing selection of *E.* × *darleyensis* with warm pink flowers, has won popularity in recent years among gardeners. Its colour does not always associate well with the carneas, which, having begun flowering last month along with cultivars of *E.* × *darleyensis*, are now in full bloom.

Forsythia ovata, the compact and precocious Korean Forsythia, is often in flower as early as February. Some forms are very good.

Garrya elliptica is an evergreen with catkins that sway in every breeze. Its provenance, California, prompts us to give it a sheltered spot. I have known large bushes, some fifteen feet wide and nearly as tall, to be badly mauled by frost and cold winds, though in sheltered gardens they are usually safe. The rather dull dark leaves make a good contrast with the pale green, fluffy catkins which may reach as much as eight or ten inches in length. Recently, the variety 'James Roof' has sprung upon us with

Daphne mezereum, a British native, valued for its frost-resistant, fragrant, early flowers

extra-long catkins, tinted with red-purple. There are also some hybrids with *G. fre-montii* named *G. × issaquahensis*. Some noted forms are 'Pat Ballard' and 'Glasnevin Wine'; while their catkins are richly tinted, they have not the elegant frilliness of *G. elliptica*. This and other species are at their greatest elegance in the male plants.

Mahonia bealei is a useful gaunt upright evergreen shrub with large, pinnate, very prickly, almost holly-like leaves and short spikes of lemon yellow bells with a delicious lily-of-the-valley fragrance—a delight usually carried into March.

Osmaronia (Nuttallia) cerasiformis is conspicuous for its dangling racemes of creamy white flowers. The sexes are on different plants; if pollinated, the females will bear strings of reddish currant-like fruits in summer.

Parrotia persica, Ironwood, is noted for long-lasting autumn colour. By February the twigs are studded with velvety brown buds opening out into bunches of crimson stamens. It is a large spreading shrub, almost tree-like and sometimes trained as a tree. It thrives on chalky and limy soils, though it is related to *Hamamelis*.

Rhododendron lutescens with pale yellow flowers and often burnished leaves. This follows the other kinds described earlier. The lower group is *Cyclamen coum.*

RHODODENDRONS

So far we have been looking at trees and shrubs with flowers that are rather small, though effective in mass; many are scented. February sees the awakening of the great genus *Rhododendron*, and those with large gardens can place some of the early plants of the race with blood-red bells on shrubs that will attain twelve feet or more, such as *R. barbatum* and *R. thomsonii* and their hybrid 'Shilsonii'. It is a startling sight to see one of the great bushes crowned with rich red flowers so early in the year. But these are for the few, where size is no deterrent. Let us consider some of modest size. Following fast upon *R. dauricum* is *R. mucronulatum* in rosy mauve, and its pure white form. Of course, being rhododendrons, they are susceptible to the least frost, but in a year free from it, they are well worth their place. This little list is but an indication of what the genus can do so early in the year. But it says enough to substantiate rhododendrons in their long-flowering period through spring and summer until August.

Rhododendron ciliatum is a lovely early flowerer in white, touched with pink.

R. × cilpinense, with blush pink flowers and darker stamens, is a somewhat later-flowering hybrid between R. ciliatum and R. moupinense. 'Tessa', also a hybrid from R. moupinense, is purplish-pink with crimson spots.

R. leucaspis, another lovely white, has contrasting chocolate anthers and handsome small leaves.

R. nobleanum 'Venustum' has during all these weeks been producing its large heads of more typical rhododendron blooms, just right for picking and opening indoors.

R. 'Praecox' is a dense, glossy-leafed bush, smothered with rosy lilac flowers, one of the most regular performers. It is a hybrid of R. dauricum with R. ciliatum. An early flowering hybrid from R. dauricum is 'Olive', in mallow purple.

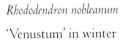

Rhododendron nobleanum
'Venustum' in winter

Stachyurus praecox, another fair-sized shrub, has racemes of cream bells hanging stiffly, very different from the lax catkins of *Garrya elliptica*.

Sycopsis sinensis is an upright evergreen whose dark brown buds are apt to be obscured by despondently pendent javelin leaves. The buds enclose bunches of crimson stamens, turning yellow much as in *Parrotia*.

Herbaceous Plants

Crocus tommasinianus seeds itself into all manner of positions in sun or shade, even in the interstices of paving and in dense shade under bushes. Luly Palmer, who gardened on chalk, called it "the prettiest weed in the garden". And so it is. One day we notice the slim little grey or buff buds, and on the next sunny morning they are all open, showing orange stamens inside lilac cups. I planted about a hundred when I moved and now after some twenty years there must be several thousand. They vary from the wild white to darkest 'Whitewell Purple' and lovely rosy lilac forms. I doubt whether other spring crocuses are ever going to make themselves so much at home.

Other willing crocuses are *C. sieberi*, which seems loath to colonise. It is rich lilac inside and out. Then there are those two species of great quality, *C. biflorus* in whites and blues, and *C. chrysanthus* in varied tones of warm yellow. Little *C. fleischeri* has such thin white segments that the stamens show through; *C. olivieri*, *C. balansae* and *C. susianus* are richly yellow-tinted. While all these species are hardy, it must be admitted that they are best in pots in a cold glasshouse or frame where winter's storms will not damage the open flowers.

ABOVE: *Crocus tommasinianus*
RIGHT: *Crocus tommasinianus* is the earliest bulb to make a spread, quickly, by seeding itself in the author's garden.

Cyclamen coum has mostly dark green leaves and chubby little rounded flowers of rich dark crimson, pink or white. Its variety *caucasicum* has most beautifully marbled leaves; in fact the whole genus is noted for its variously patterned and tinted leaves in green and grey and near white. They all thrive in almost any soil, and are quite happy when tucked under shrubs.

Eranthis hyemalis, Winter Aconite, is a golden gem with its flowers set in a toby-frill of green, smooth and gleaming. In my experience it thrives best in heavy limy soil, along with the Christmas Rose and snowdrops. It is only a few inches high but where suited under shade and trees will make an effective carpet. The cultivar 'Guinea Gold' is to be sought, for it is a large and splendid hybrid with *E. cilicica*.

Galanthus ikariae and *G. rizehensis* accompany the first scillas, as do later snowdrops such as 'Merlin' and the splendid 'Cicely Hall'.

Three early flowers:
ABOVE LEFT: *Crocus biflorus*
ABOVE RIGHT: *Crocus sieberi*
BELOW: *Cyclamen coum*

Among herbaceous plants, this month (and March) is dominated by the hellebores. There are two distinct groups: those that produce their flower stalks from ground level, and those few at the end of my list that grow leafy stems branching into heads of flowering stalks the following spring.

There is today something of a craze for double-flowered variants. To my mind a hellebore is so supremely beautiful when looked at face to face—carpels, stamens, spotting and above all shape—that I feel doubling is a retrograde step for these beautiful flowers. The sad part is to find them all nodding—but is not this an intriguing character of many most lovely flowers? Helen Ballard made great efforts to select seedlings and flowers that did not nod, so perhaps we shall see this style coming to the fore. The other great sadness is that they do not last when cut, except when single flowers (showing their greatest beauty) are floated in a bowl.

H. cyclophyllus came to me from Eliot Hodgkin, and has a fine yellow flower. It is supposed to smell of blackcurrants, but I find this elusive.

H. niger, the Christmas Rose, is seen in good and bad forms. Most will, at least, last in water, but they seldom flower before mid-February. They seem to thrive in heavy limy soil in shade.

Helleborus orientalis Early Purple Group, for years known as *H. atrorubens*, is the earliest to flower. The plants are sterile hybrids with flowers of a rich plum colour, fading paler, and are always raised from divisions.

H. orientalis guttatus has white segments usually heavily spotted with murrey-crimson, making a very handsome flower. This *H. orientalis* group can contain green, pink, murrey or white, and every conceivable intermediate tint. They are extremely beautiful, weather-resistant, long-lived and amenable to cultivation in a great variety of soils and positions. On the whole I should give them shade and a good rich soil.

H. torquatus gives us plants that are frequently purplish in bud opening to cool clean green flowers. But so variable are they all that it is best to see and select them in bloom and since they are all usually grown in containers, this is easy.

TOP: *Helleborus niger*
BOTTOM: *Helleborus niger*
'Blackthorn Group'. They are all known as Christmas Rose and thrive best in heavy limy soil, in shade.

H. argutifolius, from the Mediterranean, heads the second group, those with branching stems. It is a fine plant formerly known as *H. corsicus* (it is from that island) that will make a magnificent clump of stems some three feet across and nearly as high, with stems, leaves and flowers in shades of green. The leaves are toothed and beautifully veined, while the flowers, poised in branching heads above the leaves, are nodding and of a particularly clear pale tint. It is hardy in Surrey.

H. foetidus, a perfect study in greens, has finely fingered leaves of an exceptionally dark green, making an effectual podium for the fountain of pale green bellflowers. Various selections of this British native hellebore have been made. One of these, 'Wester Flisk', has reddish stems, but this does not attract me as much as plants with wholly pale green inflorescences.

H. lividus, another Mediterranean, this from the neighbouring island of Majorca, is not quite so hardy; in Surrey it is best grown in a cold frame or glasshouse, where, in the restricted air circulation, its delicate fragrance will be more apparent. The leaves are equally beautiful in their veining, and the flowers are often touched with pink. I showed a hybrid between this and *H. argutifolius* at a Royal Horticultural show, but it did not receive the Award of Merit; that had to wait until the following year when Sir Frederic Stern got the award with a similar plant, and the hybrid was named *H. × sternii*. Now Robin White has a hybrid strain of the same character known as the 'Blackthorn Group' that includes many fine plants. *H. argutifolius* has been crossed also with *H. niger*; the cross is known as *H. × nigericors*, and some of the results are outstanding.

Hepatica media 'Ballardii', in powder blue, is my favorite among the hepaticas, but *H. nobilis* and *H. transsilvanica* both yield a number of lovely forms. Close relatives of the anemones, hepatica flowers can be powder blue, cerise pink or white, and many intermediate shades and there are doubles as well as singles. They are best in shade with a cool root run.

Helleborus 'Bowles's Yellow' and a dark-coloured seedling of *H. orientalis*

RIGHT: *Iris unguicularis*
(*Iris stylosa*). This flowers in mild
spells from autumn until spring.
BELOW: *Leucojum vernum*

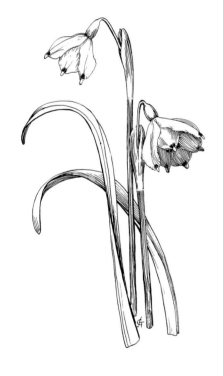

Iris unguicularis (*I. stylosa*) comes into its own in mild February days. It is a Mediterranean plant and should be planted in hot sunny places at the foot of a south-facing wall, but not left short of water, to get the best results. From the odd, errant blooms in late autumn and through to spring, there will seldom be a week when buds are not appearing, just ready to pick. Then watch the miraculous unfurling of the scented blooms indoors. Besides the two or three lilac-coloured ones that are old-established garden forms, there is the prolific 'Walter Butt', named after a noted West Country gardener; it is pale lilac. There is a white which I believe is traceable to E. A. Bowles, and several dark purple forms, such as 'Mary Barnard' and 'Bob Thompson'. As a rule they just need leaving alone, but to make things less comfortable for those vivid green caterpillars (purple inside, which gives the game away!), slugs and snails, it is advised to cut all leaves to about a third of their length in autumn. The most sumptuous dark variety I've seen was collected by Nancy Lindsay near Toulon. Its segments were grey beneath. These dark varieties seem to have narrower leaves than the ordinary kinds, and all the leaves may be expected to reach nearly two feet in length.

Leucojum vernum will by the end of the month be showing its big bellflowers over dark green, broad leaves. The flowers have six segments, as in snowdrops, but they are all of the same length with a green tip, and exhale a faint but delicious scent; like snowdrops they do best in rich, cool soil.

While there is no doubt that the hellebores as a group are pre-eminent in their varied garden value, the daffodil remains the principal spring flower. We have been fortunate over recent years in welcoming an early flowerer among the large trumpet varieties, named 'Rijnveld's Early Sensation'. Though named in Holland, where it was propagated in quantity, it was raised in Sussex. It is a typical big yellow daffodil which I have frequently had in flower in early February; in Cornwall I believe it is picked from the open fields in January. Following it is Alec Gray's exquisite 'Jana', signifying that it also flowers in January in Cornwall. I have not had it in flower before the end of February. As will be seen from my pencil drawings of it in my *Complete Paintings and Drawings* and also in *Cuttings from My Garden Notebooks*, it is a flower of great refinement.

Narcissus bulbocodium var. *romieuxii*,
an early-flowering pale yellow form
of this March-flowering species

RIGHT: Deliciously scented
small evergreen shrubs:
Sarcococca humilis (BOTTOM),
Sarcococca hookeriana
var. *digyna* (LEFT) and
Sarcococca ruscifolia (RIGHT)
BELOW: *Primula vulgaris sibthorpii*
(about twice natural size)

Primula vulgaris sibthorpii, a little primrose with flowers of soft pink, replaces the western European *P. vulgaris* in eastern European countries, and is frequently in flower before the native, in February.

Pulmonaria rubra, with flowers of coral tint, has several noted forms, none being more outstanding than 'David Ward' whose leaves have a broad white edge. It needs a cool moist place.

P. saccharata, with spotted leaves, contends with *P. rubra* for the first place in the race to flower.

Scilla bifolia praecox, which throws up a sheaf of little cobalt blue stars to about six inches, is one of the most satisfactory of early bulbs. Because other scillas are not yet in flower, there is no risk of hybridisation and it increases readily by seed.

Viola hybrids, taking all weathers, are the comparatively new winter-flowering pansies available in a good selection of self-colours that lend sunshine to the dreariest of borders.

Pulmonaria rubra
'David Ward'

MARCH

We are taught that "March winds and April showers bring forth May flowers", but the March in which I am now writing has been renowned for its still, mild weather. We have actually had four weeks in Surrey without a frost, and everything is burgeoning. It has been a wonderful month for the prunus blossom, every tree a cloud of delicate colour.

Trees

Prunus × blireana and *P. × blireana* 'Moseri' are two double-flowered hybrids with *P. mume*, the Japanese Apricot. They are longer lasting than the singles, it is true, but the trees are less beautiful, seemingly inhibited by the burden of larger blooms. Of course, they all have for the rest of the season dark murrey-coloured foliage; those with the pink flowers are darkest and are of greater consequence in summer.

  P. cerasifera 'Pissardii' and 'Pissardii Nigra' are both coppery-leafed forms of the wild, white-flowered Myrobalan (Myrobella) Plum mentioned last month, but a little later in flower. I have a weak spot in my heart for 'Pissardii' but must admit that

OPPOSITE: *Camellia × williamsii* 'Donation', the most free-flowering early Camellia
ABOVE: *Rhododendron parvifolium*, a winter-flowering species

Prunus yedoensis in the
Valley Gardens, Windsor

'Nigra' has flowers of a more decided pink. But are we ready for pink flowers so early in the year? We have them in the Almond, but it always seems to me that the faint blush of 'Pissardii' itself is more in tune with early days. In fact, I know of few spring sights so delicate and winsome as a cloud of the tiny flowers, each a quintet of little round petals, when their pale blush is seen against a grey sky. 'Nigra' can be distinguished even in winter from 'Pissardii' itself by cutting a twig—some of the foliage tint is echoed by a stain under the bark.

P. dulcis, Almond, when in bud is a favourite for cutting to open indoors. In late summer it produces hard-shelled almonds in green velvet husks. When well grown it is a beautiful small tree but is apt to suffer from silver-leaf disease. The double form is a more compact tree and flowers a week or two later. Its flowers are very beautiful and lasting.

P. subhirtella in its weeping forms, 'Pendula' and 'Pendula Rosea', both with cool pink flowers, presents one of the most delightful sights of the whole year. But avoid top-grafted trees if you can, and try to purchase one that has been grafted at ground level and trained up. The top-grafting of cherries is a particular evil because the stock (*Prunus avium*, or Gean) is much stronger than the scion and sooner or later reveals an unsightly union. It is then quite obvious that artificial means have been employed to gain the desired height. If a bottom-grafted tree is not available, you can rectify the matter to a certain extent by tying up a leading shoot to a cane attached to the stem. Then will some of the great beauty of the tree be revealed. Keep in mind, too, that the Gean is a coarse, big tree with heaving roots and thus is best kept away from lawns and paths.

P. subhirtella 'Fukubana' has the richest colour among these trees. It is not particularly vigorous, but the massed blooms so early in the year make one sit up. And be sure to keep it away from the usual reddish Japonicas (*Chaenomeles*).

P. yedoensis, a Japanese cherry also known as 'Yoshino', more than holds its own with the plums, lovely and delicate as the latter are. John Gilmour, then Director of the Royal Horticultural Society's garden at Wisley, once asked me for the most beautiful and worthy cherry to plant as an avenue. (The avenue has long since gone to make space for the Trial Ground.) My unhesitating answer was *P. yedoensis*; he had come to the same conclusion. Here is a tree with wide-spreading branches arching gently over one another and every year, giving a complete smother of blush pink, sweetly fragrant single flowers. And it has good autumn colour. I know of no other flowering tree which so consistently, year after year, gives us its unfailing spring best. But it is not for small gardens; its spreading head may reach twenty feet or more across.

Salix sepulcralis chrysocoma, Weeping Willow—long known as *S. babylonica* 'Ramulis Aureis'—when hung with pale green shoots, is one of spring's most noted harbingers. It carries on the fresh green touch throughout March into April. The earlier name refers to the bright yellowish colouring of the twigs that in turn brighten the green of the young shoots. It is a very large tree for spots not too exposed to the wind, which tends to make its lovely tresses less weeping. For small gardens, the best weeping willow is *S. caprea* 'Kilmarnock', the correct name for the most showy, male form, as opposed to the older Kilmarnock Willow, which is a rather dull female, correctly *S. caprea* 'Pendula'.

Rhododendron 'Praecox'

Shrubs

Azara microphylla, an engaging, small-leafed evergreen shrub in gardens in the milder districts of Britain, brings a whiff of vanilla to us in the March sunshine. The flowers are tiny and inconspicuous, hiding the minute yellow tassels amongst the small, dark green, glossy foliage. There is a pleasing white variegated form which will light up a sunny wall in summer.

Camellia × *williamsii* 'J. C. Williams', a single-flowered pink of a clear light tint, is one of my first choices among the *williamsii* hybrids. Another is 'Donation', perhaps the most free flowering of all the kinds, semi-double, with darker veining in the delicate pink petals. They are of a more slender and open habit than the well-known *C. japonica* varieties, which are apt to be a bit congested. All the camellias are at their best for some six weeks, joining April to March. If only they had some fragrance, like the autumn-flowering varieties, our cup would be well filled. They have, however, one very great asset: even though frost may spoil some flowers, there are always more buds to open. The same can scarcely be said of many rhododendrons. They all need lime-free soil but, unlike rhododendrons, will put up with quite severe drought.

Chaenomeles japonica (*Cydonia maulei*) is a low bushy shrub with bright, light orange-red flowers. They are followed by quantities of small, round yellow fruits in autumn that give off a lovely, pungent, quince-like odour, but unfortunately lose the flavour when cooked. On the other hand a few fruits will scent a room.

C. speciosa, commonly called Japonica, and also known as Cydonia, or quince, apart from certain rhododendrons and camellias, presents the first bit of red in the awakening year. A delight as a boy was seeing the red flowers opening on its leafless prickly twigs. It is a strange hue, near to spectrum red but dulled by a tendency towards brown. For all that, this is a most welcome hardy shrub and its buds open well indoors. It does not thrive on excessively limy soils, and in spite of its nickname is a native of China. There are many varieties: 'Nivalis', pure white, much whiter than 'Candidissima'; the beautiful 'Moerloosei', sometimes called 'Apple Blossom', whose sobriquet well describes it; 'Umbilicata', soft, rather salmon-pink, that flowers often at Christmas; 'Simonii', very dark red, and a dwarf grower; and 'Phylis Moore' (she always spelt her name with one l), with double flowers opening bright salmon-

Chaenomeles speciosa
'Phylis Moore'
(slightly enlarged)

pink, then darkening almost to vermilion. There are also hybrids with *C. japonica* classed as *C. × superba* among which 'Rowallane' is a splendid red, and 'Knap Hill Scarlet', orange-red, has a flowering period extending hesitantly into summer. But avoid 'Crimson 'n' Gold'—it generates a thicket of suckers. All of the above make fine shrubs, but 'Phylis Moore' and 'Rowallane' benefit from support of a wall or fence, where they are frequently used, ascending to some six feet.

Corylopsis pauciflora is quietly yellow, appealing to those for whom that of forsythias is too much in the early year. It is a comparatively small bush, the very quintessence of spring in its pretty form and tint. All species of *Corylopsis* have delicate creamy yellow flowers, mostly scented, borne in the form of catkins. In *C. glabrescens*, the catkins are long and more obvious. Their attractive foliage is pleasant to contemplate later in the season, which cannot be said for the forsythias.

Erica arborea, Tree Heath, at twelve feet or so, is the largest and most tender of the heaths listed here. The flowers are white, but I would choose instead *E. arborea* 'Alpina', a more compact hardy shrub that rejoices us with dense rich green foliage almost obscured by green-budded, off-white, tiny bells. It flowers for many weeks.

E. erigena (*E. mediterranea*), while not as hardy as its offspring, *E. × darleyensis*, will readily make a four-foot bush in milder districts. I have known it split with severe weather in Northumberland. Its prolific display of lilac pink flowers is well worth the risk. 'W. T. Rackliffe' is a compact, hardier white variant.

E. lusitanica, Portuguese Heath, is a little tender, but worth every endeavour, for its long spikes of pink buds open into smoky white bells in the utmost profusion. Its flowering period extends from January until May, and it can achieve five to six feet in sheltered gardens.

Forsythia × intermedia 'Spectabilis' has flowers of deep yellow that sound a harsh note and can seem rather brash among the more delicate colours of spring. *F. × intermedia* 'Spring Glory' and *F. suspensa* 'Sieboldii' have paler flowers, which I much prefer to those of 'Spectabilis'.

F. suspensa 'Atrocaulis', the queen of the tribe, has dark maroon shoots from which the 'Nymans' form produces particularly wide-petalled flowers of a bland light yellow, but it makes less of a splash than the others. Forsythias are large shrubs, and it will be found that those owning *intermedia* inheritance take two years to produce flowers from vigorous shoots which are the result of heavy pruning, whereas *F. suspensa*, though it makes long shoots after pruning, studs them with blossom every spring. It is these long wand-like growths that are so useful for cutting in yellow bud to open indoors.

Chaenomeles × superba 'Rowallane', one of the best of the "Japonicas"

ABOVE: *Pieris formosa forrestii*
'Wakehurst', showing the
colour of the young leaves

RIGHT: *Rhododendron*
'Christmas Cheer', which
in Surrey does not usually
flower before March

For lime-free soils, there is the genus *Pieris*: *P. japonica* (*P. taiwanensis*) and *P. floribunda*, their multitudes of small white bells earning them the name Lily-of-the-Valley bushes. They have been in cultivation for many years, but in recent decades several seedlings of great beauty have been raised, totally outclassing the original species. One of the selections of *P. japonica*, known as 'Grayswood', is perhaps outclassed by 'Jermyns' but this inherits an attractive brownish tinge from the stalks. Several pink forms have been named, but to my eyes they are of a muddy tone and cannot compare with the best whites. Possibly *P. floribunda* is a parent of 'White Pearl', whose flowers, instead of being borne in lax trusses, are carried in erect wide spikes and are snow-white. 'Forest Flame', a noted form that cropped up as a seedling between *P. japonica* and *P. formosa forrestii* 'Wakehurst' at Sunningdale Nursery, has inherited the admirable trait of the latter in producing young leaves of scarlet as the flowers begin to fade at the end of April. The Wakehurst plant is of course noted for the same most brilliant colour but is not reliably hardy in Surrey, except in sheltered conditions. They all thrive in soils and positions that suit rhododendrons, and their flowering period extends well into April.

Pieris formosa forrestii 'Rowallane' (TOP LEAVES) and *Pieris formosa forrestii* 'Wakehurst', both spectacular in spring

Rhododendron 'Christmas Cheer', despite the name, seldom flowers before March in Surrey. It is a tough, regular and free-flowering garden hybrid that can put up with adverse conditions, except for lime in the soil, with every prospect of success. The buds are pink, opening to almost white, and flowering begins at an early age. I know of large plants some twelve feet high and wide that remain compact and flower with great regularity in full sunlight.

R. *lutescens*, an azalea-like shrub of some size, bears dark coppery young leaves, an effective contrast to the lemon-yellow flowers. The 'Exbury' form is generally looked upon as pre-eminent. 'Bo Peep', a hybrid of this species and *R. moupinense*, is also highly desirable. Another good hybrid is × *cilpinense*.

R. sargentianum is a diminutive plant whose wide-spreading low mound of branches supports tiny dark leaves and heads of small pure white flowers of considerable quality.

R. stewartianum and *R. eclecteum*, small plants of great charm in a mild March, are both worthy of a place for their pretty rounded leaves and bell-like, pink-tinged flowers.

R. sutchuenense is a rather flat-topped, gaunt shrub, but a plant of great majesty even when not in flower. Every stout shoot bears a flat collar of long, narrow, rather light green leaves in the midst of which, in a mild season, the round head of blush pink flowers sits. More often than not frost spoils them, and we hope for better luck the next year.

Perhaps these few species and hybrids will suffice; there are many more venturing into flower, but one cannot depend entirely on rhododendrons for March, fickle as they are.

Rhododendron 'Cilpinense'

Ribes laurifolium is an unusual evergreen Flowering Currant three to four feet (0.9–1.2 m) high whose small growths disport catkins of small flowers of palest creamy green.

R. sanguineum, the well-known Flowering Currant, often opens as early as March, but it always seems to me that lovely though the crimson in the cultivar 'Pulborough Scarlet' is (and welcome also the pink and white forms), their popularity begins to pall with only the dull green leaves for the rest of the season. These are shrubs of twelve or so feet (3.6 m) and flower very freely.

Stachyurus praecox, one of the most intriguing flowers of March, is a stout-stemmed shrub with creamy little bells arranged catkin-like in hanging strings from the young shoots. Unlike the hazel catkins they hang stiffly and do not move in the breeze. When a branch is cut for indoors they only hang at their original angle, which can disconcert the fastidious arranger.

Viburnum tinus, Laurustinus, from late autumn, Christmas or early in the New Year, this old garden favourite is in flower. With the sunnier days of March it presents a good white effect, but a white which, in contrast with *Prunus* and *Pieris*, is just tinged with grey. It is a worthy old shrub that flowers freely, but both foliage and flower can be spoiled by frost. In fact, it is not quite hardy even in the south of England, and it gives off an unpleasant whiff in muggy weather from the foliage. This is a trait of many viburnums.

Perennials

March is the month not only for early flowers, but also for the first spring greenery. The hedgerows are sprouting with the fresh bright green of the Thorn or May, which along with shoots from other early leafing shrubs tends to make the evergreens appear dull; their seasons are autumn and winter. Soon after Christmas leaves are stirring from colchicums and arums, and by March their precocious, splendid, shining greenery is the brightest leafage in the garden apart from that of *Hemerocallis fulva* and its derivatives. These give us light greenery; *Colchicum speciosum* presents clumps of rich green, luxurious, aspidistra-like blades. Both these and those of *Arum*

italicum 'Marmoratum' ('Pictum') are up early in the year and last well. The latter is a prolific seeder, with many inferior forms arising from the scarlet fruits in late summer. These should be removed as soon as they have changed colour, sad though it may seem, if you want the best marbled leaves to be maintained.

Bergenia × *schmidtii* 'Ernst Schmidt', the earliest of the Megasea Saxifrages, puts up a splendid show of clear pink flower heads over the long-stalked, rounded leaves. (Other bergenias mostly have short stalks.) It was chosen by Miss Jekyll to give form and early colour in the great formal garden at Hestercombe, Somerset.

Crocus tommasinianus is no sooner over than its hybrids, such as 'Vanguard', anticipate the big Dutch crocuses that are planted so lavishly in our parks and gardens. They are descended from *C. vernus*, whose shades of purple may be seen in old gardens, such as Miss Willmott's at Warley, Essex, and at Lacock Abbey, in Wiltshire, where they sheet the ground and seed themselves lavishly. It always seems to me that

TOP: *Bergenia* × *schmidtii* 'Ernst Schmidt'
MIDDLE: *Crocus sieberi*
LEFT: *Crocus tommasinianus*, a reliable February flower

these strains of purple, lilac, striped and white are best on their own. Nobody could contemplate the white, with its dark yellow stigmata, without realising that we are looking at one of the supreme flowers of the year. The yellow Dutch crocus is best kept apart, as an underplanting to *Skimmia* 'Rubella' and red-stemmed dogwoods.

Cyclamen coum glints at us in ruby red, pink and white from the little sombre leaves; then it is the turn of *C. vernum* and others. When established from pot-grown youngsters, not dry corms, all need nothing but a dressing of leafmould and to be left alone to give us annual joy. They grow happily under shrubs and in woodland.

Cyclamen coum

Doronicum 'Miss Mason', a refined and willing daisy, is well worth growing in sun or shade and seemingly in any soil in spite of the March prevalence of yellow from daffodils. The flowers are carried well aloft on good green leaves and are set with beautiful, regular ray-florets.

Erythronium dens-canis, Dog's Tooth Violet, although not related to true violets, is one of the most exquisite of late March flowers. The lily-like nodding starry blooms of lilac-rose are borne just above leaves of soft green marbled with light maroon.

Helleborus argutifolius (*H. corsicus*) is semi-woody, and stems take two years to flower. It is a magnificent plant with a fine mass of prickly, light green leaves over which tower steeples of pale green bells. The plants may reach three feet high and wide in good conditions. *H. lividus* itself is not so tall, nor so hardy, and its scented flowers have a rosy tinge. Hybrids between the Corsican plant and the Majorcan one (*H. lividus*) have been raised (*H. × sternii*), and many are quite hardy. There are also entrancing hybrids with this group and *H. niger*, known collectively as *H. × nigristern*. All together the hellebores present a race of early-flowering, hardy plants, frost-resistant and amenable to most soils; they are particularly happy in sunless places, whether the shade be from trees, shrubs or walls.

Iberis sempervirens in sunny, dry conditions will provide a sheet of white Candytuft flowers over a sprawling, shrub-like plant that is a true evergreen. It lasts many weeks in flower, one of the best forms being known as 'Snowflake'. I like it especially when it is woken up by the brilliant orange red of the prolific *Tulipa praestans*, which reaches barely a foot in height and bears one to three flowers on a stem.

Iris 'Katharine Hodgkin', a small bulbous iris of the reticulata group, is a natural hybrid found by its namesake. It has perky flowers, delicately tinted with blue, green and grey, that open a little later than others of the group.

Lysichiton americanum, the Bog Arum, is often wrongly called Skunk Cabbage, which is a totally different plant. This name does, however, call attention to the heavy smell emitted by the great, stemless clear yellow spathes. If your garden is

ABOVE: *Iberis sempervirens* 'Snowflake'
LEFT: *Lysichiton americanum*, beautiful but offensively scented, is often called (wrongly) Skunk Cabbage.

ABOVE: *Narcissus* 'March Sunshine',
one of the most reliable of
the miniature, early daffodils

RIGHT: *Primula denticulata*

permanently moist, or even boggy, and you are not short of space, try a few plants of this. In *L. camtschatcense* the spathes are pure white, and occasionally creamy white hybrids occur. Each flower lasts about a month, and the white species is sweetly scented, whereas the yellow justifies the appellation of skunk only too well. With the flowers over, gigantic leaves grow up as large as paddles; they are inclined to flop by midsummer and may be relied on to act as efficient ground cover, controlling the coarsest of ditch weeds.

Narcissus obvallaris, the Tenby Daffodil, is a worthy addition to the list of these indispensable bulbous plants. And although they are not closely related to it, I will add the charming cultivars 'Beryl', 'March Sunshine' and 'Piper's Barn'. These bring us into the main mass of hybrids, which are more suited to the public parks and the cut flower trade than they are to decorating those pretty corners of the garden that spring has lightly touched.

Primula denticulata is called the "drumstick primula" on account of its spherical heads of small blooms borne on stout one-foot stems. But to deserve the name it must have good moist soil and some shade for the summer. In the old days the flowers were of cool lavender-blue, but the seedsmen have introduced purple, white and near crimson strains. The form 'Cashmeriana' is even more beautiful because of its powdering of white on the stems and leaves.

P. rosea, also a lover of moist ground, has shocking pink flowers assorting well with the white Bog Arum. It is a small plant that puts up a good show in really moist soil.

P. vulgaris, our native primrose, often opens flowers earlier than other primulas. In the variety *sibthorpii* those flowers may be pink or purple instead of yellow.

Pulsatilla vulgaris, Pasque Flower, used to be called *Anemone pulsatilla* before the botanists changed it on account of the hairy appendages attached to the seeds. By twisting or turning, these long awns help the seeds to enter the soil. It seeds itself freely in light soils. The whole plant is hairy—stems, divided leaves, and the outsides of the flowers. But inside they are smooth, of lilac or rich purplish colouring enhanced by a

TOP: *Narcissus hedraeanthus*
BOTTOM: *Pulsatilla vulgaris,*
Anemone pulsatilla or Pasque Flower,
a British native on chalky hills

boss of yellow stamens. There are many forms and hybrids of the Pasque Flower, including white, red, pink and all shades of purple and violet. Hybridised with related species from Eastern Europe a smaller more nodding flower has emerged in rich reds and wine colours. Once established they should be left alone, for they make deep-questing tap roots.

Symphytum grandiflorum, a relative of the pulmonarias, is ideal for the back of a shrub border in shade. It is a free-spreading ground cover bearing croziers of cream bells for many weeks, the whole not exceeding a foot in height. A little taller are the hybrids known as 'Hidcote Blue' and 'Hidcote Pink'. They completely take care of shady banks, being weed-proof, in that famous garden.

Tulipa kaufmanniana and *T. praestans* are usually the first tulips to appear. The former is available in many surprising colours; the original was creamy yellow, flushed with rose red outside but now, thanks to hybrids with *T. griegii* in red, many shades and combinations of tints are available. *T. griegii* also adds its decisive leaves, striped with maroon, to the general mélange. *T. tarda*, only a few inches high but a lovely thing, has starry white flowers with large yellow centres and looks particularly well with the purple forms of *Pulsatilla vulgaris*. Like the anemone, the tulip seeds itself freely in light soils. Other very early tulips are *T. clusiana* and its variety *chrysantha*, white and yellow respectively, flushed heavily with rose-red outside. They are slim, dainty and suitable for a cosy nook on the rock garden or elsewhere, where they will seed themselves.

Viola hybrids will seemingly grow anywhere, and they make effective ground cover in or out of flower. March is their special month. One can hardly have too many to pick of the common violet in its several purple forms. A pale blue form, which I believe to be Miss Jekyll's 'St Helena', is I find a good and free flowerer. I have not been successful for long with the one called 'Sulphurea', warm yellow, nor with 'Coeur d'Alsace', coral-rose, but the large-flowered light pink 'Rosine' presents no difficulty. What is usually looked upon as a white form of the Common Sweet Violet is no less sweet, but is, I understand, a separate species: *V. odorata*.

OPPOSITE: *Tulipa tarda*, a reliable, freely increasing early-flowering species for sunny positions
BELOW: *Rhododendron* 'Vanessa Pastel', a famous and lovely hybrid with *R. griersonianum* as one parent. It was raised at Bodnant, the garden in North Wales developed by three generations of Aberconways.

SPRING

APRIL

There is a sort of magic in the word April; it conjures up 'shoures sote' (showers sweet), according to Chaucer, the incidence of Easter, and the increasing warmth of the sun. Robert Bridges wrote:

> Wanton with long delay the gay spring leaping cometh,
> The blackthorn starreth now her bough on the eve of May.

Very often the Blackthorn's bloom coincides with bitterly cold weather and east winds, which make us realise we are not yet free of winter. The Blackthorn is, as its name suggests, a dark-twigged, large, suckering shrub. It has been preceded by wild plums, such as Myrobella (or Myrobalan) and Bullace, which are often mistaken for *Prunus spinosa* or Blackthorn.

Trees

Acer platanoides, Norway Maple, is one of the largest trees in these pages and has a clean and lovely growth with excellent autumn colour. Looking aloft this month, we are likely to see its pale greeny yellow tassels. The coppery purple forms, such as

Magnolia × soulangeana, perhaps the most popular of all magnolias and a reliable flowerer

'Crimson King', are also good in autumn; their flowers are tinted with warmer colours than those of the type species.

Other large trees to be noted are some of the most precocious of *Magnolia* species. One needs to go to the Cornish gardens to see them at their best, though the Savill Garden at Windsor and some Sussex gardens also are good homes for them. To look up to a tree in full flower, of such as *M. campbelli* in rosy pink, and its white form a little later, are well worth a long journey to see—great goblets are poised on the bare branches. With them, but usually later, are such equally famous species as *M. mollicomata, sargentiana* and *sprengeri.* Many hybrids and forms have been raised, some even of a rich plum tint. But they are for large gardens; small spaces are best furnished with one or another of the following:

M. conspicua (*M. heptapeta*) is snowy white, every flower a globe of simple purity.

M. kobus, a Japanese treasure, has, like most magnolias, a subtle fragrance. It will quickly make a slender tree, but do not expect it to flower early in its life if raised from seed.

LEFT: *Magnolia stellata*
'Waterlily', one of the
best forms of this species
BELOW: *Magnolia × soulangeana*

M. × *soulangeana*, a hybrid between *M. liliiflora* and *M. conspicua*, is the most frequently seen of magnolias. Over the south of England at least, it is a prominent free-flowering shrub of large size, the flowers being white, warmly flushed with rose. My favourite of the many named forms is 'Rustica Rubra'; they are all lovely, but often expand their flowers immediately before the arrival of the Blackthorn Winter, with dire results. As a group, magnolias also excel in fine large leaves, except *M. kobus* and *M. stellata*. They thrive best in deep loamy soil and are not so much at home in chalk.

M. *stellata* and its pink form are much smaller, though I have stood in the shade of venerable specimens in old gardens. It is generally considered that this is a free-flowering dwarf descended from *M. kobus*.

COMING DOWN IN SCALE

Amelanchier lamarckii, a small flowering tree with splendid autumn colour as well, is probably the best Mespilus. I prefer it grown as a large shrub, but it is also quite acceptable when trained to one stem. The little sprays of white flowers are borne amid pink-tinted young foliage. While many of the cherries have some autumn colour, they are beaten in that respect by this native of North America, a lover of sandy soils.

Paulownia fargesii, a tree quite on its own, is, I think, generally more satisfactory than the better known *P. imperialis*. They are both natives of Western China, and in a mild spring the furry brown buds, held through the winter, open into foxglove-like bells of lilac-blue. There is nothing like it. Even when the flowers have fallen, their sweet scent is wafted abroad. The immense leaves can be a talking point in summer, but beware—it is a fast and furious grower.

Prunus 'Accolade', one of the most elegant of hybrid cherries, is a small arching tree with light pink flowers.

P. 'Amanogawa', a fastigiate Japanese variety with double blush pink flowers, grows slenderly for a number of years and then opens out into a rather ugly, loose tree. There is a weeping variety as well, 'Kiku-Shidara-Sakura', whose large double pink flowers are rather dull. It is nearly always grafted on the top of a straight stem.

P. avium, the Gean or Wild Cherry, is a quick-growing, tall tree. Its double variety, 'Pleno', is of wondrous beauty, but is not suitable for assorting with other flowering cherries because of its size in maturity.

P. 'Kanzan' flowers well into the cherry season. This most popular of Japanese cherries has been propagated by nurseries as a best-seller for many years, and there must be as many examples of this tree about the country as of all other Japanese cherries put together. It is always—I stress the word—very free-flowering and there are about two days in every spring when its joyous plenitude of large pink blossoms delights us all. Then the foliage grows and loses its warm tint, and much of the beauty is gone. Before falling, the flowers fade and a poor colour is evident. Less vigorous and rather later is the old variety 'Fugenzo', with flowers of a better pink, though less luxurious. The scented single white 'Jo-nioi' flowers with it.

P. 'Okumiyako' (*P. serrulata longipes*) is the gem of the Japanese cherries, whose double flowers hang in lacy bunches opening blush white and turning to pure white. It is a miracle of beauty in many ways and not over-vigorous.

P. sargentii, as large a tree as *P. yedoensis* mentioned in March, has single pink flowers in abundance, followed by coppery tinted young foliage. The tree is one of the first to colour scarlet in autumn.

P. 'Shirotae', a double of snowy purity, green leaves, and rather horizontal branching, is more suitable for small gardens than is *P. avium*, mentioned above.

P. 'Tai Haku' is more upright, with warm white flowers and tinted foliage.

ABOVE: *Prunus davidiana*

OPPOSITE: The bark of *Prunus serrula*, itself a fine ornament

Iris unguicularis (TOP RIGHT) and
'Mary Barnard', and *Prunus mume*
'Omoi-no-mama', three beautiful,
scented, late winter flowers

As the cherries come and go, there is the other pageant to watch—that of the crab apples, or *Malus*. They create a froth of scented blossom, and one of the first to flower is *M. × purpurea*, which brings the first dark, rich flower colour to our garden trees. I prefer its seedling, *M.* 'Lemoinei', which is of richer, cleaner colour. When thinking of these and their relatives, we must remember that they are smaller than the cherries and also lack the characterful thrust of branches, making as they do a less interesting outline. They have other assets and disadvantages. These dark-flowered varieties have, it is true, dark-coloured crab apples, but their foliage during the summer months is nothing short of dingy. Possibly the most popular is *M. × floribunda*, which never fails to produce an excessive crop of red-budded, small white flowers among green leaves. It is a wide-spreading tree, but like all apples, withstands hard pruning in late summer. I once saw two trees pruned to beehive shapes that were spectacular in flower. The variety × *atrosanguinea* is a richer colour, but can we really claim that any flowering tree exceeds in beauty well-tinted apples such as 'Sunset', 'Arthur Turner' or 'Lord Derby'? Here we have good fragrance without stint and the promise of luscious fruit later. On the whole, from a garden point of view I think I prefer the fruiting crab apples such as 'Dartmouth', semi-weeping, with white, blush-tipped flowers and good-sized, round red fruits. 'John Downie' is another famous variety with a similar beauty in flower, pointed fruits and an upright habit. 'Red Sentinel' and the weeping 'Red Jade' are equalled in beauty by 'Golden Hornet'. But I am letting my imagination run away to autumn. They all have white or pinkish flowers and all make good small trees except the renowned 'Golden Hornet', which takes some time to make a balanced head.

Climbers

Clematis alpina and *C. macropetala*, less vigorous than *C. montana* and suitable for restricted positions, both flower well in spring and often produce scattered flowers later. The former may be described as single- and the latter as double-flowered, but they have some similarity in the colours of the flowers, being available in clear lavender blue, soft pink, white and other shades. I will leave you to find out the names from the lists; all are supremely beautiful and they will thrive in almost any position. They are indeed invaluable for adding early colour on a wall, fence or pergola. They have special uses for covering the bases of gawky shrubs and climbers that have run aloft.

C. armandii, an evergreen and truly vigorous clematis, has large, dark and shining leaves, and the new season's shoots will often exceed six feet (1.8 m) in length. It is best to let them ramble at will; I have found that wayward shoots resent being trained upwards and tend to die back. With the background of dark leaves, the masses of single white scented flowers with their conspicuous creamy stamens are startlingly beautiful. A noted variety is 'Apple Blossom', in which the buds are touched with pink.

C. cirrhosa, its variety *balearica* and the newer 'Freckles' have, during mild spells, given us pleasure from December onwards, but frequently delay the main display until April.

C. montana has white flowers delightfully vanilla scented, but it is a rampageous grower, only to be reduced immediately after flowering if necessary. Delicately pink and also scented are *rubens* and 'Elizabeth', darker is 'Tetrarose', while the variety *wilsonii* does not make such a notable spring display but continues to produce white flowers into the summer months.

BELOW LEFT: *Clematis cirrhosa balearica*
BELOW RIGHT: *Clematis armandii* 'Apple Blossom'

Coloured Leaves

Berberis thunbergii 'Atropurpurea Nana', the bigger *B. thunbergii* 'Atropurpurea' and still larger *B. × ottawensis* 'Superba' are all coppery purple shrubs whose leaves are in complete contrast to April's many fresh greens.

Euonymus fortunei towards the end of the month gives bright tints of yellow and cream in the leaves of variegated varieties such as 'Silver Queen', 'Emerald 'n' Gold' and 'Emerald Gaiety'.

Photinia × fraseri 'Red Robin' is one of the best of the evergreen photinias, many of which produce glistening young foliage in almost ruby red.

Ribes sanguineum 'Brocklebankii' and *Philadelphus coronarius* 'Aureus' have yellow-flushed leaves that are conspicuous through April and May and then begin to fade, or turn greenish.

Rosa hybrids, especially certain modern roses such as 'The Times', 'Climbing Mrs Sam McGredy' and 'Marlena' have some of the darkest, most sumptuous foliage. A visit to the Gardens of the Rose at St Albans makes a good introduction to the value of these dusky tints, rather neglected in our garden scheming.

OPPOSITE: Camellias and rhododendrons in the Savill Gardens, Windsor
BELOW: *Rhododendron* 'Seta'

Camellias and Rhododendrons

While varieties of *Camellia japonica* have been popular in our gardens since they were found to be hardy, they are all shining evergreens of the heaviest calibre. To my mind, the lighter colours—the pinks and whites—are more acceptable against the dark rich greenery, for the reds are almost too heavy by contrast, especially early in the year. There are several lovely singles, whose stamens make a projecting central collar above the petals. These can hardly be beaten for beauty, though those with petaloid stamens run them very close. Then there are those with short petals in the centre, and also the fully double ones. The selection is bewildering, with flowers in every colour from white to red, including some that are striped. The list is already too long, and we must also consider dissimilarity of growth: the bushy, the drooping and the upright. I have mentioned in previous chapters my preference for the graceful *C. × williamsii* hybrids over the *C. japonica* kinds, so I will limit myself here to naming only the cultivar 'Winton'—as far from *C. japonica* as it could get, being a hybrid between *C. cuspidata* and *C. × williamsii*. It has an open graceful growth and shuttlecock-shaped blooms of palest pink.

Having suffered a surfeit of yellow from daffodils, I welcome especially the range of near blues in the early rhododendrons. I am thinking especially of 'Blue Tit' and 'Bluebird' (whose young foliage is pleasantly yellowish); the taller 'Blue Diamond'; purple *Rhododendron russatum*; delicately tinted *R. augustinii*; *R. hippophaeoides*; and a hybrid of *R. campanulatum*, my own much larger 'Graham Thomas', a treasure to be marked that does well in my garden. It inherits the rusty back to the leaves of its parent, and the flowers, rich vinous purple on opening fading to warm amethyst-lilac, are of good size. It was raised by Gomer Waterer at Knap Hill Nursery, and named

for me by his son, Donald. Early dwarf pinks are *R. racemosum* and 'Pink Drift'. There is a whole range of bell-shaped flowers in *R. cinnabarinum* and its relatives, which usually take us into May. *R. repens* hybrids such as 'Elizabeth' bring gorgeous reds to low plants while towering above them are *R. arboreum* in blood-red and pink. Delicate blush on large shrubs is found in 'Carex' and 'Carita', and at the end of the month we may expect the lovely clear yellow bells of 'Damaris Logan' after being introduced to this colour by little 'Chikor' and 'Chink'.

Other Shrubs

Rhododendron 'Graham Thomas'

Andromeda polifolia is one of the most exquisite of small plants for peaty soils. Even the most phlegmatic mortal could hardly remain unmoved by the little pink bells hung over the rolled, narrow leaves on this little Ericaceous shrub.

Cytisus × beanii deserves a word of praise, for it is one of the first brooms to flower. It makes a splash of bright yellow over a few weeks from a low bush suitable for rock garden or ground cover.

Daphne blagayana is a gem, bearing creamy white, scented flower heads on a nearly prostrate bush. It seems to thrive best when its twigs are weighed down with large stones, but I have never been able to keep it flourishing for long.

D. × burkwoodii is one of the most satisfactory daphnes, with pinky-white flowers and a good scent.

D. × napolitana grew to a great size with me and then succumbed to old age, which commonly happens with many daphnes. They are, however, worth a lot of trouble but do not usually need it.

D. odora, *D. tangutica* and *D. mezereum*, now going over, are indispensable for the far-reaching scent from their tiny blooms.

Fothergilla major and its relatives, so showy when capped with bottlebrushes of pure white stamens, are plants for moist, lime-free soil. They are invaluable too for autumn colour.

Kerria japonica, especially in its lanky, invasive, double form, I at one time positively disliked. But if we can forgive its wayward habit, its flowers are wonderfully soft orange, a scarce colour at any time. Less invasive and a lot shorter is *K. japonica* 'Golden Guinea', a single of undoubted charm. The variegated form of the species, 'Picta' ('Variegata'), is a pleasing variant, very beautiful in its summer growth. They have no scent.

Mahonia aquifolium, Oregon Grape, may be found in most gardens, sown by birds attracted in summer to its nearly black, bloomy berries. These are good as a substitute for blackcurrants in making a piquant jelly. Its bunches of bright yellow, small, scented flowers are very cheering. There are several forms and hybrids of excellence such as 'Apollo' and 'Atropurpurea'. So valuable for their handsome evergreen foliage, pinnate and shiny, all are equally as garden worthy as viburnums, although I understand that in some parts of the world, seedlings escaping from gardens have formed unwelcome thickets of growth in the wild.

M. japonica, with handsome, prickly leaves, will still be spreading fragrance from its yellow flowers as late as April.

Two deliciously scented shrubs:
ABOVE: *Daphne odora*,
a low evergreen
BELOW: *Mahonia japonica*,
a large shrub, wonderful
in every way—foliage,
flower and fragrance—
that thrives in shade

Daphne laureola, a low
shrub, a study in green

M. × *wagneri* 'Undulata' is a fine erect shrub achieving six to seven feet (1.8–2.2 m), with extra good glossy leaves and plentiful flowers, but it does not bear berries. *M.* × *wagneri* 'Moseri' is compact in growth and showy in its yellow flowers and foliage of pale yellow turning to coral.

Osmanthus delavayi is one of the choicest shrubs ever to come out of China. It is attractive through the year because of its small round leaves in darkest green. Against these, the multitudinous little white trumpet flowers held in bunches, and with a sweet, delicate scent, have the ideal setting. A hybrid, *O.* × *burkwoodii* (at one time called *Osmarea* × *burkwoodii*), though more vigorous, hardier and earlier, has not the quality of *Osmanthus delavayi*. The only trouble to us gardeners is that this species is very slow growing to start with, but eventually it makes a large bush.

Paeonia delavayi, whose shining dark red flowers are half-hidden in the foliage, quickly makes a big gaunt shrub. Its flowers are soon over, but the blue-green, fingered leaves remain an asset through the season.

Prunus tenella, dwarf Russian Almond, of which the form 'Fire Hill' is the most desirable, is for a brief two weeks in spring one of the brightest of garden plants, seldom attaining more than three feet (0.9 m). Unfortunately, if on its own roots, it is of a wandering nature.

Rosmarinus officinalis, Rosemary, is another good evergreen that I should not like to be without. I keep a plant in a sunny position near the garden door where it is handy for use in the kitchen. There are several forms with flowers of dark or light blue; as a general rule, the dark blues are less hardy than the pale ones. I grow 'Sissinghurst Blue', which is good and hardy, having originated as a self-sown seedling in that famous garden.

Salix hastata 'Wehrhahnii', a willow of considerable beauty, is a fairly upright shrub not distinguished by handsome foliage later, but wonderful in early spring in its silvery white catkins turning to yellow.

S. lanata 'Stuartii' is not only conspicuous in a similar way at flowering time, but has handsome, rounded grey leaves and is not without beauty from its twigs and buds even in winter. It makes a low spreading shrub and, like the other, needs damp soil.

Spiraea thunbergii is scarcely past its best before *S. arguta* in a similarly pure white takes over, with wiry sprays studded with tiny flowers. *S.* × *vanhouttei* is larger and later. These are unfussy plants able to thrive anywhere.

Viburnums

It would be difficult to fill a garden of some size without including at least one representative of the genus *Viburnum*. Between the many species, they contribute to the garden at all seasons as evergreen and deciduous shrubs with excellence in leaf and autumn colour, flower and fruit in one season after another. We have already looked at *V. tinus* (Laurustinus) and we should keep in mind that the offensive smell of the shrub, especially on a moist day after frost damage, is found in a number of species, so it is well to place them away from the house and from sitting places. Fortunately, the old favourite, *V. carlesii*, and its forms and hybrids do not have this defect.

Soon after the daffodils are past their peak, the flowers may be expected on small viburnums—bunches of white, pink-touched in the bud, beckoning with a ravishing scent not unlike that of clove pinks. *V. carlesii* itself, though very beautiful in flower and in dark autumn leaf colour, is prone to black aphides and I think should give way to 'Fulbrook', a hybrid with the species *V. bitchiuense*. It is a similar and more graceful shrub with equal fragrance; it is as well to pinch out the tips of leading,

Viburnum carlesii with *V.* × *burkwoodii* beyond, both well scented

leafy shoots of young plants to make them more bushy. 'Juddii' is another good hybrid from America and does not suffer from aphides. Apart from several named forms of the original *V. carlesii*, some, like 'Aurora', with crimson buds, there are also the two hybrids with the evergreen *V. utile*, *V. × burkwoodii* and its subsidiary, 'Park Farm Hybrid', both raised by Mr Burkwood. Of the two I prefer the second; it is rather more graceful and pink in the bud, though neither has quite the scent of *V. carlesii*.

Two very early flowering species with rounded heads of tiny creamy flowers are *V. furcatum* and *V. lantanoides* (*V. alnifolium* of gardens). Both have large rounded leaves, resplendent in autumn colour. While *V. lantanoides* is a very vigorous spreading bush, *V. furcatum* is a good, compact garden shrub.

Perennials

Hepatica transsilvanica

Anemone nemorosa, Wood Anemone, is a native of many European countries, including Britain, and I know few more rewarding little plants. They take two or three years to get thoroughly established and then run with a will, threading through the ground under shrubs or indeed in almost any position and soil. Each little bloom has a long life, about a month, and they may be white or touched with pink or some shade of mauve or blue. All are charming, and there are two doubles, 'Vestal', with its centre densely packed with small segments and another equally double with a blue eye. As a tribe, they have undoubted charm. *A. apennina* and *A. blanda* are other good blue-flowered anemones that please greatly in my spring garden. The first has a good white variety, but the latter is available in white and cerise, in various tones, 'White Splendour' being especially good. They revel in limy soil in almost any position and, when suited, seed about and increase freely. Much larger and a little later is *A. coronaria*, with parsley leaves and flowers of brilliant colouring red, pink, purple, almost blue and cream, and all are offset by central stamens of bluish tint. They also increase freely in stiff limy soil in sunny dry positions and will even seed themselves in turf. They have a long flowering period extending into May.

Bergenia ciliata, perhaps the handsomest of Megasea saxifrages, has large hairy foliage and white flowers from ruddy calyces, but is not to be trusted in cold gardens.

LEFT: *Bergenia* 'Sunningdale'

BELOW: *Petasites fragrans*, an arrant spreader for waste places, but richly fragrant

B. cordifolia 'Purpurea' takes some beating for foliage effect, and its tall red stems develop branching heads of magenta flowers. As are most bergenias, it is a *par excellence* noble-leafed ground cover and the one least maligned by those who deride them as "elephant's ears".

B. crassifolia is less cabbagy, with lilac-pink flowers.

B. purpurascens, noted for its dark purplish red leaf-colour, is gorgeous red at the back. It has tall red stems and magenta flowers but, its leaf blades being held erect, it is not so satisfactory as a ground cover as the others.

B. stracheyi has quite small leaves; the flowers may be pink or white.

Bergenia hybrids: One of the most splendid is 'Ballawley' with extra large leaves. 'Eric Smith', 'Margery Fish' and 'Sunningdale' are all good, but a special prize must be reserved for 'Morgenröte', which has the invaluable asset of producing a second crop of flowers in June. For a tall white, I pick 'Silberlicht', and for a clear pink I like 'Rose Klose'. In shady positions they remain green throughout the year, but in full exposure usually develop in winter-rich, burnished leaf colour, red at the back, particularly noticeable in 'Sunningdale'.

Cardamine pentaphyllos and *C. heptaphylla* are two more of the garden toys that gladden our eyes in the early year. The former is short with lilac flowers, the latter a good upstanding plant with white flowers in short spikes. Some of the cardamines are arrant spreaders and should be avoided. But these two, which used to be called *Dentaria*, are good stay-at-homes. They thrive anywhere except in dry ground and appreciate some shade.

Chionodoxa forbesii (*C. luciliae*) is taller than *C. sardensis*, with larger white centres to the somewhat paler blue flowers. It spreads just as freely from seeds. There are pink and also white forms, and a larger-flowered one now labelled *C. luciliae gigantea*. Though it has larger flowers, it bears fewer on the stem, and they are of lilac-tinted blue.

Chionodoxa sardensis has the best blue effect among the chionodoxas, collectively known as Glory of the Snow. It has a small white centre to the starry flowers, produced six or more at a time on the stems of five inches (13 cm) or so. Like scillas, they have two dark green leaves.

× *Chionoscilla allenii*, a bigeneric hybrid, is a real startler of bright cobalt blue with no white centre. It does not spread by seeds and pays for division every few years.

Narcissus from Christmas until mid May: 'Jana' in January–February (TOP LEFT), 'Folly' in April (TOP RIGHT), 'Cedric Morris' in December (BOTTOM LEFT) and *poeticus* var. *recurvus* in May (BOTTOM RIGHT)

DAFFODILS

April is the main month for daffodils. We looked at a few in March, and to my mind nothing surpasses those early ones. Mainly before us in April are the multi-coloured hybrids, so popular these days with the municipal authorities. There are flowers with big trumpets, wholly yellow or delectably near-white; there are short trumpets of yellow, pink or white; and small cupped varieties which we call "narcissi" (though all daffodils belong botanically to the genus *Narcissus*). Many of these have a rim of orange-red to their cups; in fact, the diversity of colours is extraordinary. It has all been brought about by hybridising the yellow trumpets with *N. ornatus* and other species. And all have strong, upstanding stems and good foliage. But I question whether they are suitable for naturalising in grass. Surely their place is in the formal garden or the kitchen garden from where they can be cut for the house. I do not think that Shakespeare or Wordsworth would have been inspired to write their immortal couplets after contemplating an array of these modern grandifloras. Their words were wrung forth by the meek Lent Lily, *N. pseudonarcissus*.

Doronicum 'Excelsum', following on from 'Miss Mason' in March, provides the best bright yellow daisies of all. Many other selections from *D. carpetanum* and *D. pardalianches* add to the collection, so we need not look far for this colour. And they are all easy growers.

EPIMEDIUMS

It always amazes me what imperturbable plants the epimediums are. In heavy or light soil, in sun or preferably in shade, these worthy ground coverers are lastingly at home and no weeds penetrate them. Some of the most successful are *Epimedium perralderianum* and its hybrid with *E. pinnatum colchicum*: *E. × perralchicum*. Leafy plants with a variety of tints at each end of the year, their thick verdure is decked with airy flights of bright yellow small flowers for weeks. Their enemy is spring frost, which will destroy all buds and blooms. Some gardeners cut down the foliage in February to make way for the flowers. This is more desirable with *E. grandiflorum* 'Rose Queen' and *E. rubrum*, and also with *E. × versicolor* 'Sulphureum', whose foliage is not so evergreen as those above. These all run through the soft colours, but *E. × warleyense* is orange red and not so dense growing. There are several new Chinese species becoming known and grown, but these must wait for another chapter or book.

ERYTHRONIUMS

Some of the most exquisite flowers of the whole year are found among the American species of *Erythronium*, so misleadingly called Dog's Tooth Violet. They do not resemble violets, nor are they related to them, but are members of the Lily Family. The name of Dog's Tooth refers to the shape of the corm or tuber. Their other name of Trout Lily is readily understood on looking at the (usually) marbled leaves of which there are two for each flower stem. Two or three flowers are poised on thin stalks well above the foliage. They resemble a Turk's Cap Lily in their nodding way, with finely drawn, recurving, pointed segments with stamens dangling

ABOVE: *Adonis volgensis*, bright yellow and parsley-green
BELOW: *Erythronium revolutum*, a real gem of spring

Erythronium
'White Beauty'

below. Two very early ones (following on from *E. dens-canis* from March) are *E. citrinum* and *E. californicum* in creamy yellows. Then go to the Savill Garden in Windsor Great Park to see the rose-pink *E. revolutum* in their thousands. Look carefully and you will see also another gem, *E. hendersonii* in palest mauve with a dark eye. Hybridists have been busy and there are two good soft yellow ones, 'Pagoda' and 'Kondo', of great vigour and beauty. They inherit their vigour from the yellow *E. tuolumnense*; this species has also shown the need of dividing the congested clumps after flowering. They all seem to thrive in lime-free, sandy, damp soil in part shade. 'White Beauty' is classed as a form of *Erythronium oregonum* and is a first-rate garden plant.

Euphorbia robbiae and *E. myrsinites*, two splendid evergreens, bring us yellow tints muted by green. But beware of the former; it is a ready spreader and will infiltrate the densest of other plants and shrubs. It may, however, be forgiven this trait for the perennial beauty of its handsome dark green leaf-rosettes, above which are poised in the early year the slender spires of greeny yellow stars. *E. myrsinites* is quite different, though of equally perennial attraction. Its stems are procumbent, clad neatly in small glaucous leaves, each ending in a head of greeny yellow blooms. As they age and turn to seed pods, they develop pink tinges, at which time the new season's trail is advancing. My third, *E. polychroma*, is bright, unalloyed yellow, and quite deciduous, arising afresh every spring to a foot or more and lasting, like the others, for an astonishing time in beauty. But I avoid *E. cyparissias*; although lovely in flower and autumn colour, it is a rapid spreader.

FRITILLARIAS

There comes a time, usually in late April, when, confronted by a Crown Imperial, we realise that this is the tallest plant that has grown up from the soil in the spring weeks. It gladdened the eyes of John Parkinson prior to 1629, so that he placed it foremost in his great book *Paradisi in Sole Paradisus Terrestris*. There is something infinitely imposing in its ruff of green leaves supporting a naked stem atop which, some three feet (0.9 m) from the ground, are hung the floral bells in yellow or shades of brick red and orange, crowned with a further tuft of leaves. Inside the bells are large drops of sweet liquid. This is *Fritillaria imperialis*, a native of the Himalaya. A close relative, though not as imposing, is *F. raddeana*,

Fritillaria imperialis

with greenish-yellow bells. With the special exception of the Crown Imperial, the fritillarias are mostly of rather subdued colouring. But this should not prevent us from enjoying the murrey-coloured bells borne all up the tall stems of *F. persica*, in which we have an especially good form in 'Adiyaman'. And we must not forget our own native *F. meleagris*, the Snakeshead Lily, in chequered chocolate or white. *F. pallidiflora* and *F. verticillata* charm in greeny cream. They all seem to grow best in a stiff, but well-drained, limy soil in sun.

Iris hybrids, the bearded kinds, are making themselves felt with their striking vertical grey-green leaves. They are mainly the dwarf and intermediate ones at present, giving us a foretaste of the glories of May and June, when the magnificent tall bearded irises reach their peak at the crown of the year.

RIGHT: *Fritillaria meleagris* prefers a heavy, limy soil, where it will seed itself freely.
BELOW: *Primula vulgaris*, the common Primrose, a wonderful April flower that seeds itself freely in cool gardens

Muscari moschatum, among the last of the blue spring bulbs to go over, lingers in rich blue, or creamy yellow, with a ravishing scent.

Oxalis acetosella (Wood Sorrel), a pretty little native spring flowerer in pearly white, is charming grown under shrubs; there is a pleasing pink variety and also a larger species from North America, *O. oregana*, with rich rose flowers. All three will thread their way among other plants in part shade.

PRIMROSES

April is undoubtedly the month for primroses. They seed themselves with abandon and nearly always in the least expected places. But they are never in the way, giving us a mental uplift and a promise that spring is really here. Nothing to my mind exceeds the beauty of the cool yellow of the common species *Primula acaulis*, though one can have great joy from a bunch of mixed colours—lilac, blue, purplish reds and creamy pinks. They all seed themselves with abandon, I find, except the true blues, which need nurturing. Some of the reddish colours approach *P. × juliana* and 'Wanda'. The Garryarde strain of primroses tends to have coppery foliage and is the more remarkable for it; their floral colours are intriguing. Then there are the wonderful auriculas with their velvet colours, pasty faces and, I may add, lovely fragrance. They need heavier soil than mine. The 'bunch flowered primroses' or polyanthuses are perfect for lasting spring bedding (extending into May), but excepting the attraction of their warm scent, I find I can do without them.

Primula 'Wanda', a good, short, free-flowering hybrid in rich crimson-purple

Ranunculus constantinopolitanus 'Plenus' (*R. speciosus plenus*), a lovely large double buttercup, is a good hearty plant for a damp position, and of course for really wet conditions there are the calthas or marsh marigolds. The usual species, *Caltha palustris*, is a magnificent plant when doing well. In the form 'Flore Pleno', the segments are doubled very fully, making a brilliant blob of yellow. This is the best species for smaller gardens, while *C. polypetala* is a rampageous spreader with the same lovely big leaves and yellow flowers. I have not much use for the white flowered species.

ABOVE: *Scilla sibirica*

RIGHT: *Caltha palustris*,
Marsh Marigold

Scilla sibirica continues the season begun in March, in which we rejoice in the yellow of daffodils accompanied by the blue of scillas. We looked then at *Scilla bifolia praecox*, and there is also the normal blue to follow, with 'Rosea', a subdued pale pink. Now we have the normal short blue *S. sibirica*, quickly followed by 'Spring Beauty'. This is a splendid selection rising to six to eight inches (16–20 cm), and each bulb produces more than one stem. The colour, rich ultramarine blue, can be the most satisfying thing in the garden. It is the queen of the tribe, an opinion shared, unfortunately, by birds, some of which tend to peck the flowers. But they thrive and increase mightily. *Scilla messeniaca*, a little free-spreader in cool blue, brings up the rear.

TRILLIUMS

In the shade under shrubs, if you have no woodland, there are few plants to equal the Wood Lily, or *Trillium* species, natives of North America. The long-lasting flowers of *T. chloropetalum* are usually the first to appear. They are good stalwart perenni-

LEFT: *Trillium grandiflorum*, which thrives in cool, moist, humus-rich soils
ABOVE: *Trillium grandiflorum* 'Roseum' in flower growing with *Dicentra*

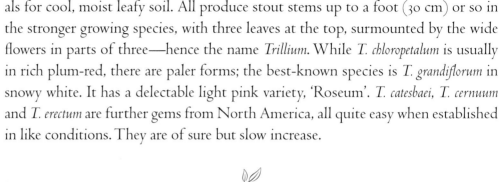

TOP: *Trillium grandiflorum*
'Flore Pleno'

BOTTOM: *Aurinia saxatilis*
'Dudley Neville Variegated'

als for cool, moist leafy soil. All produce stout stems up to a foot (30 cm) or so in the stronger growing species, with three leaves at the top, surmounted by the wide flowers in parts of three—hence the name *Trillium*. While *T. chloropetalum* is usually in rich plum-red, there are paler forms; the best-known species is *T. grandiflorum* in snowy white. It has a delectable light pink variety, 'Roseum'. *T. catesbaei*, *T. cernuum* and *T. erectum* are further gems from North America, all quite easy when established in like conditions. They are of sure but slow increase.

Valeriana phu 'Aurea' also provides a patch of bright yellow, but in its leaves. Later it has heads of small white stars.

Waldsteinia ternata is in effect a shining evergreen strawberry with, for a week or two, particularly bright yellow flowers. In full or part sun, there are few better evergreen carpeters than this. Its relative, *W. geoides*, has hairy leaves, is clump-forming and for a few weeks delights us with small yellow flowers.

Bedding Plants

At the end of April we are of course entering the spring bedding plant season, and wallflowers and double daisies continue to enchant for the coming weeks when the tulips, in great array, encourage us in delicate or rich colour schemes. The good old wallflower with its delicious scent reigns supreme over other bedding plants. But they are having a severe knock from winter-flowering pansies, in season as they are from October onwards, ending the spring with a veritable flush of bloom in all colours. Two special favourites of mine among the rock-garden pansies are 'Hunter-combe Purple', a vibrant, rich colour, and 'Molly Sanderson' in dusky velvet, almost black.

As I have mentioned the rock garden, this is the place to call to mind the usual combination of aubrietas and *Alyssum saxatile*, which has now been rechristened *Aurinia saxatilis*. It is hard to think of a rock garden without these two. The variety of *Aurinia saxatilis* called 'Citrina' is a cool clear colour and is easier for blending with aubrietas as well as alpine phloxes, which flower at the same time. Both make wide, floriferous mats, but the aubrietas last longer in flower than the phloxes. It was something of a shock to me to read in the invaluable *Plant Finder* that *Aubrieta* 'Dr Mules' had received the Award of Garden Merit from the Royal Horticultural Society: it was among the first six rock plants that I purchased as a schoolboy about 1924. This must be something of a record in delayed recognition. Aubrietas are available in purple, lavender, pink and crimson; the phloxes mostly in cooler colours. They all make good edging plants for borders on reasonably light soils. Another plant in the long-ago-purchased half-dozen was *Saxifraga* 'Bathoniensis', a good, crimson, mossy saxifrage. I still grow it. There are many other varieties from white to darkest crimson.

ABOVE: *Aubrieta* flowing
over a low wall
LEFT: *Viola* 'Huntercombe Purple'
BELOW: *Viola* 'Molly Sanderson'

MAY

By early May, half the trees and hedges are partially fledged with young leaves. Our gardens, like the countryside, are then more subtly beautiful than later when fully filled with greenery. To watch a beech hedge first throwing off its old leaves, then elongating its pointed buds and sending forth its silky young leaves is a miracle that rewards a contemplative pause.

Trees

Aesculus × carnea, the Pink Chestnut, serves to remind us of the great Horse Chestnut, *Aesculus hippocastanum*, one of the earliest trees in leaf. It is a monster of a tree, but who is not struck afresh every year by the sight of its candles of white flowers? Sometimes it is planted in a row alternating with the pink one, but the planting carries with it disappointment in time, for the pink hybrid is not nearly so vigorous as *A. hippocastanum*. The best form of this, *Aesculus × carnea*, is the richly coloured 'Briotii'. Do not worry if the trunks of your trees develop cankerous holes; they do not seem to harm the trees.

OPPOSITE: *Prunus subhirtella* 'Pendula'
BELOW: The evergreen shrub *Sycopsis sinensis*, the flowers of which are bunches of colorful stamens enclosed in furry brown scales. A winter flower of some charm, and evergreen

TOP: *Aesculus × carnea*
'Briotti', the Pink Chestnut
BOTTOM: *Crataegus
laevigata* 'Punicea'

Cercis siliquastrum, Judas Tree, has the curious habit of flowering all over young or old branches, straight from the bark. The pea-flowers are of some shade of pink, or white, and give rise to red brown pea pods later. It is a somewhat procumbent tree in old age, and thrives on any well-drained soil in full sun.

CORNELS

We must not overlook the Cornels, despite difficulties in their cultivation. *Cornus nuttallii* is the most imposing, but is not always a success; from observation I would recommend a light, gravelly, lime-free soil. The tall growth, with tabular branches set out with the large, four-bracted white flowers, is very striking in the landscape of the garden.

C. florida, more of a shrub, but often trained as a small tree, is best in its warm pink form 'Rubra'. This also requires lime-free soil and is easy to propagate by layering. 'Eddie's White Wonder', from Canada, is a comparatively new hybrid with *C. nuttallii* that bids fair to become a large and popular tree of well-rounded habit. It is a wonderful sight in flower, the array of branches being smothered with white flowers, each composed of four large bracts. It excels in leaf colour in autumn and seems to thrive in any well-drained soil. A similar plant from the same parents, 'Ormonde', is perhaps less desirable on account of the compact, upright growth of the former.

CRATAEGUS, OR HAWTHORN

"Cast not a clout till May be out" is an old and oft-quoted saying, but a poorly understood one. Does it refer to the month or the tree? The May Tree or Hawthorn (*Crataegus laevigata* and *C. oxyacantha*) is frequently in flower as early as April, and we should find it irksome not to cast a clout in some of the hot spells that occur in May. The snowy flowering of the tree is a welcome sight in the countryside; each flower a perfect array of five white petals, held in loose bunches. It has sported a number of coloured forms such as 'Masekii' in salmon-pink, 'Rosea Flore Pleno' and 'Paul's Scarlet'. All are double-flowered and do not give rise to red haws in autumn. 'Punicea' is a single crimson with a somewhat weeping habit, and there is also a double white, 'Plena'. They are all harbingers of summer fullness and cast a rich, and to some, cloying, scent abroad. They are all apt to be loose-rooted, with the result that they tend to lean with age and are thus not suitable for formal planting. There are innumerable other species, many from America, and among them may be singled out the small-growing *C. laciniata* (*C. orientalis*) with deeply cut leaves, greyish, and large orange-red haws, and the well-known *C. × lavallei* 'Carrierei', whose large white flowers are conspicuous amongst the good broad foliage of darkest green, which does not fall until autumn is well advanced to reveal the large and showy orange-red haws. *C. durobrivensis*, *C. × prunifolia* and *C. crus-galli* are noted for

their wide-awake white flowers and large red haws, also for their large curved prickles. They all have splendid autumn colour. *C. tanacetifolia* is much larger in its characterful growth, greyish leaves and large, edible orange haws, but it is not really a tree for small gardens.

ABOVE: *Crataegus laevigata* 'Paul's Scarlet' and 'Rosea Flore Pleno'
BELOW: *Davidia involucrata*

Davidia vilmoriniana, the queen of all flowering trees at this time of the year, over long observation seems to me to be more resistant to spring frosts than the better-known *D. involucrata*. To stand under one of these trees when hung all along the branches with large white bracts, which earn it the name Handkerchief Tree, is an experience worth a long journey. They grow best in rich deep loam.

Drimys winteri, a native of South America, has many forms and cultivars. They grow best in the milder West and South, on any deep soil, including those over limestone, where they bring the majesty of evergreen trees to our gardens. I hesitate to mention *D. winteri* because those of us in less salubrious climates are denied these splendours. But it is probable that those trees with glaucous undersides to their long leaves are the hardiest, and a few gardeners may like to risk an experiment with them. Those same trees mostly have purer, whiter flowers of starry crystalline quality as well, which may be added encouragement to the adventurous.

Embothrium coccineum, Chilean Fire Bush, has flowers of fierce orange-red that clashes with most other trees and shrubs, leaving me a little diffident in writing about it. There are several at Bodnant, where they have for companions the silvery grey of the Blue Cedar, *Cedrus atlantica* 'Glauca'; elsewhere, but always on lime-free soils, I have seen them toned down with coppery purple foliage. *E. coccineum lanceolatum* 'Norquinco' is about the best one to get.

Halesia carolina (*H. tetraptera*), best known of the aptly named Snowdrop Trees, is seldom seen as a bold tree; rather, it is often a large and wayward shrub. The flowers are outclassed by those of *H. monticola*, which is a more tree-like species, especially lovely in its variety *vestita*; the flowers are creamy white and hung all along the branches, pink-flushed in the form 'Rosea'. To come upon one of these trees a-dangle with "snowdrops" is one of the most appealing sights of the year. They prefer lime-free soils and shelter from winds.

Laburnum vulgare, Golden Chain Tree, usually flowering early in the month, is not really worth a place in our gardens. By waiting until the end of the month, we may have *L. alpinum* and the famous hybrid *L.* × *watereri* 'Vossii', with long, elegant racemes of brighter colour. Laburnums are usually of a rather stiff and upright form, except of course the two weeping varieties. These are, however, forms of *L. vulgare* and not of much account. In my boyhood, before the advent of so many cherries and crabs, it was a fashion to plant the crimson or pink May trees with laburnums. Some gardeners liked the clash of colours. To appreciate to the full the beauty of laburnums, plant them in leafy groves where their growth will be more graceful and their greenish-tinted yellow flowers will merge better with the background. A warm and lovely scent pervades them. There is a curiosity, not particularly beautiful but a great talking point, in + *Laburnocytisus adamii*. This originated as a graft hybrid, the result of grafting the mauve-pink little shrub *Cytisus purpureus* onto rootstock of *Laburnum vulgare*. The strange result is a tree bearing not only yellow laburnum flowers, but also tufts of the mauve cytisus and intermediates.

Magnolia veitchii, of rapid growth and great size, echoes the beauty of the tree magnolias referred to in April. Its large flowers are of rosy white, and it has very fine foliage as befits so large a tree. Much smaller is *M. liliiflora*, whose wine-pink flowers rejoice us when all the Soulangiana varieties are over.

Malus hupehensis, one of the few flowering crab apples blooming into May, is a smother of scented pure white flowers. And in autumn, there are small red fruits. It is a fairly large tree as crabs go.

Embothrium coccineum 'Norquinco'

ABOVE: *Halesia carolina*
RIGHT: *Halesia monticola* 'Rosea'.
While the former is usually
a shrubby tree, the latter achieves
real tree-like proportion.
Both are best on lime-free soil.

ABOVE: *Magnolia liliiflora*

RIGHT: *Malus hupehensis*, one of
the last crab apples to flower

Malus ioensis 'Plena'

M. ioensis 'Plena', even later, is semi-double, with rather globular, blush pink flowers as fragrant as a bunch of violets. It does not thrive everywhere; the best tree I know is on limy gravelly soil. A larger, more vigorous version is *M.* 'Charlottae', also with semi-double pink flowers, but they are not produced freely until the tree is of some size.

Prunus cerasus, Morello Cherry, in the form 'Rhexii', has extremely neat, very double, white blooms appearing when all others are over. The Morello itself is single-flowered and, of course, highly esteemed for its fruit, but I often wonder whether we are not neglecting it as an ornamental tree. I know of few plants of any kind that have flowers of such a cold pure white.

P. serrulata 'Albo Plena' is quite different from the Morello, although in the same season is regaling us with its double white flowers borne thickly along the nearly horizontal branches. It is a wide-spreading, low tree of great character.

Salix triandra, a little-known native willow, has conspicuous, very fragrant yellow catkins. As its leaves are not without beauty and hang on long into the autumn, it is worthy of more than a glance. It is, however, a flowering tree or large shrub, eminent among willows, and easy to strike from hardwood cuttings in winter.

Tilia oliveri: among our greater trees only the Lime, or Linden, equals the beech in early beauty, and of the many limes none to me equals the appeal of zig-zag, velvety shoots hung so lavishly with cool shining green leaves, white beneath, as seen in *T. oliveri*. Though not overlarge as limes go, it is rather beyond the space available in the average garden. We should be better advised to plant *T. chinensis*—similar in beauty and often with the luxury of rosy bracts.

Trees for Foliage

The list of flowering trees about exhausts the subject for May, but in this month especially, foliage is much to the fore. There are few flowering trees to rival the two Sycamore variants, *Acer pseudoplatanus* 'Brilliantissimum' and 'Prinz Handjery'; in the former, of very slow growth, the young foliage is a brilliant shrimp-pink, and in the latter rather darker. Both lose their colour as summer advances, turning to light green. It is an exception to see either over twenty-five feet (7.5 m) in height. Rivaling them in early colour is the remarkable Chestnut, *Aesculus neglecta* 'Erythroblastos', again a bright shining pink in spring turning to pale green. It is also a slow grower and thus may, with discretion, be planted in small gardens.

One of the most popular of trees for gardens large and small is the Willow-leafed Pear, *Pyrus salicifolia* 'Pendula'. There is an upright *P. salicifolia*, an example of which I once saw in a garden in Ireland, but, strangely, only the weeping form is generally seen. The weeping habit is really its undoing, for it develops into a dense, shapeless mass. Its silvery, narrow leaves and plenteous white flowers endear it to all of us, but if you want to see it at its best, be hard hearted with the pruners. Keep cutting away all the shoots and branches under the head. The result will be a much taller tree in time with a unique line and deportment. A much larger tree of similar leaf colour in spring is *Sorbus aria* 'Lutescens', whose budding

ABOVE: *Acer pseudoplatanus* 'Brilliantissimum', a compact small tree
RIGHT: *Pyrus salicifolia* 'Pendula', with *Acer pseudoplatanus* 'Brilliantissimum' beyond, at Knightshayes Court, Devon

branches recall a magnolia in early spring, opening out into lovely rounded leaves of pale sulphur grey colouring, gradually becoming more green later. Though often recommended for small gardens, it is not really suitable for them because it is quick growing and can easily reach fifty feet (15 m) in height and two-thirds as wide. I have not seen it in flower; the foliage alone commends it.

Shrubs

Berberis darwinii and its forms and hybrids are difficult to place in gardens. Their hot orange yellow can be upsetting unless given a foil of coppery purple leaves. *B.* × *stenophylla* is graceful and fragrant, and flowers abundantly in a cooler tint; against this is a lack of the blue berries in August that make *B. darwinii* so valuable. 'Irwinii' is another hybrid of this species of fairly compact growth, cooler colour, but no berries. There are some pale yellow species with charming nodding blooms, among which I should select *B. calliantha*, whose dark shining leaves are white beneath, a character which is also found in the compact *B. verruculosa* and its hybrid *B.* × *chenaultii*. But all these are horribly prickly.

CEANOTHUS, THE BLUE-FLOWERED SHRUBS

The so-called California lilacs have nothing to do with *Syringa*, being found under *Ceanothus*, a fact reminding us of the extraordinary confusion there is in the term "blue". There are no blue lilacs, whereas many species and varieties of *Ceanothus* have blue flowers. Coming as they do mostly from California, they are not altogether hardy in Britain, and as a consequence are often given the benefit of a sunny wall. They appear to thrive in any well-drained soil, but preferably not on chalk. Fifty years ago, only a few species appeared in nursery lists, such as *C. dentatus*, *C. floribundus*, 'Russellianus' and 'Veitchianus', and these of doubtful provenance, but they are outclassed by many new hybrids. Already famous among these are 'Concha', 'Cascade', 'Delight', 'Italian Skies', 'Puget Blue' and 'Southmead'. They are all upstanding bushes well suited to wall training. There are some interesting semi-prostrate kinds such as 'Emily Brown' and the paler

Ceanothus 'Cascade', a true-blue evergreen shrub

RIGHT: *Daphne cneorum*
'Eximia' shown life-size
BELOW: *Daphne* ×
burkwoodii 'Somerset'

C. thyrsiflorus repens. These all flower in May or soon after, bringing that rare colour, true blue, to our gardens, though indeed some are richly tinted with purple. These spring-flowering kinds should be pruned, if necessary, immediately the flowers are over. Other sections of the genus will be found under later months.

Choisya ternata is a handsome and popular evergreen for a sheltered spot. The scented white flowers (Mexican Orange is its popular name) look well against the shining, dark green, fragrant leaves, but on the yellow-leafed cultivar 'Sundance', they are lost. As to the new hybrid 'Aztec Pearl', I can see little to recommend it.

Cytisus ardoinii, a diminutive broom in dazzling yellow; the graceful, almost prostrate *C.* × *kewensis* in creamy yellow; the much bigger *C.* × *praecox* 'Warminster' in lemon yellow, as well as its parent, *C. purgans* in bolder yellow, are all to the fore. *Cytisus albus*, the White Spanish Broom, is now correctly labelled *C. multiflorus*. It is a tall shrub with multitudes of small, creamy, warm white flowers. It is a lanky grower and should be hard pruned immediately after flowering. The same treatment should be given to the Warminster Broom.

Daphne cneorum, once displayed in every Chelsea rock garden, suddenly developed a disease and died out. Fortunately, my old friend A. T. Johnson acquired a form of it now known as 'Eximia' from stock collected in the wild, and this is grown widely today. The small green leaves on their low branches can be completely covered with the neat heads of rich pink, tiny flowers, smelling so much like 'Mrs Sinkins' pinks.

D. tangutica, its purplish buds opening into crystalline white flowers with a wonderful scent, does better with me than did *D. × napolitana*. In this and all respects, it is echoed by the much smaller *D. retusa*. 'Somerset', a form of that strong hybrid *D. × burkwoodii*, is a good hearty plant as a rule, and the near-white flowers from pink buds are as prodigal of their scent as the other daphnes.

Deutzia kalmiiflora we may expect to be at its best, although most deutzias belong to the summer months. If thinned after flowering, the result will be a gracefully arching bush heavily hung with small light pink flowers.

Dipelta floribunda, related to the weigelas, is a noble shrub with attractive peeling bark and tubular flowers somewhere between white and pink, with yellow throats.

Enkianthus perulatus is a large, elegant shrub hung with white bell-like flowers, although in others of the genus, the flowers are rosy fawn. All prefer lime-free soils and yield good autumn colour.

Exochorda racemosa, a most graceful, open shrub of some size, decorates every branch with single, snow-white flowers not unlike little roses, which is not altogether surprising since it belongs to the Rose Family. It needs full sun and lime-free soil, but there are several other species of *Exochorda* less particular about soil. Among the hybrids is 'The Bride', a spectacular shrub of spreading, weeping habit which needs a large space unless it be trained on a wall or pergola.

ABOVE: *Clematis* 'Étoile Rose' and *Clematis viticella* 'Plena Elegans'
LEFT: *Exochorda* 'The Bride'

Fabiana imbricata, that strange Chilean shrub so smothered in little white trumpets, and in *F. imbricata violacea* flushed with violet, is, except in very sheltered conditions, best on a warm wall. They have much of the appearance of heather in their tiny leaves.

Genista lydia and *G. pilosa* are two low-growing brooms for this season. The former is captivating in its arching, mound-forming growth and clear yellow pea-flowers. The second is mat-forming with flowers of darker yellow.

Leucothöe davisiae is a good compact evergreen for lime-free soils, its growths capped with racemes of white bells.

TOP: *Paeonia rockii* 'Joseph Rock'
BOTTOM: *Paeonia* 'Souvenir de Maxime Cornu'

L. fontanesiana, whose racemes of creamy bells are hung amongst the handsome leafage, is in complete contrast to the two big heaths of April, *Erica arborea* 'Alpina' and *E. australis*, which will still be in flower. Though good arching evergreens to about three feet (0.9 m) on lime-free soil, their leaves assume rich colours where exposed later in the year. They thrive in shady places.

TREE PEONIES

Among shrubs, only one genus has flowers of a size so spectacular as to allow them to be compared with magnolias and rhododendrons—and that is *Paeonia*. Erroneously called tree peonies, the shrubby species are woody plants making, in time, large bushes. The great flowers of the numerous hybrids raised in China and Japan are fleeting in their season, but we may rely on their good foliage for many months. They thrive in full sun on well-drained soil, even on chalk, and seem impervious to drought. Nomenclature among the numerous hybrids is confused, and I think it best to avoid being dogmatic about them. They come in a wide range of colours, white, pink, purple, murrey, and include as well yellow. Several good yellow-toned varieties have French names, such as 'L'Espérance' (one of the best) and 'Souvenir de Maxime Cornu' with 'Madame Louis Henri' in copper colour. The yellows owe their tint to *P. lutea*, a Chinese species of which *P. lutea ludlowii* is the finest form, but the flowers are small compared with the above hybrids, and forms of *P. suffruticosa*, often called Moutan. Of this species, I grow *P. rockii* 'Joseph Rock', a wonderful plant for a week or two

when displaying its great white blooms with five almost black blotches and a tuft of yellow stamens. It appears that seeds are formed only when a flower of a different individual is brought into play. Apart from *P. lutea ludlowii*, with comparatively small flowers, there is also the willing, vigorous *P. delavayi*, a noble shrub with leaden green leaves and dark crimson, shining flowers a few inches across. It seems a likely parent, and hybrids have already occurred. Quite a dwarf compared with these giants is *P. potaninii*; although usually under a foot in height and in spite of its small, nodding flowers, white, yellow or reddish, it has lovely fingered leaves that last until autumn. It spreads mildly by underground shoots.

Paeonia rockii 'Joseph Rock' in the author's garden

Philadelphus
coronarius 'Aureus'

Philadelphus coronarius claims attention at the end of the month because of the glorious scent from its cream flowers. Nor may its lovely yellow-leafed form, 'Aureus', be ignored; it looks well with the coppery leaves of *Photinia fraseri* 'Red Robin'. At the same time there is the freer-growing *Philadelphus magdalenae* with equally fragrant, pure white, scented blooms. It is a larger, more graceful bush than *P. coronarius*.

RHODODENDRONS AND AZALEAS

We have had rhododendrons in flower since the winter, but May really sees the great awakening of the genus. Botanically speaking, the old segregation of the genus into azaleas and rhododendrons does not hold good: they are all really rhododendrons. There are multitudes of species and hybrids that make their devotees think no other plants are needed in the garden. They are available in all shapes and sizes, from mat-forming prostrate plants to free-flowering bushes of a foot or two and tree-like monsters such as one sees in the sheltered coombs of Cornwall and the west of Scotland. The genus owes much of its popularity to the Kurume and related azaleas, those small bushes which are laden every year with a prolificity of bloom not equalled by any others. Of the original early introductions from China, none has equalled 'Hinomayo' in clear pink with an annual superabundance of small flowers. Modern hybridising has resulted in larger flowers with frilly petals and startling colours. There are pinks and whites, flames and reds, and crimsons and lilacs of all possible hues, and they flower in their different sorts from early May until mid-June, finishing with 'Mikado' and the dainty 'Naomi'.

Early in the month, we are usually greeted with the first of the Mollis azaleas; though there are good yellows among them, the prevailing colour is glowing salmon-red typified by 'Koster's Brilliant Red'. In spite of much hybridising and selection among the deciduous azaleas, none to my mind excels in beauty and scent the so-called Occidentale hybrids such as 'Exquisitum', 'Delicatissimum' and 'Superbum', flowering at the end of May, even into June, and, like the Mollis group, giving us also good autumn colour.

Rhododendron schlippenbachii, if you get a good form, can surpass all other azaleas in beauty, with its broad leaves and shapely flowers. Also with elegant long stamens is *R. vaseyi* in delicate pink; both have good autumn colour. For general reliability, rich yellow colouring, a far-carrying sweet scent and blazing autumn colour, we must turn to *R. luteum* (*Azalea pontica*). It ushers in resplendent hybrids and forms bred at Knap Hill Nursery and at Exbury, embracing every possible shade of white, yellow, salmon and pink and fiery reds. And they are all splendid again in autumn.

Among the species of rhododendrons, we get great satisfaction from the early lavender-blues such as *R. augustinii* and its cousin 'Electra'. But be sure you get a green-eyed form of the former; those with pink or red eyes are not nearly so effective. They make large bushes with small fragrant leaves. In this same category is *R. yunnanense*, in lilac or white, usually with red-brown spotting in the throat. Like the azaleas it is regularly well flowered and makes a large bush.

The huge number of rhododendrons introduced from the Far East has changed

ABOVE: *Rhododendron schlippenbachii*, one of the most exquisite of all azaleas
LEFT: *Rhododendron luteum* in the Savill Garden, Windsor

TOP: *Rhododendron orbiculare*

BOTTOM: *Rhododendron* 'May Day'

our conception of the accepted form of these plants in our gardens. There are prostrate growing species with bell-shaped flowers of glowing red and scarlet of the *R. forrestii* Repens Group, and the same handsome globular shape is found in the flowers of many larger species and hybrids in pinks and reds—witness *R. orbiculare* (outstanding for foliage as well), 'Hummingbird', 'Penjerrick', 'May Day', 'Winsome' and scores of others. Since this great influx, we have been treated to yellow bell-shaped blooms from *R. cinnabarinum* Concatenans Group, *R. wardii* and indeed the aforementioned 'Penjerrick'. Apart from true spectrum blue, the genus can show us every colour under the sun, including that rare hue among flowers—orange. This is found in *R. dichroanthum*, one of a few species that have cup-and-saucer flowers, and it has been a potent parent in hybridising. It flowers rather later than most of those I am mentioning for May.

'Yellow Hammer' is a unique plant with small, creamy yellow, tubular flowers, tiny leaves and an upright habit which has the double value of producing a second crop of blooms in November. This it has done regularly in my garden for many years. It flowers with the dwarf-growing, nearly blue *R. scintillans*.

May is definitely the month for the beautiful lavender blue 'Susan', though it is sparing of blooms in alternate years. We are now approaching rhododendrons of the accepted, popular, June-flowering style. Forerunners, with the redoubtable 'Pink Pearl' in the lead, are such as 'Daydream' (rather a lanky grower), the almost equally famous 'Loder's White', 'Raoul Millais' and 'Unique'. These will lead us on to June, and enough has been said of these shrubs to act as an introduction to their manifold beauties for the month of May.

EARLY ROSES

We may now mention the rose family, which includes some of the most widely used plants in gardens everywhere. Early shrub roses generally produce flowers in the south of England by mid-May. On sheltered walls of considerable height, there is the beautiful Banksian Rose. In warm districts we can venture to try the small double white *Rosa banksiae* 'Albo Plena', which has a pronounced and delicious scent; there are also a single white and a single yellow, also very fragrant, but the most often seen is the double yellow, *R. banksiae* 'Lutea' of cool butter colour. It is fragrant, like primroses, but less strong than the others. Banksian roses flower on the second-year side shoots and thus require intelligent pruning.

Among early roses usually flowering before the end of May is the renowned *Rosa moyesii*. This is a giant Chinese species reaching twelve feet (3.6 m) in good conditions. I prefer its seedling 'Geranium', raised at Wisley, which is more compact in growth and has better, fresher green leaves and brilliant red flowers. They are followed in late summer and early autumn by the flagon-shaped, scarlet heps. It is a two-seasons shrub of great value. *R. rugosa* will also be in evidence. The species is a good compact bush with very prickly stems and good foliage turning yellow in autumn when the large tomato-red heps clash with purplish pink flowers. This can be avoided by choosing the superlative white variety 'Alba' or 'Fru Dagmar Hastrup', whose clear, pale pink flowers are accompanied by crimson heps, or indeed selecting one of the doubles such as 'Roseraie de l'Haÿ', which seldom produces heps. They all flower from late May onwards and are thus invaluable garden plants, but are not good on very limy soils.

The great single white rose, 'Nevada', will be showing its early blooms, and the Burnet or Scots briars are always among the first roses to bloom. They are very prone to suckering, so beware, but their miniature blooms, single or double in a variety of colours, and revivifying scent are a great joy on the prickly thickets. If unpruned, *R. chinensis* 'Mutabilis' will be starting its display of multicolored blooms. It is a large grower in warm districts. Some of the single yellow species and hybrids, such as 'Canary Bird', *R. hugonis*, *R. ecae*, 'Cantabrigiensis' and 'Headleyensis' are a foretaste of the glories to come, and the splendid hybrid 'Frühlingsgold' combines so many good points—free growth, large flowers and warm fragrance—that it is difficult to imagine a garden without it. Though also good, its sister seedlings ('Frühlingsmorgen',

TOP: *Rosa rugosa* 'Alba',
one of the purest white roses
ABOVE: *Rosa rugosa*
'Roseraie de l'Haÿ'

'Frühlingsduft' and 'Frühlingsanfang') have never quite hit the headlines as triumphantly as the first named. They are all spring-flowering shrubs, though 'Frühlingsmorgen' occasionally produces later flowers.

Rubus deliciosus, with arching branches displaying lovely, large, single white flowers, though not prickly, resembles a species of *Rosa* to which *Rubus* is closely related. The hybrid of it, *R.* 'Benenden' (*R.* × *tridel*), is similar but larger growing. Both have a rare elegance, as does what may be called a pink relative, 'Walberton', a hybrid with *R. odoratus* with soft mauve-pink flowers in bunches.

Spiraea × *vanhouttei*, a large bush covered in pure white flowers like a small thorn tree, follows *S. thunbergii* and *S. arguta*, which flowered in the preceding months. There is also for May the charming *S. prunifolia* 'Plena' whose arching wands are studded with clusters of neat rosette-flowers—and we must not forget it is a two-seasons shrub, splendid in autumn colour. Through the long spring months and into summer, we can always have spiraeas in flower.

Staphylea × *elegans* is not often seen and that surprises me. It is a tall shrub like its brethren, but unlike them has long, hanging racemes of white flowers. I consider it the queen of the tribe, despite the claims of *S. colchica* and the pretty pink form of *S. holocarpa*. I believe *S.* × *elegans* to be synonymous with *S.* × *hessei* and *S. coulombieri grandiflora*.

OPPOSITE: The rambler rose 'Phyllis Bide' at Sudeley Castle, Gloucestershire. It flowers early and carries on to September.

BELOW: *Spiraea* × *vanhouttei*

Despite waning beauty from the flowering trees and the upsurge of the flowering shrubs, to me May is the special month for tulips, wallflowers and lilacs, three of the loveliest flowers of the year. To let a season go by without inhaling the heady perfume of lilac is a sad omission.

The French took up the hybridising and selecting of lilacs late in the nineteenth century and continued with the work into the twentieth, and the varieties they produced have not been surpassed. We owe the majority of them to the famous firm of Lemoine, at Nancy, though possibly the most valuable of all is of Berlin origin, 'Andenken an Ludwig Späth' ('Souvenir de Louis Spaeth'). This, in its rich colour and evenly spaced flower spikes, always produced lavishly, is indeed the standard by which all others are judged. And these others are many: single and double, from white through all shades of typical lilac colour to rich wine-lilac, as in the Berlin variety. Fortunately the doubles are just as fragrant as the singles, proving that the scent emanates from the petals. Apart from some wonderful whites, the selection has brought forth very beautiful flowers, almost true blue from rich pink buds, such as 'Olivier de Serres' and 'Président Grévy', with 'Belle de Nancy' the nearest to pink.

The season really opens with the Common Lilac, *Syringa vulgaris,* mainly in white and normal lilac tint. It is a strong suckering shrub with greedy roots and not really suitable for small gardens. The same may be said of the named forms. At one time these used to be budded onto Common Lilac rootstocks, which meant that before long you had a thicket of the common one around the cherished named form. They have also been grown on roots of privet, which does away with this nuisance. Nowadays they are mostly grown from cuttings, which means that all suckers are of the right kind. From Common Lilac seed shrubs of any tint may arise, and on the whole, white-flowered forms have pale green buds in winter, whereas those with purplish buds will have tinted flowers. But they all have that delicious scent. What is known as *S. × chinensis* is a much more graceful plant than the above kinds, and did not originate in China, being a hybrid between *S. laciniata*

Syringa 'Président Grévy'

and *S. vulgaris*. It was raised at Rouen and is thus known as the Rouen Lilac. Its branches weep with the weight of the floral trusses spread along the branches, a cool lilac colour. It has a more reddish variant, 'Saugeana'.

Weigela 'Abel Carrière' and *W.* 'Le Printemps' give us good pink flowers now, and these are followed by many others, including the crimson of 'Bristol Ruby' and 'Eva Rathke' in June. I wish the tubular-flowered *W. middendorffiana* was not so frost-tender in flower; it is a good free-growing shrub with cool, pale yellow blooms.

Xanthoceras sorbifolium is seldom seen, but I recommend it for a sunny position on any soil. It should perhaps be classed as a small tree, but it is usually seen as a shrub in the warmer, drier parts of the country. Its white flowers emerge in bunches early with the pinnate leaves, at first yellow-tinted, with crimson eyes. It is easy to raise from seeds, which it sets freely in good seasons.

Xanthoceras sorbifolium

Perennials

I think we may say that while the early year was greatly concerned with bulbous plants, by May and June the flowering shrubs and trees have reached their apogee and that thereafter the herbaceous plants gradually take over, giving rise to that splendour of our summer gardens, the herbaceous border. By May they are making themselves felt. I mentioned wallflowers and tulips earlier. The former today are treated like biennials, though in hungry soil they can reach a woody old age. Is there any fragrance so appealing as a whiff of wallflowers on a warm sunny day? And their colours together with the tulips give us the first chance to indulge in colour scheming. I need not dwell on seed strains here; they are to the fore in every park and public place, and all are fragrant.

Aquilegia hybrids follow the daffodils, along with *Brunnera* and *Camassia*. I think all aquilegias are beautiful, except the 'Clematiflora' strain, which some unthinking seedsman bred without spurs. The spurs are just what make these flowers so

ABOVE: *Camassia leichtlinii*
'Eve Price', a useful successor
to daffodils in May, raised
at Wakehurst Place, Sussex
BELOW: *Dicentra spectabilis*

beautiful. They represent the necks of the eagle or dove which the flowers resemble: eagle = aquila; dove = columba in Columbine, that lovely name for these cherished plants. The tight little Granny's Bonnets of the garden forms of *Aquilegia vulgaris* in their dull purples and pinks must now give way to the more open strain bred from *A. alpina*. Then there are the multicoloured, long-spur strains of great beauty. There are many species besides these but none is long-lived, making the raising of fresh stock from seed essential.

Brunnera macrophylla is a free-seeding plant of which you may get too many, but try to forgive it; its blue forget-me-nots are so fresh and bright, and it lasts in flower for weeks. The foliage is large and coarse, and it prefers a cool spot in any soil.

Camassia leichtlinii 'Eve Price' is dark blue, but others are cream or greyish blue. There is a large pale lilac-blue named 'Electra' which will reach four feet (1.2 m), as will the double cream 'Plena'. Camassias are tuberous or bulbous plants with long untidy leaves, but the slender spires of starry flowers come just right in the awakening season. It is best to place them among plants that will hide their foliage.

Convallaria majalis, Lily of the Valley, has roots that travel underground. They are arrant spreaders when suited, and the foliage lasts in beauty till late summer. By putting them in various positions, some in sunshine and some in shade, a flowering period of some six weeks can be realised. By the time they are all established, you will probably have more than you want. From a large group, the ravishing scent will reach up to you as you pass by, but of course it is as a cut flower that we think of them most, though they are not long lasting in water. The season usually starts in my little garden with the lilac-pink form. It is quite different in shape and poise from the usual white, and I wish I knew where it originated. It is followed by the normal kinds, and the flowering season finishes with the large-belled 'Fortin's Giant'.

Dicentra spectabilis, to my mind one of the supreme beauties of the year, flowers with the late narcissi. It is a plant for a cool sheltered position to protect its dangling flowers and succulent growths, though it is quite hardy. The sight of its "Bleeding Hearts", "Ladies' Lockets" or "Dutchman's Breeches" speaks for its endearing floral shape; picked and turned up, the rosy envelopes pulled apart, it reveals a "Lady in a Bath". Lovely also though the all-white variety may be, I do not feel it is much of a rival to the rosy wonder.

Dodecatheon meadia, the aptly named Shooting Star, should thrive in cool, moist, lime-free soil, sending stout stems above primula-like leaves bearing dozens of little nodding flowers, pink, with other subtle tints, like cyclamens. There are several species of the genus from North America, all with the family likeness.

DRY BORDERS

It sometimes happens that shrubs grow so thickly at the back of a border that nothing much but spring bulbs can be used, and even these will be obscured by the shrubs. I have one such border shaded by neighbours' trees and a fence, and made dry by a public footpath two feet (0.6 m) below the fence. The border is therefore both shady and dry, a combination that makes gardening difficult, but the common Male Fern (*Dryopteris filix-mas*) is a safe bet, as also are the creeping symphytums. I have in mind *Symphytum grandiflorum* and its two relatives 'Hidcote Blue' and 'Hidcote Pink'. These I found growing on shady banks in that famous garden, and named them thus. They are greedy surface spreaders and have large hairy leaves making effective ground cover. Throughout May and June, they produce croziers about two feet (0.6 m) high of (respectively) cream, pale blue and creamy pink. They save all work except trimming back the forward shoots so that they do not swallow up the entire border.

Endymion nonscripta, our own native, much loved Bluebell, and the even more prolific Spanish Bluebell, *E. hispanicus*, seem to do best when there is a little shade. The latter will grow anywhere, but let me issue a note of warning about both; if allowed to seed, the progeny becomes multitudinous in a few years. It is wise to remove the old flowering stems soon after the blooms have gone, to guard against this increase. The bulbs also have a habit of increasing on their own. The native has a somewhat nodding habit and tubular, dark blue flowers, whereas the Spanish species is lighter in colour, upright with almost cup-shaped flowers. They both vary to white and soft pink. Particularly attractive with them is that lovely yellow daisy *Doronicum* 'Excelsum', which can ascend to nearly three feet (0.9 m) and is best divided in early autumn.

Dicentra macrantha (FIRST STEM), light yellow, *Dicentra formosa* (SECOND STEM), pink, *Dicentra eximia* (THIRD STEM), also pink, and *Dicentra spectabilis* (FLOWER), for comparison. All are suitable for cool moist places in the late spring garden.

With us for many months, from spring till late summer, the euphorbias or spurges have a uniformity of spikes or heads of cup-shaped small flowers nearly always of a "greenery-yallery" tone but not the less captivating for that. And they last a long time in flower, the earliest contrasting with the true blue of forget-me-nots, *Omphalodes*, *Brunnera* and *Anchusa*. We have already looked at *Euphorbia myrsinites* and *E. robbiae* in April; others follow fast.

Euphorbia wulfenii, now so well-known, is classed as a variety of *E. characias*; the latter has green plumes of flowers with brown eyes. I should go for *E. wulfenii*, whose flowers are bright greenish yellow in the best forms, descended, I believe, from the plant known to me as *E. sibthorpii*. 'Lambrook Gold' and 'John Tomlinson' are two very bright cultivars. They are all dignified plants; the many woody stems spend their first year in making lovely narrow leaves like a bottlebrush up to some three feet (0.9 m) that in the following spring nod and then turn up into a wide spike of flowers. They seed themselves gently; if in the wrong place transplanting while quite small is best. There are several variegated forms coming on the market that add considerably to this little selection. These are the giants of spring; lower plants of long-lasting beauty are *E. polychroma* and much taller *E. palustris*. They will all grow in any normal, drained soil. A rich bit of reddish colour is provided by the young foliage of *E. griffithii*, but we shall be looking at this later in flower.

Gentiana acaulis, whose huge incomparably blue, almost stemless flowers are so magnificent over the tufts of leaves, remains an enigma. It won't do anything for me. Lime is not the answer; I don't know what is. I have seen it resplendent in bloom in gardens as far apart as Ireland, Wales and eastern Britain and cannot find amongst them any real reason for success except sun and fresh air. I had some success in an open field with *G. angustifolia*, which is the Pyrenean variant of the eminently Swiss alpine jewel.

Geranium malviflorum has lavender blue blooms held well above the foliage. The leaves arrived in autumn from bare ground, deeply incised or fingered, and have been beautiful through the winter. But alas, they do not linger for long in spring, for they are already turning yellow at flowering time. Clear these away and sow an annual crop of such as *Lobularia maritima*. But perhaps you will not want the geranium; it spreads rapidly by little tubers. On the other hand, the other earliest geranium, *G. sylvaticum*, is a stay-at-home with beautiful lavender blue, white-eyed flowers on stems of about two feet (0.6 m) above good foliage. There are pleasing white and pink forms.

G. monacense, which used to be called *G. punctatum*, is sitting up and has in early spring lovely leaves of primrose yellow with five reddish spots. It is one of the *G. phaeum* group with flowers in June.

IRISES

The main flowering of bearded irises occurs in June, but May sees their introduction through dwarf varieties such as 'Austrian Sky', and a little later the intermediates, of which I find the pure purple 'Annikins' a reliable flowerer. There is much to be said for flowers of one colour; they are more telling in the garden than bicolours. In no group of plants is this so true as in irises, in which the upper three segments are different (often paler) in colour from the lower three segments. Though these two-tone effects add some charm in their blend of tints, they have a less marked effect in the border than do flowers of one colour. Usually before May is over, the common so-called German Flag is in flower, together with the white *Iris florentina*, dark purple *I. kochii* and even *I. pallida dalmatica*. These few are what I was brought up with and tried to render in watercolours at about the age of fifteen. The painting was a failure; the shape of the blooms, no less than their veining and colours, defeated me.

Lathyrus vernus is a dense, clump-forming little plant for sunny positions. The heads of small purple pea-flowers are held above the divided leaves and turn to blue on fading. There are charming variants in pink-and-white and blue-and-white which are more compact and slow of increase. There is also the much larger *L. aureus* with flowers of a strange brownish yellow.

Lithospermum purpureocaeruleum (now to be called *Buglossoides purpureocaerulea*) rambling through the May geraniums will be rooting its

Two-toned bearded iris hybrid with well-shaped flowers raised in the early 1900s

threading stems as it goes and pleasing us with starry blue flowers at every tip. It is a rapid surface creeper.

Lunaria annua, Honesty, is one of the most valuable plants for filling the gap made by the passing of the daffodils. It does best with a little shade. My choice would be the 'Munstead' strain, which has branching stems up to four feet (1.2 m) of rich crimson-purple flowers. The normal type is pale magenta, and there is a variegated form of this, and also a pure white. But they interbreed rather much, and it is best to be ruthless and settle for one or another. They are free-seeding plants flowering the year after germinating—what we call biennials. Another species, *L. rediviva*, is a true perennial in lilac-white. The resulting seed pods give the name of Moonwort to the biennial, whereas the perennial might be called Halfmoonwort; its pods are elliptical. Seeds of all self-sow anywhere.

Milium effusum 'Aureum', Bowles's Golden Grass, seeds about fairly freely, but I have never found it a nuisance, and its brilliant yellow leaves look wonderful with *Omphalodes cappadocica*. It has airy sprays of flowers of the same yellow colouring. Apart from the golden-leafed form of *Philadelphus coronarius*, there are few brighter things in the May garden—in June as well. There is also a peculiarity, common, presumably, to all miliums: each leaf turns over so that its underside is presented uppermost. I can offer no explanation, but it is possibly something to do with the stomata.

Narcissus poeticus recurvus, or Late Pheasant's Eye, pure white with a red "eye", is one of the most loved of May flowers, renowned for its penetrating sweet scent. It has a neat double form, *N. poeticus* 'Plenus', which does well in soft western climates but never flowers with me in harsh Surrey. Of late-flowering hybrid narcissi, a few of my favourites are 'Silver Chimes' and 'Thalia', both creamy with two or three flowers per stem, as indeed has the yellow 'Tittle Tattle' and also the miniature 'Hawera'. These are all of modest size; there are plenty of "Grandifloras" of every conceivable mixture of colours, but with them my enthusiasm wanes.

HERBACEOUS PEONIES

Together with the irises—long favourites of mine for their scent as well as their shape and colouring—come the very earliest of herbaceous peonies, starting regularly in my garden with the American hybrid 'Early Bird', a single gorgeous red with narrow leaflets inherited from *Paeonia tenuifolia*, a parent also of the later, larger *P.* × *smouthii*. *P. tenuifolia* is a rare plant these days; its almost hair-fine leaf segments set it apart from all others. There are three kinds to search for, single crimson, single pink and also the double crimson. All are choice plants and very beautiful. I suppose the most sought-after of all peonies is *P. mlokosewitschii* in clear light yellow. It makes things easier among friends if you call it "Mollie the Witch". Few can resist its attractions, but it hybridises easily, and plants true to name may be hard to find. 'Avant Garde' is one of several hybrids of *P. wittmanniana*, which is a coarser, paler version of Mollie; the hybrid is a fine upstanding plant with violaceous young foliage and peachy pink flowers. I think my favourite of all these early peonies is the light pink 'Mother of Pearl', a form of the magenta *P. arietina*; the foliage has a downy grey tint over the green which tones so well with the flowers.

Ranunculus aconitifolius is a charmer needing moist, cool spots. The single form is beautiful, throwing up wide-branching stems over handsome lobed leaves on stems about three feet (0.9 m) when well suited. The flowers are small buttercups in pure white. The double form, in spite of the opprobrium cast by Reginald Farrer, has earned the name of Fair Maids of France and is to me even more beautiful. While the single can be raised from seeds, the double must be increased by division, which is a slow job.

Smilacina racemosa, False Spikenard, bears a decided resemblance to Solomon's Seal in spring, but the image is shattered when fluffy white, fragrant flowers appear at the ends of the shoots. It is a noble plant that builds up slowly into a big clump when provided with moist lime-free soil with humus. But beware of its invasive, less beautiful relative, *S. stellata*.

Trollius europaeus, the British native Globe Flower, has stems of about two feet (0.6 m) over dark green divided leaves. The flowers are buttercup-like, of a moony pale yellow and very distinguished. There is nothing to beat the wild pale yellow for colouring, but if you prefer something warmer there are good orange forms such as *T. × cultorum* 'Orange Princess'. For those of us blessed with a wet patch in our gardens, I can think of few more rewarding plants for it than trollius. Other richly coloured species will be seen in June.

Paeonia mlokosewitschii

TULIPS

Tulips are available in a very wide range of seasons, shapes and colours. Apart from some exciting species of various shapes and attractions, tulips can be classed as "early flowering", about a foot high in many colours; I especially favour 'Generaal de Wet', a pure yellow with a sweet fragrance that reaches up to you. As with other groups there are doubles as well as singles, and the former tend to last longer in flower, though they lose the classic shape. After these earlies there are the taller, globular Darwin hybrids and other groups such as the lily-flowered and various striped and feathered varieties. But save me from those untidy abortions, the Parrot tulips; the tulip has a classic satisfying shape which should be preserved. And we do not want bigger flowers; the neat old varieties such as 'Clara Butt' stand the weather better. Tulips are best planted deeply, quite six inches down, so that there is less likelihood of their splitting into small bulbs the year after flowering, which can be so disappointing.

OPPOSITE TOP: *Smilacina racemosa*
OPPOSITE BOTTOM: *Tulipa* 'Queen of Sheba',
an example of the lily-flowered group
LEFT: *Meconopsis chelidoniifolia*, a pale yellow
perennial for cool, moist, lime-free soils

JUNE

laming June does not come without hesitancy. It may be late in the month before summer is really with us. To the gardener a dry June is a real trial. Just when the garden has reached its full flush of greenery, as likely as not a drought will set in, inhibiting the growth of all perennials, and, indeed, tender bedding plants that were planted at the end of May. It is left to the trees and shrubs to show their independence.

There is no lack of flowering shrubs for June, but flowering trees are getting scarce. Of the largest trees we only have left the Sweet or Spanish Chestnut (*Castanea sativa*), but this is scarcely a garden tree, rather, one for park or woodland. The Horse Chestnut has an appealing relative in *Aesculus flava*, a comparatively small tree with smooth bark and neat leaves; the flowers, borne terminally, are small, but of butter-yellow. Much larger is *Aesculus indica*, which echoes the Horse Chestnut in light pink three or four weeks later. An especially good form was selected at Kew and named after the then Curator, 'Sidney Pearce'. It has fine spikes of pink flowers. Though they all grow into handsome trees, I find that in the young stage they are very susceptible to spring frosts.

Just when we find that we are being enveloped in uniform greenery, two trees are

OPPOSITE: A "great moment in the year's beauties"—the flowering in late spring of *Styrax japonica* 'Pink Chimes' (enlarged)
BELOW: *Hypericum forrestii*, which starts to flower in June

outstanding in their efforts to recapture the lively spring tints. They are the Red Oak, *Quercus rubra*, and the Ash called *Fraxinus excelsior* 'Jaspidea'. Both have young foliage of a marked pale yellowish green and are conspicuous for a few weeks, until they join the uniform greenery. The ash has yellowish twigs in winter, but both trees are rather large for the average garden.

Robinia pseudacacia 'Frisia'. Its brilliant yellow foliage gets rather boring through the summer.

Trees

Fraxinus ornus, Flowering Ash, is a lovely thing for June, with fluffy, white, tiny flowers held in large heads. It will achieve some thirty feet (9.0 m), while *F. sieboldiana* is smaller, with the same pretty flowers and more handsome leaves.

Ptelea trifoliata is grown as much for the sweet scent of the flowers as for its arboreal attraction. It is a small tree or large shrub, and its dainty flowers delight the nose more than the eye. My preference would be for the form with yellowish leaves, 'Aurea', which carries on the colour after the flowers have gone.

Robinia pseudacacia, Honey Locust, the commonest of a group of comparatively small trees, so often called acacia, is coarse of growth but is, nevertheless, capable of developing into a tree of great character. In a way, it can be likened to a white Laburnum. The scented flowers are hung profusely from the outmost twigs, well-clothed in fresh, green, pinnate foliage. It has some pretty varieties, such as 'Rosynskiana' and 'Tortuosa', also one called 'Bessoniana'. All are late to start into growth, and the last two named seldom if ever flower. *R.* × *ambigua* 'Decaisneana' might be looked upon as a delicate pink form of *R. pseudacacia*; though a hybrid, it is less vigorous, but a charmer. The common species unfortunately has a running root system, and new trunks frequently arise some distance from the parent tree. Because it is easy to raise from seeds, it is used as an understock for grafting the choice, large pink-flowered species, all of which emanate like the common one from North America. The most tree-like of these is *R. kelseyi* in lilac pink; others are *R. hispida rosea*, *R. boyntonii*, and 'Hillieri'. *R. hispida* 'Macrophylla' is one of the most appealing, though it lacks the bristly, colourful stems. The flowers of all are of great beauty, but the plants are of brittle growth and benefit from wall-training. There is nothing like them in June or at any other time.

Styrax japonica, the well-known Snowdrop Tree, is best placed where you can look up at the horizontal branches a-dangle with crowds of white four-petalled bells. There is an exquisite form, 'Pink Chimes', with flowers of light clear pink. With large rounded foliage on an upstanding tree of medium height, *S. obassia* has flowers borne on outward-facing racemes. *S. hemsleyana* is equally beautiful. All species of this choice and uncommon genus need good, lime-free moist soils and are ideal in thin woodland.

Climbers

Clematis 'Nellie Moser', with large, lilac-pink flowers with red bars at the centre of each petal is, deservedly, a most popular hybrid in a race often called the Queen of Climbers. There are many more in every colour, from white to pink, crimson, lilac and purple, and we go further into them later. Meanwhile, I think it best to refer you to my book *Ornamental Shrubs, Climbers and Bamboos*, not only for descriptions of clematis but also for the pruning required for each section.

Lonicera periclymenum 'Belgica', the so-called 'Early Dutch', is the first honeysuckle to flower. It is a strong grower with well-scented flowers of cream and pink appearing all at once in a single flush. *L. tellmanniana* is yellow, without scent, as is the magnificent *L. tragophylla*; this is best in shade. *L. heckrottii* has scented flowers of an orange-flame tint. They all look best when encouraged to grow through gawky shrubs; on the other hand if trained on wall or fence, the resulting short shoots will be well supplied with flowers.

Rosa hybrids, including well-tried old favourites such as 'Albertine', 'Gloire de Dijon', 'Mme Grégoire Staechelin', 'Mme Alfred Carrière', 'Mme de Sombreuil', and 'Mme Caroline Testout', climbing on sunny walls may be expected to flower in a warm June. Roses are such very special things that places should be reserved for them as climbers for walls, ramblers for pillars, arches, swags and for running into and over trees. In addition, there are the new, so-called ground-cover roses, though until they breed them without prickles, hand-weeding among the young shoots is an irksome task.

Schisandra rubriflora is the most conspicuous in a genus of twining plants with smooth leaves and stems. Its glowing crimson buds open to wide-petalled flowers, followed by fruits like redcurrants. It and its relatives, of which there are sev-

Lonicera periclymenum 'Belgica'

eral, seem to prefer walls with a cool aspect, or may be grown on arches and pergolas.

Wisteria sinensis, the most usual of this genus of climbers, is in many ways the most beautiful, but be sure to get a young plant vegetatively propagated; if raised from seed the quality of bloom will vary, and it may be many years before flowers are produced to reveal the mistake. *W. venusta*, a plant of great beauty, has shorter racemes, and the flowers are white. *W. floribunda macrobotrys* (*W. multijuga*) has much longer racemes, but the flowers do not all open at once, as they do in *W. sinensis*, so that some of the beauty is lost. *W. sinensis* has flowers of clear lavender blue; *W. floribunda* is inclined to be two-toned; they both have superb white varieties, and the second species in particular has many colour forms. All are immensely vigorous and can smother a large tree if left to grow at will, but they also lend themselves to pruning and with suitable cutting at the right time will settle down and flower freely into old age, even when kept down to a few feet. The secret is to remove all the long lanky shoots in summer, and thus to encourage the short side shoots to produce flower buds. On a wall the same treatment will ensure abundant blossom.

Shrubs

Brachyglottis 'Dunedin Sunshine' (which we all used to know as *Senecio greyi* or *S. laxifolius*) has a moment, perhaps a fortnight, when it is superb. That is when it is covered in snow-white buds. It is then a lovely contrast to irises; it thrives on hot sunny banks and quickly makes a wide smother of handsome silver grey leaves. The flowers are daisy-like, of brilliant light yellow. As soon as they are over, it is advisable to remove them and shorten wayward branches since the bushes soon become loose and ungainly.

Carpenteria californica is an evergreen shrub of some size which, as the name suggests, enjoys all the sun it can get. When in flower, it presents a wonderful sight if you get the large-flowered 'Ladhams' Variety'. The snow-white blooms make a wonderful show, but as an evergreen it is disappointing unless in very favourable conditions. It is a close relative of the Mock Orange or *Philadelphus*, but is practically scent-

ABOVE: *Wisteria floribunda macrobotrys*
OPPOSITE TOP:
Cistus × *cyprius*
OPPOSITE BOTTOM:
Cistus 'Silver Pink'

less. With age the shrubs need a little pruning after flowering to remove exhausted weak twigs.

Cistus × corbariensis is a good hardy Rock Rose with a dense habit and abundant pure white flowers.

C. × cyprius, one of the giants among Rock Roses and a reputed hybrid between *C. ladanifer* and *C. laurifolius*, is named after the island of Cyprus and yet, oddly, these species are not known to grow on the island. *C. laurifolius* is possibly the hardiest species, which is fortunate because *C. ladanifer* is tender, but *C. × cyprius* has all the good points of the latter and is a really splendid shrub, with dark narrow leaves and large flowers of white, yellow in the centre and blotched with murrey-crimson. The leaves inherit the parents' sticky laudanum and give off a delightful whiff of it when picked and put in water in a warm room in winter.

C. × pulverulentus has grey-green leaves and flowers of flaming magenta. All Rock Roses are lovers of hot sunny slopes on well-drained soils. Their silken flowers open fresh every morning, usually to drop in the afternoon. But when the day's perfection is repeated for many days, who cares? Pruning where necessary should be done after flowering, in August.

C. × purpureus is usually the first of the Rock Roses to open; each big pink flower is like crumpled silk, with five dark blotches towards the centre. In fact, many kinds have these dark blotches.

C. salviifolius 'Prostratus' is one of the meritorious dwarfs among Rock Roses.

C. 'Silver Pink' has a delicacy and charm matched by few of the many species, varieties, and hybrids among Rock Roses.

Cotoneaster multiflorus is spectacular in flower but unfortunately sends forth a rather strong odour; it is best to place it well away from one's daily itinerary and grow it for its plentiful large berries in autumn. I would not place it in the forefront of flowering shrubs, but it is an outstanding member of the Rose Family.

Cytisus scoparius provides forms and hybrids from plain yellow to flame, pink, mahogany and plum, many of them exhibiting two colours. I do not find that these bicolours are as effective in the garden as the self-colours, however fascinating they may be near at hand. At the distance of a few yards they present a medley of colours, and do not blend with anything. There are early and late varieties in all colours. It is important to keep them bushy by removing much of the growth that has flowered as soon as it is past its best, because brooms do not sprout well from old wood.

Dendromecon rigidum, Bush or Tree Poppy, a California relative of the poppies capable of reaching nine feet (2.7 m) or more, has clusters of bright yellow four-petalled flowers held prominently among glaucous leaves. They appear for many weeks intermittently when given a sunny place in any well-drained soil.

Diervilla sessilifolia is related to *Weigela*; it has small tubular yellow flowers, but it also has colourful spring foliage in light khaki-green.

Fremontodendron 'California Glory' has furry lobed leaves that are a splendid background for the large yellow flowers, which turn to orange-brown on fading. Starting in June, they continue in production until late summer. It is a rapid grower and also, sadly, usually has a short life, and we have to start all over again. No matter where we live in Britain, there are few plants to the north of us, with the result that we covet all the tender things from the south. A warm sunny wall, a wonderful asset to a garden, is the best site for some of our southern plants, but so often the tender plant will thrive for a few years, and then a severe winter brings disaster. But isn't the temporary triumph worth the sadness of eventual loss? 'California Glory' is not particular about soil so long as it is well drained.

Genista cinerea, perhaps the most spectacular of all brooms, makes a large lax bush with silvery young shoots. At flowering time it can easily be the most impressive plant in the garden. The flowers are small, borne in incredible profusion, of a brilliant light yellow, and scented. While it can be pruned as for other brooms, to try to keep it compact will destroy its wayward charm. No brooms are suitable for transplanting. Their special uses in the garden are for temporary enjoyment, while young; being quick of growth, they can be looked on as expendable luxuries.

Hebe 'Fairfieldii', a relative of the better-known but tender *H. hulkeana*, is the first of three hebes that should be brought in here. It is a small shrub with abundant heads of tiny lilac-pink flowers; another is the excellent, very glaucous carpeter *H. pinguifolia* 'Pagei' with heads of tiny white flowers; the third is *H. macrantha*, another small plant, but with surprisingly large snow-white blooms at the top of every green-leafed shoot. They all enjoy as much sunshine as available, and the only pruning required is done after flowering to keep them in shape. I find 'Pagei' just the thing to give relief and contrast to the winter-flowering ericas, and it is especially lovely when covered with dew or hoarfrost.

Fremontodendron 'California Glory' trained on a sunny wall

Kolkwitzia amabilis

Kolkwitzia amabilis, a relative of *Weigela*, is a commanding object when in full flower, and deserving of the vernacular name used in America, Beauty Bush. The plant is completely smothered with little pink tubular flowers with orange throats. 'Pink Cloud' is a noted form raised at Wisley.

Magnolia liliiflora 'Nigra' (*M.* × *soulangeana* 'Nigra'), a compact small bush, follows its late May display with those astonishing deep plum-coloured blooms through June and even later. The great value of the few kinds that I mention now is that they flower, usually, when frosts have gone. The much neglected *M.* × *thompsoniana* has highly scented, large cream flowers all over a rather lax bush with good leaves, glaucous beneath—a character inherited from *M. virginiana*, which we shall be considering in July. Then there is the sumptuous *M.* × *wieseneri* (*M.* × *watsonii*), so prodigal of scent from large cream flowers with conspicuous reddish stamens. It is a large thrusting shrub, almost a small tree. The hybrid 'Charles Coates', raised at Kew, has worthy late-season cream flowers, too.

Neillia thibetica (*N. longiracemosa*), another member of the Rose Family, has graceful growths and attractive leaves that are foils for the dainty terminal sprays of tiny pink flowers.

Summer is almost here when the mock oranges flower. They are usually at their best at the crown of the year, the end of June, and along with the bean fields and the Lime, or Linden, trees and roses flood the air with perfume. After *Philadelphus coronarius*, which we looked at in late May, some of the most fragrant, such as the favourite 'Belle Étoile', are touched with mauve pink in the centre. This colouring is due to the influence of *P. mexicanus*, and they are all extra fragrant. *P. delavayi* is one rather on its own; if you can get a plant of the 'Nymans Variety' (which has purple calyces), nodding flowers on the high bushes will enchant you. Other early flowering kinds are 'Conquette' and 'Enchantment', but we will leave the main collection until July.

Phlomis fruticosa, Jerusalem Sage, has few equals for furnishing a dry bank in full sun, on poor soil. Along with lavenders and santolinas, it has woolly, greyish leaves and abundant stems bearing heads of gay yellow nettle-flowers. It can be reduced after flowering if necessary but usually makes a good clump.

    Potentilla fruticosa, Shrubby Cinquefoil, a native of Britain and elsewhere, has given rise to a great many varieties, forms and hybrids. Most have a long flowering period and are invaluable for the front of borders and larger rock gardens. They all make dense little bushes, smothered with flower for weeks and months in reasonably moist ground. But they present a rather fussy appearance on account of their small divided leaves and small flowers. I find them a trifle boring, though I grow several sorts in my garden. There are good whites and creams, and since the advent of 'Red Ace', pink tones are cropping up, but the yellows are rather shrill. Some, like 'Floppy Disc' and 'Manchu' (pink and white, respectively), are semi-prostrate and merge well with other plants in the heather garden; others may ascend to four feet (1.2 m). They require no pruning but a good chop back in spring will rejuvenate old bushes.

Philadelphus 'Belle Étoile'

It is the time of the popular old Hardy Hybrid rhododendrons, which thrive even in full sun provided the ground is reasonably moist. The champion, 'Pink Pearl', is over, but all the old Waterer clan are in full swing. 'Lady Clementine Mitford', in clear pink, is a favourite of mine on account of its silvery young foliage. After the main mass is over, embracing many colours except yellow and orange, there are several later varieties that should be considered: the blush 'Gomer Waterer', with its stocky habit and bold foliage, is a wonderful old variety, and 'The Warrior', very dark crimson. Winding up the whole collection, in pink, is 'Mrs John Kelk'.

When we turn to the newer, woodland hybrids, the palette is greatly extended in what we might call "azalea colours". It is important that these newer kinds be separated from the Hardy Hybrids, as the sharper colours war with them. Dazzling 'Fabia', glowing 'Fairy Light' and 'Vanessa Pastel' assort better with the late flowering azaleas themselves; very dark murrey-colour is found in 'Impi', a small grower, while 'Moser's Maroon' has dark foliage as well as dark flowers, but sprawling growth. Rich reds are found in 'Grosclaude', 'Lava Flow' and 'May Day', while 'Albatross' is supreme in white, and the 'Angelo' forms echo the beauty of the earlier 'Loderi' group. For really sheltered woodland, there is the imperious 'Azor', owing much of its beauty to the parent of several of the above: *R. griersonianum*, a wonderful plant and potent parent.

In spite of the fact that azaleas are on the whole flowers of April and May, there are some worthy species for June. *R. arborescens* is one, with good foliage and scented pinky-white flowers with a yellow eye. It is a large grower. Much more compact is *R. viscosum*, of which I esteem the variety 'Glaucum'. The grey foliage and white flowers, its delicious fragrance and the autumn colour have endeared it to me. It prefers a damp spot. Time was, when azaleas were considered distinct from rhododendrons, that the term Azaleodendron was coined for hybrids between them. They are mostly striking in colour, but they have a spindly habit, except 'Fragrans', which with 'Govenianum' is a worthy scented mauve flower; both are reliable growers.

Rhododendron 'Moser's Maroon'

Viburnum sargentii
'Onondaga'

Solanum crispum, from Chile, is often planted against a wall for shelter and warmth. It needs a lot of space and ascends to some eighteen feet (5.4 m), the thick woody stems producing cluster after cluster of pale lavender-blue potato-flowers for several weeks. I think I prefer its colour to that of its variety 'Glasnevin' ('Autumnale'), which lasts in flower much longer, but the subdued soft violet flowers do not make so distinct a contrast to the foliage. But do give both of them plenty of space.

Spartium junceum, Spanish Broom, is a very large plant which needs the same pruning as *Cytisus* to prevent it from getting lanky. The large yellow flowers are particularly handsome, almost flamboyant.

Viburnum opulus, our native Guelder, is at its best this month, though why a term from the Netherlands should be applied to this shrub is a mystery. Not only its rounded clusters of white flowers—the "snowballs" of the sterile form, so misleadingly called 'Roseum' nowadays—but also the single form gives rise to shining scarlet berries in autumn, at which time the foliage turns to rich red. It seems to thrive on any soil, but keep it well away from the dwelling, for in damp autumn weather it gives off an unpleasant smell. *V. sargentii*, a related species, has given rise to 'Onondaga', which has murrey-coloured young foliage; moreover, the flowers are red-tinted, surrounded by a conspicuous ring of white sterile flowers; it has rich autumn colour. Although the many species of Viburnum do not approach in majesty the flowers of rhododendrons, peonies and magnolias, they stand very high when their two or three seasons of beauty are considered.

Weigela cultivars began flowering in May, but June is really the month for them. There are many varieties in pink and crimson making large shrubs and asking for hard pruning directly after the flowers have faded. They have no particular beauty of summer or autumn foliage, but there is no denying the grace of the arching branches which so well display the tubular flowers. Among the many pinks, I place first the extra strong growing 'Conquête'; there are several good crimsons, 'Bristol Ruby' being about the best. 'Rubidor' has the doubtful advantage of having rich crimson flowers contrasted by yellowish foliage. There are two good variegated forms; one is *W. florida* 'Variegata' with creamy yellow edges to the leaves and pink flowers, but I prefer *W. praecox* 'Variegata' with whiter edges and crimson-pink flowers. An unusual form is *W. florida* 'Foliis Purpureis', whose soft purplish foliage tones go well with the dusky pink flowers, making it a valuable adjunct for the softer colour schemes.

Perennials

Alchemilla mollis, Lady's Mantle, will seed itself prolifically if the flowering stems are not removed before the flowers turn brownish. The leaves alone are enough to make us all want to grow it—mantle-shaped with velvety surfaces on which raindrops appear like quicksilver. Over this clump of cool green, airy sprays of greeny-yellow arise. While we may glory in strong colours there is no doubt that they do not make a restful garden. This, then, is the plant *par excellence* for blending fighting colours.

Allium cernuum makes an excellent companion for *Rhazya orientalis*. Both grow to about eighteen inches (0.46 m); their foliage is nothing special but the head of grey blue stars on the latter is just right to set off the former's subdued pink flowers in a hanging bunch at the top of the stalk. While I admire and like allium flowers, it must be admitted that they can become terrible weeds, seeding about freely. And they have an irritating habit of letting their leaves die just when the flowers are opening. The

ABOVE: Rose 'Nevada', one of the great glories of June with some flowers appearing into early autumn; the flowers can be four inches across

LEFT: *Alchemilla mollis*

seeding of course can be controlled by cutting down the flowering stems, but who grows alliums solely for their flowers? The seed heads are among summer's joys. Fortunately, there is a period of several weeks between the dropping of the flowers and the formation of the black seeds. One of the most splendid is *A. christophii* (*A. albopilosum*), whose large round heads of amethyst stars quite put the earlier *A. aflatunense* to shame, though *A. hollandicum* 'Purple Sensation' is very good. *A. schubertii* echoes *A. christophii* in size and colour, but has the intriguing character of florets on stalks of different lengths, giving an exploding rocket effect.

Anchusa italica, an old favourite in the Borage Family, is much to the fore when it comes to true blue flowers. But on account of its rather floppy stems, it is best passed over in favour of the cultivar 'Loddon Royalist'. There is also the old 'Opal', a light blue of great appeal to me. Other borage flowers are found in *Lindelofia longiflora* and *Cynoglossum nervosum*, both good blues.

Aruncus dioicus, Goats' Beard, a large and imposing plant, is a relative of the spiraeas and makes a great clump of elegant divided foliage over which are disposed big plumes of tiny cream

ABOVE: *Allium christophii* with *Berberis thunbergii* 'Atropurpurea Nana'

flowers. Be sure to get a male plant; the plumes are more handsome, besides which self-sown seedlings will not appear. Perhaps because of its relationships with spiraeas and apparent relationship with *Astilbe*, it is often given a damp spot, which it scarcely needs. As soon as the flowers are over, they can be removed, and you can enjoy the great clump of leaves to the full for the rest of the summer.

Baptisia australis is a sound perennial of the lupin persuasion with stately spikes of light, indigo-blue pea-flowers. The latter epithet means "from the south", i.e., the Mediterranean region, not Australia. Here, as with Dittany, the autumn display is worth watching: the pods turn to dark grey and the leaves, after frost, to coal black. Both this and the Dittany make deep tap roots, and, once established in good deep soil, should not be disturbed.

Campanula persicifolia, the Peach-leafed Bellflower, is one of the first of its kind to flower. Like *C. latiloba*, which we shall come to next, it has good winter rosettes of leaves. In *C. persicifolia*, they are of dark shining green, and the wiry flower stalks ascend to some three or four feet (0.9–1.2 m); one flower at the top always opens first, followed down the stem by the lower ones. All have a purity of shape, if single, in warm lilac or purest white ('Alba'). I should not like to have a summer without them. The old 'Telham Beauty', with light lilac flowers, has never been surpassed for size.

There are doubles in either colour, but to my mind they are unattractive. *C. latiloba*, on the other hand, has produced no doubles; it lacks the grace of the former, because its flowers are placed, stalkless, on stiff erect stems. But besides the normal rich violet-blue one, there is 'Hidcote Amethyst', which I found in that superb garden and named appropriately, the darker 'Highcliffe Variety' and the pure white 'Alba'. These two campanulas excel in the purity of their white forms, accentuated by the three-pronged cream stigma. *C. latifolia* and its colour varieties, purple, lilac and white, are alluring plants in a woodland glade, but do not last long in flower. *C. sarmatica* is a great favourite of mine; its hairy flowers of cool light lilac are held well above the leaf-rosettes, while the rich dark purple flowers of the invasive *C. glomerata* are borne in dense heads. There are several named forms which should be sought, being, on the whole, less invasive.

Cardiocrinum giganteum, from the Himalaya, is, I think, the grandest of all perennial plants. Because the bulb dies after flowering, its offsets need lifting in September and replanting in fresh ground. It should be prepared in a moist sheltered spot in partial shade and enriched with all the best leafmould and old rotted manure you can find. Then, and then only, will the spikes achieve that dignity that is theirs alone; they ascend, when each bulb has built up sufficient strength, perhaps to eight to ten feet (2.4–3.0 m). The stem at the base may be four inches (10 cm) thick, carrying huge rounded or heart-shaped leaves of shining dark green until the flowers appear nearing the top. They are large, long, white and trumpet-shaped with reddish murrey marks in the throat and a strong scent. *C. giganteum yunnanense* is only a little less majestic; its stems are maroon and the flowers smaller and creamy green. They both call for as many superlatives on paper as are required in the preparation of the site.

Cephalaria gigantea (*C. tatarica*) is a lovely relative of *Scabiosa* whose lemon-yellow flowers give a long display. I like to place it with *Crambe cordifolia*; it is the same height and has handsome divided foliage.

Codonopsis clematidea appears to be a rather ordinary plant at first sight, dangling its pale blue bells from a swaying stem of one or two feet (0.3–0.6 m); they surmount small rounded leaves which have a foetid odour when bruised. But look inside the bells, and you will find them most beautifully marked with orange and dark blue. They are plants easily raised from seed and prefer a cool aspect and no disturbance of their fleshy roots.

Cardiocrinum giganteum

Crambe cordifolia, its great airy mass of tiny white flowers so like a giant *Gypsophila*, decorates the garden for weeks. It is somewhat surprising that its great height, six to eight feet (1.8–2.4 m), should be achieved by some perennials so recently merely tufts at ground level. But there they are—vigorous expressions of seasonal energy. The crambe needs a space of some six feet (1.8 m) in width. You can cut it down after flowering to reveal the large dark green leaves or leave the stems to display their tiny seed pods later.

Dactylorhiza braunii, *D. majalis* and *D. foliosa*, the kinds of orchids I grow, all thrive with little attention, but need splitting when they get congested and need replanting in autumn. In colour they are rich crimson-purple in the first two, paler in the third. *D. majalis* has very distinctly spotted foliage. In not-too-dry borders in part shade, they present no trouble, but I cannot speak about their progress on chalk. *Orchis mascula*, on the other hand, needs more moisture.

Dictamnus albus, Dittany, is, like Baptisia, a strangely neglected plant. It is unusual to find the white variant defining the species, but in this case it does so, and the Dittany with mauve pink flowers is thus called *D. albus purpureus*. The common name, Dittany, is simply a contraction of the Latin. Both white- and mauve-flowered plants have elegant spires of bloom up to four feet (1.2 m) or so, each flower being decorated with long stamens, the petals green-veined in the white, red-purple in the other. They are held well above lobed, dark green, fragrant foliage. With advancing summer the red-brown seed pods mature, exuding volatile oil on hot days, and if a lighted match is held below them, they will produce a puff of flame and smoke, earning the name of "burning bush". Picked for drying, they crackle and explode. But it is a lovely garden plant that deserves more recognition.

Digitalis purpurea, Common Foxglove, is thought of as a shade-lover but it will also give a good performance in sun. Much as I love the pinky mauve of the normal type,

I tend to limit mine to the white forms. The old original white forms still have that delightful one-sided spike, so much more appealing than the multi-spotted 'Excelsior' strain with flowers all round the spike like those of a Hollyhock. They are all biennials but will seed themselves—often almost too freely. I keep stressing the value of pale yellow as a useful blending tint in the garden, and there is a splendid soft light yellow Foxglove, more or less perennial, called *Digitalis grandiflora*. It is only half the height of the ordinary foxgloves. There is a hybrid between the two called *D.* × *mertonensis*, a perennial with flowers of a curious soft rosy mauve shot with coppery buff. It has to be divided in early September to keep it in good health. The others all come readily from seed.

DROUGHT LOVERS

There are several good things for dry sunny places, especially on limy soils. How often we see the common Valerian, *Centranthus ruber*, thriving on old walls. Its subdued pink puts up a fine show with innumerable tiny flowers, but I prefer not only the richer-toned 'Atrococcineus' form, but also the white, 'Albus'. They seed themselves, often where they are not wanted; apart from the June flush, they will flower again later if cut over. For any hot sunny exposed spot on (preferably) limy soil, the wild Seakale (*Crambe maritima*) of our coasts is unbeatable for its lobed and convoluted large grey leaves, intensely glaucous. It is of course used as a vegetable by gently forcing the leaves under cover, but I find the young flower heads, green or purplish, are very palatable when cooked. And the later leaves are just as good for contrast in the garden. For dry sunny places, there is possibly nothing better than the low-growing *Erigeron glaucus*; its lilac daisies are very trim and neat, and it has a warm-coloured variant in 'Elstead Pink'. I have seen them thriving in dust-dry conditions. Almost the same may be said of certain Pinks; the seed-raised single Pinks, mostly with dark eyes, are wonderfully thrifty and easy. They may be seen growing in the mortar of old walls. Besides their colours, they have, like all Pinks, a delicious clove scent. Named varieties are a little more particular, but they all need sun and perfect drainage; they have usually finished flowering by July, but their blue-grey tumps of leaves keep them respectable. There are hundreds of varieties, which have to be increased by cuttings or layering. Among many favourites of mine are 'White Ladies' (superior to 'Mrs Sinkins'), 'Highland Queen' (single, dark pink), 'Thomas' (double, deep copper colour), 'Bat's Red' (crimson-pink), 'Cocken-

Dianthus plumarius 'Thomas' in the garden at Mottisfont Abbey, Hampshire zie' (fringed, crimson-pink) and 'Musgrave's Pink' (single, white with a green eye). The last three are old, treasured varieties.

And the catmints (*Nepeta*): where would June borders be without them? Again sun-lovers for dry soil, they have only one disadvantage—cats love to roll on them. (This is easily cured with a few prickly shrub prunings tucked in among the shoots.) Another point: though hardy and thrifty on drained soil, they resent being cut down in autumn. Besides the well-known *Nepeta* × *faassenii* (which we once knew as *N. mussinii*), there is also the hardier and much larger plant, 'Six Hills Giant'. There are many intermediates due to impatient nurserymen raising them from seed.

For equally drained frontal places, there are the thrifts (*Armeria*), among which none is finer than the vivid, tall 'Bees' Ruby'. But the ordinary *A. maritima* in pink or white is not to be despised; it makes a good mossy edging when not in flower and of course can be used on the rock garden. The almost brick-red *A. corsica* is good as a young division or seedling but seems to forget to flower when older. There are some good taller, larger kinds in white and pink raised from other species.

Among taller plants there is that intriguing, imposing, fragrant-leafed perennial *Morina longifolia*, which is most at home in the milder and damper west of Britain. The thistle-like leaves give rise to a tall stem set with prickly whorls of small tubular flowers, white turning to pink and then to crimson. It is something all on its own. As a

Phlomis russeliana

companion, I can think of nothing better than *Phlomis russeliana*. In complete contrast, this has softly hairy, plain, basal leaves with whorls of very soft, creamy yellow nettle-flowers borne on stout stems. They stay aloft long after the flowers have gone, making a statuesque perch for hoarfrost. *Centaurea ruthenica* is one of those useful pale yellow flowers that blend so well with almost anything. It is a Knapweed relative with attractive flowers and good, divided dark green leaves and prefers a sunny position. The handsome plant we used to call *C.* 'Pulchra Major' is now given the name *Leuzea centauroides*. Few perennials have more assets or beauty. The leafy clump is composed of long, deeply indented leaves, almost white beneath, and is well overtopped by globular heads of papery buff bracts holding pink Knapweed flowers. It is an altogether very fine plant and I am glad that its right name has been published in *The Plant Finder*.

Eremurus elwesii, E. olgae and *E. robustus* are the tallest of the lily relatives known as Foxtail Lily. Some may reach as much as eight feet (2.4 m). The foliage is long and limp and lies around over the tuberous roots which may be likened to a large starfish, just under the surface of the soil, so handle your tools with care. It is as well to mark the positions of the crowns with a stout peg. They need sun and perfect drainage and thrive on chalky and sandy soils in a variety of cool pinks, buff and white. Much shorter and more vivid in colour are some of the hybrids such as the Ruiter's and Shelford Hybrids and *E. stenophyllus* itself.

Eryngium giganteum, known as Miss Willmott's Ghost, is, except for the foxgloves, the only biennial in these pages and is well worth growing. It readily seeds itself, yielding basal rosettes of greenery and stalwart stems bearing thistle heads of steely white, prickly, with a knob of blue flowers in the middle. Of late years, another form of the same species has been introduced from Asia Minor which has been dubbed 'Silver Ghost'; it usefully flowers a fortnight later than the original. With them *E. tripartitum* is turning from green to intense blue, bearing masses of miniature thistles with prickly ruffs. It is a good perennial when once established and is propagated mainly from root cuttings. Few plants give such a long-lasting and delightful effect at midsummer and onwards.

Eryngium giganteum

Festuca glauca, a grass that thrives in any sunny spot, makes small tuffets (much loved by ants) of very thin blue-green leaves with sprays of blue-green flowers above. It is not invasive.

Filipendula hexapetala, another British native on limestone and chalk, is a matformer whose rather invasive roots are difficult to eradicate, but who would not wish to grow the substantial double form 'Flore Pleno'? Its carrot-like leaves clothe the ground thickly, and it is a good frontal plant even on dry soils, though then its foothigh flower stems tend to get mildew. The dense, flat heads of tiny creamy flowers make good effect. It is easy from division.

Geranium pratense, Meadow Cranesbill, can be seen in the more northerly counties of England, mainly on the limestone, often showing its lovely lavender-blue flowers in patches along the roadside, regardless of coarse grasses and other plants. It is a refreshing sight in the wild and in the garden, seeding itself avidly, reaching some three feet (0.9 m) and offering considerable variation in flower from white and greywhite to pale and dark colours. But beware, cut it down before the seeds set to invade the garden, and you can then admire to the full the handsome clump of fingered

leaves that last until autumn and often assume bright colours. There are fortunately three doubles that do not set seed: *G. pratense* 'Plenum Caeruleum' in light blue and 'Plenum Violaceum' which has perfect rosette-flowers of rich colour. There is also a white 'Plenum Album', but this is not very impressive. The hybrid 'Johnson's Blue' is a winner of less stature and a very worthy garden plant with a long flowering period. Like the doubles noted above, it must be increased from division.

Geranium psilostemon (*G. armenum*), perhaps the most splendid of hardy geraniums flowering now, makes a great clump of handsome divided leaves overtopped by flowers of flaming, richest magenta. A saving grace is their black eye. Another asset of this plant is its autumn foliage, which often assumes rich tints. If vivid magenta is too much for you, try 'Bressingham Flair', which is softer. Other geraniums are following fast. There is the splendid *G. himalayense* (*G. grandiflorum*) in either its rich blue form or the paler 'Irish Blue'. They are runners in the garden, but welcome even so. *G. endressii* follows in pink, both "shocking" pink and salmon-pink or merely paler, and they go on flowering for weeks. *G. sanguineum* is a clump-former with spreading roots and a tendency to sow itself. It is a British native and varies from strong crimson-purple to the almost rose-pink 'Glenluce'. There is also a white, 'Album'. All have extra dark, fingered leaves.

Geum 'Mrs Bradshaw' in fiery red, and her counterpart 'Lady Stratheden' in rich yellow are the famous pair in a group remarkable for their bold leaves and brilliant double flowers. 'Princess Juliana' and 'Fire Opal' are midway in colour, and all are derived from *Geum chiloense*. There is yet another with brilliant orange single flowers and shorter stature, but still with good leaves. It is the hybrid *G. × borisii*.

Gillenia trifoliata, an unexpected member of the Rose Family, has wiry, branching stems, sparsely leafed, and carries airy sprays of small, white flowers for many weeks.

ABOVE: *Gladiolus papilio*, a hardy species whose flowers contain a medley of strange colours
RIGHT: *Geranium* 'Johnson's Blue'

Colour is given by the bracts and calyces which are richly reddish. It presents no difficulty in cultivation, but does, I find, prefer cool conditions.

Gladiolus byzantinus, a hardy native of southern Europe with intriguingly marked purplish flowers, is almost impossible to describe. One needs his paint box to recall the medley of tints—purple, crimson, brown, pink and allied shades all being present in the intriguing, dainty flowers. They readily increase by offsets or seed in any sunny spot and are of wondrous beauty. It is just the thing to wake up a border where subdued hues are too well represented.

Helianthemum, whose several species have given us a wide range of colours, many with silvery or grey foliage, are really shrubs, but this seems the right place to mention them. They do not usually exceed one foot (0.3 m) in height but may spread to several feet in well-drained, sunny places. They are easy to strike from cuttings taken as soft tips in summer. They range in colours from white to pale and dark pink and crimson on the one hand, to brilliant yellows through brick-red and flame on the other. There are a few doubles which, though they lose some of the charm of the singles, are a blessing for those who must leave their gardens for much of the day, since they retain their petals long after the singles have dropped—perhaps as early as mid-afternoon.

Hemerocallis dumortieri and *H. middendorfii* are usually first among the day lilies to flower; both have their flowers at the top of a stout stem. The former is bright yellow, the latter almost orange-yellow, and both are flushed with brown in the bud and have some scent. They are much the same in size as *H. lilioasphodelus*, about two feet (0.6 m), and all have lovely, arching, folded, grassy leaves of bright green which remain in beauty long after the flowers have fallen. This last used to be called *H. flava* and has loose heads of clear yellow flowers with a delicious scent. They are easy plants to grow, the last being invasive.

Heuchera has many named forms and hybrids. Some really bright ones are 'Sparkler', with seedlings of *H. sanguinea* like 'Red Spangles' and 'Bressingham Blaze'. *Heuchera* also provides the ideal foil for all these strong colours in 'Palace Purple', a silly name for the coppery, murrey-coloured leaf form of *H. micrantha diversifolia*. The flowers are of little account; it is grown solely for its leaves. All of these are ideal frontal plants, usually under two feet (0.6 m) in height and creating an airy-fairy

Gladiolus byzantinus, or a close relative

Hosta sieboldiana
'Frances Williams'
with *Carex stricta*
'Bowles's Golden Sedge'

effect. They are not difficult to please in any drained soil, appreciate sun and are best divided in early autumn with firm, deep planting. The leaves of some are prettily marbled.

Hosta fortunei albopicta, with its yellow variegation, is just the thing to place with blue poppies. Some fifty years ago, hostas were practically unknown, especially the variegated forms. Now it may be asked how we could garden without them. Other numerous variegated forms have taken hosta lovers by storm. One of the latest I have seen is 'June Beauty', in which the leaves are partly grey blue and partly creamy yellow. 'Wide Brim', 'Francee' and 'Gold Standard' represent years of selection and cultivation, but I think the palm must be given to 'Frances Williams', a form of *H. sieboldiana* in grey-blue and green that takes some beating. Then there are the miniatures which can assuage a collector's desire for a bigger garden. Charming though the miniatures may be, to my mind it is the large-leafed forms that are the greatest sobering effect in gardens. The great rounded glaucous leaves of *H. sieboldiana elegans* will hold their own with the garden's greatest plants and shrubs. In addition, their glaucous grey-blue tone is wonderful for adding apparent distance to a view. 'Halcyon' will do the same for smaller gardens. But I was not intending to write about hosta leaves: everyone knows their value. Most produce flowers during July, but the white-edged *H. crispula* has elegant spires of pale lilac lily-flowers above the foliage in late June, at which time the stumpy off-white heads of *H. sieboldiana* buds will be emerging from their mound of leaves. Slugs and snails are the enemies which in a few nights can reduce what was a pile of beautiful leaves to a shredded horror. And hostas don't bless us with a second crop. Slug pellets cause death, but I believe the corpses are the result of the scarcity of thrushes. The answer is shredded bark or nut shells over which the marauders can get no grip. Hostas are easy to increase by cutting out a section of root as if it were a round cake, and infilling with good soil. It can be done at almost any time of the year, and the sections re-establish quickly.

Incarvillea delavayi, though usually classed as hardy, has failed to come up after a sharp winter in my garden. Perhaps this is not surprising because it belongs to a mainly tropical family, *Bignoniaceae*. In fact, the splendid flowers of warm rose-pink atop their stems a foot or more high resemble closely those of the Trumpet Vine, *Bignonia*. The leaves, too, are pinnate. There is a lovely white form. It is a noble plant with some dwarf variants, *I. mairei* among them.

IRISES

The great bearded irises run peonies close in colours, with the added luxury of yellow but to the exclusion of red. I find myself at odds with iris breeders today. The modern large-flowered, bearded irises are available in many lovely colours, but they have lost the classic shape (like two capital letters R back to back) through extravagant frilling and ruffling in the petals. In the 1920s, the falls (the lower segments) were weak, limp and poor. This was altered through breeding, and a superior shape, along with glorious colours, was reached during the 1930s. With the impetus in breeding after 1950, this new-found luxuriance of ruffling ran riot. It is claimed that ruffled petals are stronger and better able to resist damage from wind, but enthusiasm among breeders for ruffles has gone far beyond increased strength; some ruffled iris flowers, with undulating petals interlocked in the bud, have difficulty opening. There are few flowers with such undisputed beauty of shape, glistening texture and colour range as irises. Why then spoil them with a superabundance of ruffles?

There is also the new fashion for "flaring" falls: lower segments held horizontally, or nearly so, instead of remaining perpendicular. This fashion leaves the upper segments perched on the lower like a dumpling on a plate, and does away with half the colour surface of the flower when viewed a few yards away. These evils are even creeping into modern *Iris sibirica* hybrids that are in other respects such a marked improvement on older kinds. We are glad to find Siberian irises with more flowers to the stem and a longer season of display, but in achieving this, must we lose the

Irises of the "classic shape" with foxgloves

slenderness of the old, and the movement they bring to the landscape as they lean to the wind? The colours of Siberian irises are not so varied as with the bearded varieties, ringing the changes between white, lavender blue and darkest violet, with a few pinks and yellows in recent years. What they lose in size and colour is made up in part by the sheaves of narrow, arching, green leaves, so appealing at the waterside. The great bearded irises, on the other hand, prefer a dry, drained soil and like the sun to penetrate to their rhizomes. They do not enjoy neighbouring ground-cover plants. I think the leaves of the Siberian irises last in beauty longer than those of the bearded varieties, except the aforementioned (May) *Iris pallida dalmatica*, which is always the plant to be chosen for foliage effect.

Less well known are the Orientalis irises to be considered for late June: *I. spuria*, soft lavender-blue and of medium height; *I. orientalis*, reaching to four feet (1.2 m); and the splendid *I. × ochraurea* overtopping them both. This last, with crisp delightful shape and strongly recurving falls, is a study in yellow and white. These plants, with their narrow, erect, sword-like foliage, play a strong part in the June and July borders. Of more recent breeding are vigorous varieties with perhaps as many as a dozen flowers on a stem. Unfortunately, the colours have become confused: yellows are mixed with smoky lilacs and brownish purples. I cannot think these colours are much use in gardens.

I. kerneriana, a charming relative of *I. orientalis*, is a perfect miniature of this group, growing only to about a foot (0.3 m) or more, with grassy leaves and pale yellow flowers of remarkable shape. The strongly recurved falls almost make a circle. All of these irises thrive in sun in any well-drained soil. I particularly like the contrast afforded by the big rounded leaf-blades of bergenias and any iris. *Bergenia* 'Morgenröte' has, besides its April flowers, the inestimable asset of always flowering again in June, with good heads of rosy red.

Iris laevigata is one of the last irises to flower and likes a really wet place, even with its toes in water. (Unlike the better-known *I. ensata* [*I. kaempferi*], which, though often immersed for effect at flowering time, flourishes quite happily most of the year in rich moist soil.) Over the slim, sword-like leaves, the comparatively flat flowers of *I. laevigata* are of strong violet-blue. There are also white, pale and particoloured forms, as well as a hybrid with *I. ensata* in soft rose-pink known as 'Rose Queen'. It doesn't need so wet a place.

Kniphofia 'Atlanta', the earliest Red Hot Poker, is a three-foot (0.9 m) stalwart in bright red and yellow.

Lathyrus grandiflorus, the true Everlasting Pea, is distinct from the Perennial Pea, *L. latifolius*, which flowers in July or later. *L. grandiflorus* has larger flowers, two or three on a stalk, of magenta-pink with a murrey-red keel. They appear over sparse glaucous foliage. *L. rotundifolius* is taller and equally invasive in some forms; the flowers are variable, coppery pink to almost brick colour. *L. undulatus* is somewhat similar in magenta-crimson. They are all from southern Europe, deciduous, and more or less invasive at the root. Their value is in clambering over a shrub no longer in flower, or with the aid of a few pea sticks, forming an unemphatic pillar among lower plants. The display continues for several weeks in any normal soil, but the flowers are not scented.

LILIES

July is really the month for lilies, but a few early ones which usually flower in June are *Lilium hansonii, L. martagon, L. pyrenaicum* and the group which used to be called *L. umbellatum. L. pyrenaicum* is usually first, narrow-leafed and bearing a flight of small

Lilium 'Enchantment', bright orange-red

yellow Turk's Cap flowers spotted with black and with a strong scent. This coloured form is now called *L. pyrenaicum pyrenaicum* to differentiate it from the brick-red type. They flower with *Philadelphus coronarius* and puff a tremendous scent across the garden. It will stand full sun and is easily grown, whereas *L. martagon* and *L. hansonii* prefer some shade. They are also heavily scented, and their leaves are in whorls up the stems which overtop those of *L. pyrenaicum* by two to three feet (0.6–0.9 m).

L. martagon is a native of Britain and does well in retentive, rich soils, being available in white (*album*), muddy pinks and dark murrey colours (*cattaniae* or *dalmaticum*). Their strongly recurving segments are glossy. *L. hansonii* is similar in all but colour, which is warm dark yellow. Hybrids between the two have been raised and all are easy to grow, but the colours are not to everyone's taste. Something quite different is found among the many selected forms of what used to be called *L. umbellatum* (*L. hollandicum*), with comparatively narrow leaves and umbels of upright flowers of bright red, orange and yellow. They are scentless but good colour givers in cultivars such as 'Enchantment'. *L. monadelphum* (*L. szovitsianum*) is a great beauty with huge flowers, nodding and clear yellow. It seems to thrive especially in heavy limy soils. Lilies will thrive in my rather light soil only if split and moved on in early autumn into soil well enriched with leafmould and bone meal. None of those mentioned above object to lime, except perhaps *L. hansonii*.

Linum perenne in sky blue and its more stocky relative *L. narbonense*, whose blue is rich and rare, make a good effect in the mornings but are apt to drop petals later in the day. The former is a graceful willowy plant, the latter almost shrub-like in a dwarf way. There seems to be some connection between true blue flowers and limy and chalky soils; this is where they thrive. In fact, of late years I have noted the farmers' return to the cultivation of *L. usitatissimum* on chalky fields in our southern counties for the production of linen and linseed oil. As you pass by in the morning, all is green but the flowers open facing the sun, and the whole field turns to blue, dropping in the afternoon.

   Lupinus hybrids were, during the twentieth century, developed into untold variations, and now that clever seedsmen have perfected the colour strains, young, vigorous plants are always available; we need no longer purchase the heavy old roots propagated from cuttings. This wide variety of colours has come about partly from the

Lupinus 'Russell Hybrids'

Meconopsis × sheldonii

blue *Lupinus polyphyllus*, which over the years of seed raising appeared in pink, purple and multicolours and became sharpened with yellow from an infusion of *L. arboreus*. A good bed of mixed lupin hybrids in full flower is one of the great sights of the year; nor has their fragrance been lost in the breeding. Being deep rooters, lupins should be placed while young and not transplanted. Perhaps *L. arboreus*, being somewhat woody, should have been included in the shrub paragraph. Crowning every branch with a fragrant spike of light, bright yellow, it is one of the most refreshing sights and smells of the garden.

Lychnis chalcedonica, with which we leave the pinks, mauves and lilacs far behind, confronts us with a tall plant bearing at the top of its stems a rounded head of small flowers of arrogant, staring vermilion. It is an old favourite of the June border that can be used only with yellows. It is an early summer plant and soon over. There is a double variety, several pale pinks and salmons and a good white. The perennial potentillas in some of the yellows, and perhaps the deep brownish reds, provide suitable companions for the lychnis, but not 'Gibson's Scarlet', which would shriek in disagreement.

Lychnis viscaria, in penetrating pink, is a somewhat greyish-leafed plant suitable for the border front. It produces its flat round flowers, like pinks, for several weeks.

Lychnis × walkeri 'Abbotswood Rose' was raised at Abbotswood, a famous Gloucestershire garden. The leaves are grey and felted, a fitting basal setting for the felted branching stems, which bear flowers of really dazzling magenta-crimson. It lasts several weeks in flower, putting most others to shame, and serves as well as the hardy gladiolus among softer hues.

Meconopsis grandis and some of its hybrids with the later *M. betonicifolia*, called *M. × sheldonii*, are wonderful plants for lime-free soils. *M. grandis* is, of course, a magnificent plant with each remarkable butterfly blue flower borne on a long stalk well above the basal hairy leaves. These plants are the despair of gardeners like myself who live in regions too warm and dry for them; besides moisture and leafmould at the root, they demand cool, moist air. There is then nothing like them for beauty. The hybrid × *sheldonii* is to my mind at its best in the form known as 'Slieve Donard'. The colour is superb, far more brilliant than the first-known perennial blue poppy, *M. betonicifolia*. In connection with these plants, I use the word "perennial" with some reserve, because only when they are growing well are they likely to produce extra rosettes at the base to provide divisions. September is a good month for this work. An old favourite of mine is *M. quintuplinervia*, which, like the above, hails from the damp hinterland of China. It makes copious leaves a few inches high, over which hover the nodding flowers of light lavender-blue with a dark eye and cream stamens. It is easy to grow and divide so long as it has moisture and part shade.

Meconopsis × sheldonii

There are some delightful pale yellow species such as *M. integrifolia*, which assort well with the blues, but they are not perennials. And remember all of these poppies need lime-free soil. We might slip in a word here about leafmould made from trees on limy soil or on any soil overlying chalk: it will not do for these plants, for it contains lime brought up to the leaves by deep roots; we therefore have to resort to peat and peat substitutes.

Mertensia virginica can well hold its own in the beauty of the nodding, pale blue, tubular flowers and greyish leaves. For more blue flowers, go to the Flax plants (*Linum*), borages (*Anchusa*) and veronicas.

Papaver orientale, a poppy with huge, vibrant red flowers on three- to four-foot stems (0.9–1.2 m), usually needs staking. But the flowers have so little staying power that they are a flash in the pan—here today and gone tomorrow. There are some magnificent things among them, both the old 'Beauty of Livermere', in rich dark red, and some prettily fringed varieties. But I am glad to see that the breeders of these delights are turning their attention to dwarfer plants with softer, pastel flowers. Perhaps they have a great future before them. And don't forget Miss Jekyll's trick of growing *Gypsophila paniculata* behind them to fill the empty space when the foliage has died down. There are, however, other perennial poppies to be considered. *P. pilosum* is the largest of a little group of tangerine-orange colouring. It is a good leafy plant and, like *P. atlanticum*, will go on flowering for weeks if the pods are picked off. They are graceful plants, unlike *P. spicatum*, whose flowers emerging from hoary white buds closely stud the stem. All of these are quite easy to grow in any drained soil.

Paradisea liliastrum, St Bruno's Lily, is one of two similar Swiss plants that I should not like to be without. Both have pure white, somewhat trumpet-shaped flowers with conspicuous yellow stamens at the top of stems of a foot or so, over limp, narrow, greyish floppy leaves. This has the larger flower, but I have not found it easy to establish. The other is St Bernard's Lily (*Anthericum liliago*) which, on the other hand, presents no difficulty, and if you can get hold of the form 'Major', you are likely to be well pleased. It and the others breed true from seeds.

Penstemon ovatus, though not a sound perennial, is easy to raise from seeds. The broad basal leaves also ascend the stem which bears heads of true blue, tubular flowers. Less known but equally easy from seed is *P. pubescens*, whose longer flowers are a delicate mixture of cream and lilac.

PEONIES

The month brings the flamboyant and imposing peonies to perfection. Some of them anticipated June by flowering partly in May, but now, with such famous varieties as 'Globe of Light', 'Lady Alexandra Duff' and many other famous British-raised varieties crowding the lists, the air is filled with fragrance. The palm has passed from Europe to the United States, where the firm of Klehm, in Illinois, now raises many new peonies, particularly compact varieties. The variations of peony colours through white and pink to darkest crimson give us something which has no equal in our gardens and for cutting for the house: they are good lasters.

Peony 'Rubyette', a modern hybrid from the United States, introduced by Roy Klehm

Persicaria macrophylla, once known as *Polygonum sphaerostachyum*, over a goodly clump of leaves produces rosy pink spikes of tiny blooms for a long period. It is a moisture lover I should not like to be without.

Phalaris arundinacea 'Picta', Gardener's Garters, a white-striped grass, is of great beauty in June, but invasive.

Polemonium caeruleum is the best-known and tallest of a group that, though not excessively tall, seldom topping four feet (1.2 m), is known for some obscure reason as Jacob's Ladder. Its pinnate leaves are attractive, and so are the pale lilac-blue (or darker), cupped flowers borne at the top of the stems. There are several shorter named variants, some decidedly of a pink tone, worth searching for.

Potentilla argyrophylla (yellow) and *P. atrosanguinea* (red) are two good single-flowered species. There is also a wealth of named varieties, including some rich velvety doubles, such as 'Gloire de Nancy' and 'Monsieur Rouillard'.

Salvia pratensis haematodes gives us a long display on many spikes of small light lavender-blue flowers. If your garden is warm and sheltered, you could try the

Potentilla 'Gibson's Scarlet', a valuable pure red flower

statuesque *S. interrupta*. This is a big plant with heads of hooded lavender-blue flowers all the way up the tall stems. And at its foot, for contrast, use the hybrid *S.* 'Mainacht', a good solid effect in intense violet-purple. It is one of the most arresting plants of the season.

Scabiosa caucasica and its several named forms were noted in May; it goes on flowering during June and indeed until the autumn stops it.

Scilla peruviana, from the Mediterranean region, got this name from having been shipwrecked on a cargo boat named "Peru". The sprawling basal leaves give rise to slightly domed heads of rich blue or white stars, no mean effect being achieved. It is bulbous and likes a warm corner.

Selinum tenuifolium, once known as *Oreochome candollei*, is seldom seen. According to William Robinson (*The English Flower Garden*), it was used as a lawn specimen. Admittedly the feathery foliage makes a most attractive clump when overtopped by the elegant white Cow Parsley flowers, but I think it would be necessary to bury a barrow load of manure beneath it for it to reach the proportions of a lawn specimen.

Sisyrinchium striatum, a slender iris-like plant with sword-like grey leaves and tall spikes of small pale yellow flowers, renewed daily, is the ideal complement for true blue in gardens. 'Aunt May' has cream-striped leaves.

Stachys macrantha has softly hairy clumps of crenate leaves that make a good mound over which the stout, four-sided stems arise, bearing whorl upon whorl of hooded, soft pink flowers. This ardent sun-lover is a splendid companion for the soft colours of alliums and bellflowers.

Stipa gigantea is a wide clump-forming grass that I saw some fifty years ago in Oxford University Botanic Garden. I was given a root, and I believe the results are now almost everywhere, but it is not invasive. The flowering stems rise to some five feet (1.5 m), like a giant oat, glistening purple at first, turning to harvest colour and last-

ABOVE: *Salvia involucrata* 'Bethellii' showing its unusual cup-shaped calyx lobes
RIGHT: *Zantedeschia aethiopica* 'Green Goddess'

ing through till autumn without staking. It is not wise to divide grasses in autumn; they often fail. Late spring is best.

Thalictrum flavum glaucum (*T. speciosissimum*), in clear sulphur-yellow, is a noble plant with delicate, divided foliage. The flower stems reach to some six feet (1.8 m), and when over they can be cut off, leaving the sturdy stems with their lovely greyish leaves lasting through summer. Less glaucous, but no less appealing, is the foliage of *T. aquilegiifolium*; its flowers can be rich lilac or paler, or white, and all are beautiful.

Tropaeolum polyphyllum, a trailing "nasturtium", studs its branches with glaucous folded leaves. Sometimes the whole trail can be covered with pairs of warm yellow nasturtium-like flowers. It grows from tuberous roots which are not always easy to establish. I think they thrive best in stiff limy soils, and when once established, it is a pity to disturb them.

Verbascum 'Gainsborough', a Mullein, has large, woolly grey leaves. The flowers, which last well on the spikes, are of a particularly cool, bland yellow. Its relatives, the 'Cotswold' varieties, are of strange coppery yellow colouring, while 'Pink Domino' is a cold pink. They all need propagating from root cuttings from time to time to keep the plants vigorous.

Veronica teucrium has slender spikes of flowers of good clear blue. I like especially 'True Blue', 'Royal Blue' and 'Crater Lake Blue'. With them comes that lovely plant *V. incana*, which adds grey foliage to the blue. These are all short growers, but in *V. longifolia* and *V. exaltata*, you have plants up to three feet (0.9 m) with good compound spikes of flowers on top.

Zantedeschia aethiopica 'Crowborough' I found in an open border in a garden at Crowborough, Sussex. To all intents and purposes, it is what we should call an Arum Lily (though an Aroid, not a true lily) which will thrive in any moist sunny border. Whether the normal greenhouse type would do the same, I know not; before getting its fang-like roots well down into the soil, it may succumb to winter cold. But there is no denying the majesty of the deep shining green of the huge leaves and the beauty of the creamy white spathes. There is a closely allied form, 'White Sail' and the unique 'Green Goddess', whose flower spathes are light green and most useful for cutting as they do not show up well in the garden.

Dianthus 'Hidcote', valuable for its long flowering period on the rock garden

SUMMER

JULY

By the time July arrives, it is nice to feel that the chilly airs of spring are well and truly past. Some years when June has not been "flaming", just the opposite obtains. And we should not be surprised; the cold spells that seem to beset us in Britain were charted by a certain Dr Buchan in Scotland over some 70 years. His findings led him to conclude that in Scotland at least the period June 29 to July 4 is often cool and wet. It is by no means as well marked as May 11–13 which often brings frost; this is a period well marked on the Continent as the "Three Ice Men". These cold spells are variable with the current air streams and the latitude, but over many years I have been convinced that they warrant careful attention.

So we cannot welcome July and its implied summery warmth with open arms, and must take the vagaries of the weather as they come. At least the chill air of evening has usually gone, and as the month progresses, increasing warmth day and night may be expected. Our gardens are mostly filled in July with flowers from perennials and annuals, roses, certain other shrubs and just a few trees.

OPPOSITE: Rose garden at Frith Hill, Sussex, with 'Buff Beauty' and 'Cornelia' prominent

BELOW: *Hypericum kouytchense*

Trees

Apart from certain magnolias such as *Magnolia obovata*, *M. × thompsoniana* and *M. × wiesneri* (the last two are really shrubs), it is the genus *Catalpa* that keeps the flag flying during July, the later ones lasting sometimes into August. They are magnificent, large-leafed trees of considerable weight in the landscape. Their flowers, which are borne freely in warm sunny climates, are little short of imposing—great heads of lipped flowers arranged in a spike as in *Aesculus* or Horse Chestnut. They are slightly scented, but that is not an outstanding attraction. Close inspection of the flowers reveals an intriguing shape and wonderful markings. Mainly some tone of pale pink in *C. speciosa* (the first to bloom), they also have white and orange in their palettes. *C. speciosa* is a fairly compact, though large and upright tree, while the best known, *C. bignonioides*, is wide-spreading. There is a form of the latter with yellow-flushed leaves called 'Aurea', but however bold and magnificent the tree, it will be understood from my suggestion of the colour of the flowers that it is not at its best at flowering time. On the other hand, *C. erubescens* 'Purpurea', with dark foliage, sets off the delicate floral colours to advantage. There are several other kinds with flowers of rose pink flushed with purple, including *C. fargesii* and its variety *duclouxii*. These should be sought diligently; although less vigorous, they can well hold their own amongst all summer's riches. These two are Chinese trees; the earlier two are from the United States. They all need all the sun they can get in Britain.

Cladrastis sinensis, a member of the Pea Family, is a little-known small to medium tree with pretty pinnate leaves. When well established, it delights us with clouds of small creamy flowers usually in late July. It is especially interesting in the way it covers the incipient shoots with its leaf bases.

Fraxinus spaethiana, a Flowering Ash to follow those of June, has a froth of small creamy white flowers after midsummer. The leaves are pinnate as in all the species.

Genista aetnensis, the largest growing Broom, also flowers in July. It should be planted when quite small—one year old from seed—so that its roots can get a good hold on the soil to support the twenty or so feet (6.0 m) of arching branches. Every whippy twig is covered in summer with small pea-flowers of bright yellow, deliciously scented. It gives the appearance of a shower of yellow rain. It is best in deep sandy soil or good loam and does not take kindly to chalk and clay.

Hoheria lyallii and *H. glabrata*, deserving attention from all who garden in a warm, sunny district, are the best-known New Zealand members of the Mallow Family. The flowers of all are white, prolific and fragrant; some other species go on flowering into autumn. They are tall shrubs or small trees and have luxuriant foliage.

Stewartia malacodendron,

notable for its blue anthers

Magnolia grandiflora usually starts to flower in July. It is a noble-leafed evergreen and is usually seen trained against a south wall on some large building. The rattling of its leaves on a windy night has sometimes kept me awake, but picking one of those great cream goblets to scent the room was a compensating joy; they have a rich aroma of lemon. It is important to get vegetatively propagated stock rather than seed-raised, which might take many years to flower. This is a simple matter because the best named forms are always grown from cuttings. I rank 'Goliath' one of the very best, but better known perhaps are 'Exmouth Variety', 'Ferruginea' and 'Gallisonnière'. Of late years hybrids have been raised with another Eastern States species, *M. virginiana*, a shrub with small globular blooms of cream and an equally delicious scent. The leaves are brightly glaucous beneath, and the cream goblets appear for weeks on end, as in *M. grandiflora*. Those who are yearly disappointed by frost on the spring-flowering kinds should take note. It is not truly evergreen, but the progeny have inherited some of that quality from *M. grandiflora*, the best known of which are 'Maryland' and 'Freeman'. The former seems the more satisfactory, and a twenty-year-old tree in my garden is about twelve feet (3.6 m) high and wide, and flowers freely. The flowers are slightly smaller than those of *M. grandiflora*, but equally noble and well scented.

Magnolia × *thompsoniana*, another beautiful summer-flowering hybrid of *M. virginiana*

M. obovata is a tree-like species carrying good foliage and sumptuous cream flowers with plum-coloured stamens. It can easily attain thirty feet (10.0 m) on good soil, as can *M. tripetala*, with less conspicuous flowers.

Stewartia pseudocamellia, best known of the stewartias, is a slender tree of medium height with lovely, flaking, tinted bark. The comparatively large flowers only last for a day or two, but there is a succession of them. They are like single camellias, and indeed they belong to the same botanical family. *S. sinensis* is another good species, but perhaps the choicest of all is *S. malacodendron*; this is more of a shrub and is noted for its late display of flowers made conspicuous by the blue anthers. There are few others with more appeal in summer. All excel in autumn colour.

Tilia chinensis, *T. miqueliana* and *T. mongolica* are Limes, or Lindens, with which you can be sure of the scent without the disadvantage of huge growth. The best known are very tall trees suitable only for parks and roadside planting, and we must be grateful for the few small enough for some gardens; July would be the poorer were it not for their far-reaching sweet scent.

Shrubs

Abelia floribunda is usually the first abelia to flower, but I should add, if you garden in a warm climate. It is a rare treat to come across this species in a sheltered Cornish or Irish garden, hung lavishly with its crimson, tubular flowers. Theirs is a richness apart. It seems perfectly happy in any fertile soil and has a good three to four weeks of bloom.

Abutilon vitifolium is a rapid grower with velvety, vine-like leaves and glorious yellow-eyed flowers of lavender or white, not unlike those of hollyhocks, to which they are closely related. Time was when we wrestled with this and other abutilons, lovely things though they are, but found them not reliably hardy in Surrey. They are from the southern hemisphere and need all the sun they can get. Then the hybrid *A.* × *suntense* came on the market. It has darker flowers, seems hardier, and quickly reaches six feet (1.8 m) or more even in dry soils. Quite a different thing is *A. megapotamicum*, which may sometimes be seen against a hot sunny wall, dangling its yellow bells in crimson calyces from late summer onwards.

Chionanthus retusus, the Chinese species, has more or less upright panicles of blossom, whereas the North American, *C. virginicus*, bears them drooping and has larger leaves. Both are known as Fringe Tree, with flowers, although small, noteworthy for their quantity and fragrance. If you are in a sunny, warm climate, you might find the Fringe Trees a great asset, but they require a good baking to make them flower freely. When they do, these large shrubs can be pictures of beauty.

Clematis 'Étoile Rose' nearly became extinct until I rescued it from the garden at Abbotswood, Gloucestershire. It is a triple hybrid with the red bellflowered species *C. texensis*, and has inherited wider flowers from *C. viticella*. They are nodding or more or less upright and rosy red. My painting of it is on page 81. I find it a hardy satisfactory plant achieving some eight feet (2.4 m). I cut it to within a foot of ground level every year, and it scrambles through a Deutzia that flowered in May. Other clematises are beginning to open, particularly some early viticella varieties like 'Minuet'. But we will leave them all till August.

Deutzia monbeigii, one of the later deutzias, is a dainty floriferous shrub of some size, producing among its dark green leaves small snow-white flowers, creating a lovely spectacle.

Abutilon × *suntense*

ABOVE: *Chionanthus retusus*

LEFT: *Clematis* 'Étoile Rose',
a hybrid of *C. texensis*

D. setchuenensis corymbiflora is slightly later than *D. monbeigii*, but equally snow-white with a long flowering period. Each corymb of blossom takes several weeks to complete its display. This species requires adequate moisture, and I have not found it particularly hardy, but there is no denying its value and charm. There are other species coming into flower, such as *D. pulchra* and *D. chunii*, both valuable additions to our July list, and the few large flowered hybrids such as 'Magicien', 'Contraste' and 'Mont Rose'; all have exquisite blooms of a warm lilac-pink. Their growth is stiff, and they pay well for systematic pruning immediately after flowering—which is necessary with all deutzias. To these may be added that glory *D. longifolia* 'Veitchii', a superlative rose-pink flower in generous bunches. Glorious though many deutzias are in flower, and welcome though they are in the waning summer, they have no further beauty to give us in autumn. *D. compacta* and its possible form 'Lilac Time' wind up the season with flowers of white and lilac respectively, held in bunches like those of Hawthorn.

Escallonia rubra macrantha produces a long succession of sprays of pink or crimson bells among shining dark foliage. 'Red Hedger' and 'Crimson Spire' are two noted bushy kinds, but if I were limited to one cultivar, I think I should choose *E.* 'Edinensis' for it is hardy and graceful—just right for training on any support—and the little pink stars show up well against the greenery. They all make sizeable shrubs when established, take hard pruning with impunity and are easy to root from cuttings, but are best in the warmer districts, particularly in maritime locations.

Hebe pinguifolia 'Pagei', whose glaucous grey leaves scintillate in mist or hoarfrost, is quite hardy with me. It is an admirable carpeter and among the excellent, mostly dwarf hebes with white flowers suitable for the outskirts of the rock garden, the heath garden and the fronts of borders. Equally prostrate is 'Sussex Carpet', which originated at Wakehurst, Sussex. It is a forward pointing grey plant. Rather larger, also greyish, is *H. albicans*, whose variety 'Red Edge' has its leaves so marked. Bright green is found in *H. rakaiensis*, which makes a first-rate low, bushy, ground cover studded with short spikes of white flowers. I prefer to clip mine in spring, which does away with the flowers and the brown pods. It makes a lovely low hedge. Then there is a much taller shrub, *H. cupressoides*, very like a fragrant conifer in foliage; it ascends to some four feet (1.2 m), is tolerably hardy, and is smothered in tiny lilac-white flowers in July. *H. brachysiphon*, for many years known as *Veronica traversii*, is an example of the not-so-desirable taller species that gradually get leggy. A very bushy larger leafed plant is *H. × franciscana*, a hybrid of *H. speciosa* but tolerably hardy, seen all round our coasts in the form known as 'Blue Gem'. Then there are the fairly hardy 'whipcord' kinds, with tiny leaves appressed to the twigs; examples are the green *H. hectorii* and the startling yellowish brown *H. ochracea*, of which 'James Stirling' is a noted form.

Hebe speciosa 'Great Orme'

H. salicifolia is potentially large, with notably drooping flower spikes of white, whereas the others mentioned have perky, erect, often short spikes. Taking in also those treated in June, the comparatively large flowered *H. hulkeana* and 'Fairfieldii', it is a big and varied group with great garden value, able to thrive in limy or acid soil, needing at the same time full sunshine and adequate moisture. They are all easy from cuttings and present an absorbing study.

H. speciosa, the finest and most showy of the genus, which mainly comes from New Zealand, is native to the North Island, and therefore of doubtful hardiness in our gardens. It has given rise to some of the finest garden hebes—striking shrubs with shining, dark, pointed leaves and big spikes of tiny flowers over a long period, many continuing until the autumn. Some famous varieties are 'Gauntlettii' (pink), 'La Séduisante' (crimson-purple), 'Midsummer Beauty', 'Hidcote' (lilac) and 'Simon Deleaux' (crimson-violet). These are the queens of the tribe, but there are princesses, among them 'Autumn Glory' (procumbent, violet blue, with burnished leaves), 'Carnea', 'Great Orme' (pink) and many more. As a general rule the larger the leaf, the more tender the plant proves.

Hedysarum multijugum has cool green leaves, elegant and pinnate, providing the perfect setting for vertical racemes of glowing crimson-purple flowers throughout the summer. It is seldom seen, but is a worthy sprawling shrub that flowers well in full sun, but not until fully established.

Hydrangea paniculata 'Praecox' is a big, angular, Japanese shrub that flowers earlier than most and, with its pointed panicles of cream flowers, indicates the glories that are to come from others of its kind. To get good panicles, some hard spring pruning is indicated. There are two lesser species which put up a good show towards the end of the month: *H. arborescens* and *H. arborescens discolor* (*H. cinerea*). In the fertile or lace cap forms, these species have little garden value, but in common with many others, they have been treasured through the ages in sterile forms known as 'Grandiflora' and 'Sterilis', respectively. And their greenish white is very cooling and refreshing, turning to creamy white and, in autumn, to snuff brown. The species is inclined to be floppy, but *discolor* is a good upstanding shrub with larger heads of smaller flowers. All prefer lime-free soil and moisture.

Hypericum androsaemum, Tutsan, I have come to regard as a true friend, though its progeny can be a nuisance if you don't pick off its seed pods when they turn from red-brown to black. But the plant is so charming in its foliage tints and neat flowers produced alongside the fruits that I tolerate its prolificity. The name Tutsan derives from *tout sain*, "cure all". It will grow anywhere, short of a bog, and by cutting it right down in spring, a very long period of flower is achieved. There are dusky and variegated forms.

Hypericum calycinum

H. bellum has a form, unnamed, with burnished, slightly undulate leaves; the pale yellow flowers are also a welcome change.

H. calycinum, that ardent coloniser of rough ground, is perhaps the most neglected and beautiful of the shrubby hypericums, known collectively as St John's wort. They begin their long flowering period in July. Theirs is a lovely warm yellow, and the bunches of stamens add greatly to their charm. Each flower is a miracle of beauty. But I do not recommend *H. calycinum* for the garden proper; every bit of root will grow and it becomes invasive. I always regret the day when I left some roots in my new garden. They have since taken over square yards. Even so, for some rough bank in sun or shade, it can prove a wonderful ground cover. It is known as Rose of Sharon, perhaps wrongly.

H. 'Hidcote', the famous variety whose flowers are produced occasionally after the main crop, must not be overlooked, nor must the superb 'Rowallane'. But this is not quite as hardy as the others, often being cut to the ground by winter frosts. For all that it will sprout up and produce its great globes of orange-tinted deep yellow until the frosts come again. It is the most beautiful of all but needs a warm corner. 'Eastleigh Gold' is equally prolific over a long period.

H. × *inodorum* is closely related to *H. androsaemum* and resembles it in all respects except for the fruits, which are bright scarlet. It suffers in some gardens from rust on the leaves, a failing with the other two species also. Rust does not seem to attack well-nurtured plants. Whether the specific epithet refers to the lack of scent in the flowers (hypericums are not noted for fragrance) or the leaves I have not discovered. Crushed leaves of all other species release a scent reminiscent of lemon.

H. patulum and its relatives are a great group that takes some beating, coming into flower when few other shrubs are showing colour. Their only shortcoming is in the compact little bunches of stamens, which are, like the petals, yellow; in *H. calycinum* the stamens are red and the contrast is telling. Reddish stamens are found also in the very worthy *H.* × *moserianum*, which is like a compact *H. patulum*, nearly evergreen and flowering from July onwards. The flowering period of the patulums can be lengthened by severe pruning back of all flowering shoots in spring. That is what I do every year to one of my plants of *H. kouytchense*; the other I leave alone to flower early. I could go on commenting on Asiatic species, but the list would be long, and I think I have written enough to satisfy you that these are shrubs of small to medium height, easy to strike from cuttings and happy in any fertile soil in sun or shade. There are a few American species, markedly different: small-leafed and with small flowers usually of rich orange-yellow, such as *H. frondosum* (*H. aureum*).

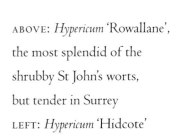

ABOVE: *Hypericum* 'Rowallane', the most splendid of the shrubby St John's worts, but tender in Surrey
LEFT: *Hypericum* 'Hidcote'

Indigofera amblyantha is useful for carrying on the floral flag from July onwards, its spikes of flowers being almost of a salmon tone displayed against pretty pinnate leaves. There are other species of similar habit and leafage, but usually with subdued, mauve-purple flowers. *I. heterantha* (*I. gerardiana*) is one of the best known, and deservedly so, while *I. hebepetala* is distinct in its two-toned flowers of pink and crimson. These all are best grown on sunny positions and will make fair-sized shrubs in time or may be cut to the ground in spring and enjoyed as we do fuchsias. *I. decora* is much smaller, almost herbaceous, with larger flowers in pink or white. They may all be raised from seeds.

Kalmia latifolia
'Clementine Churchill'

Kalmia latifolia has, as its name suggests, the largest leaves of the genus, although they fall short of the majesty of some rhododendrons. They are shiny and smooth and make an excellent contrast to fascinating flowers, which are held in bunches, and when in bud, resemble nothing so much as fancy icing on a cake. They open to little cups, and the cusps around the bud contain decurved stamens which emerge and spring to attention when visited by a bee. Numerous colour forms have been separated, embracing near white, various pinks to near crimson and almost a chocolate tint. None, however, surpasses the rosy beauty of 'Clementine Churchill'. They are raised from cuttings, or by seed from a sowing of which all sorts of tints will appear. The lesser species, *K. angustifolia* and *K. polifolia*, are rather earlier flowering and not without charm. The latter needs a moist spot, and the former has rich dark pink ('Rubra') and white ('Candida') forms. It often repeats its late spring bloom with autumn blossom. All thrive best in acid soil and in gardens are frequently the companions of rhododendrons, to which they are close botanical relatives.

Lavandula (Lavender) 'Munstead', in darkish purple, and the lighter 'Folgate' are among the first of these unthirsty plants to flower. Then comes *L. angustfolia*, of which the best-known clone is 'Hidcote', followed by 'Hidcote Pink' and 'Loddon Pink'; the dwarf 'Nana Alba' is white and suitable for knot gardens. 'Twickel Purple' is I think my favourite of them all. It carries its flower stalks all over and round the bushes and is a compact grower of good colour and scent. 'Hidcote Giant' is a compact, dwarf bush with long stems bearing large, conical, light purple flowers. We end the display with the clone known as 'Dutch'. This has good grey foliage and will go on flowering into September. 'Richard Gray' is a hybrid of the very dark purple *L. incana*, with extra grey leaves. *L. incana* has not proved hardy with me. While it is good in the interest of tidiness to remove the old flowering shoots, on no account clip the bushes until spring is well advanced. They are all easy to root from cuttings.

Lonicera americana, or the plant that in gardens goes by this name, benefits greatly from spring pruning. It may throw out long new shoots with quite a plume of blossoms at the end, as well as on all the short shoots. It makes a lovely climber for an arch or pole, but I have also seen it kept as a large shrub. The flowers are like the Woodbine but of warm rosy pink. I place it very high among honeysuckles.

L. etrusca, more of a shrub than a climber, is certainly not a twiner. The normal form in our gardens, distinguished by the epithet 'Superba', is warm yellow. My old friend Donald Waterer found a rich crimson form in Spain, and this is known under his name.

L. heckrottii is interesting for its scented flowers of a curious creamy salmon-red. It is a vigorous twiner. And then there is that rich orange-yellow *L. tellmanniana*, without scent, and the giant of the hardier types, *L. tragophylla* with very large bunches of yellow trumpets. It seems to prefer part shade. Lastly there is a group of American species, forms or hybrids known as *L. sempervirens* or *L. brownii*. The splendid flowers are of bright coral-red but not scented. Somehow I feel that a honeysuckle without scent is not the real thing.

L. japonica 'Halliana' stands on each side of my front door so that visitors in summer and autumn may enjoy and be beguiled by its fragrance. By keeping the plants well in hand by hard spring pruning, this variety will go on flowering until frosts call a halt. Its creamy flowers are produced from every leaf joint, hence the value of hard pruning. It is virtually evergreen and produces shiny black berries late in the year.

L. periclymenum 'Serotina', the Late Dutch Honeysuckle, is well worth a space. It does not have just one flush of bloom but, if spring-pruned, will continue to produce fresh flowers, crimson-tubed, until autumn. By training up a single strong shoot to a stake and pruning the top unmercifully in early spring, a charming standard can be made (with the flowers at nose level, too). But do not expect them to give their best scent until the evening, for they are pollinated by moths with long tongues, and after pollination the flowers, white inside, turn yellow, as in most species. In a totally different tint is my own namesake *L. periclymenum* 'Graham Thomas'. This I found in a Warwickshire copse one October flowering merrily though it certainly had not been pruned. It is a strong grower with fine heads of white flowers turning to creamy yellow, and a marked fragrance in the evening.

Lonicera periclymenum 'Graham Thomas' at the Savill Gardens, Windsor

Mahonia aquifolium in fruit

L. similis delavayi was found in China long ago, and I am surprised it is not better known. It is semi-evergreen, more of a dense shrub than a climber and produces masses of small, scented, creamy white flowers from July onwards.

Mahonia japonica and its hybrid *H. × media* varieties, having flowered in winter and early spring, are ready to give us joy from their strings of pale blue fruits. The Oregon Grape, *M. aquifolium*, too, can be quite a picture with its bunches of fruits, to which the birds are inconsistently partial. An especially attractive contrast is found in *M. × wagneri* 'Moseri', where sky blue fruits show against the pale young foliage. The berries of all are near black but with a waxy coating; it was Rowland Jackman who told me that they make excellent jelly, like that from blackcurrants.

Neillia thibetica used to be called *N. longiracemosa*. The graceful branches bear elegant lobed leaves and terminal spires of tiny pink flowers. It is hardier than the greatly admired *Abelia floribunda* and serves in its stead where frost is frequent.

Ononis fruticosa, a small sun-loving shrub with small leaves and a dense twiggy habit, displays its bunches of small clear pink pea-flowers to advantage for many weeks. I know bushes of some two to three feet (0.6–0.9 m) that give relief from the many midsummer yellows in a border, and are a great joy.

Philadelphus 'Virginal', large and double, is I suppose the most popular of the many hybrids of this often strongly scented and usually white-flowered group. But those with rosy mauve central markings like 'Sybille' and the beautiful arching 'Beauclerk' are regular July performers, as is their doubly fragrant forbear *P. × purpureo maculatus*. At the end of the month appears *P. incanus*, snow-white, with greyish leaves. They come just as summer is bursting upon us, and with their pure white flowers make a

LEFT: *Potentilla* 'Red Ace'

BELOW: *Rhododendron* 'Conroy',
a June-flowering orange-red hybrid

rare contrast to the many colours that beset us. Some six weeks of glory in all, and they have gone.

Potentilla fruticosa and its many relatives give us a contrast to all the warm yellows of hypericums. 'Red Ace' and one or two others were mentioned in June, but there are innumerable yellow forms and hybrids, usually on the cool side, one of the best being 'Elizabeth'. Of whites there are also several, 'Abbotswood' and the dwarf 'Mandschurica' standing pre-eminent. There are some pretty creamy ones which are so useful for colour grouping, and also the tall-growing, silvery-leafed 'Vilmoriniana', which has sulphur yellow flowers, a plant of great appeal. There is another excellent silvery-leafed one, a form of *P. arbuscula* named 'Beesii' ('Nana Argentea') with flowers of extra bright yellow borne more or less continuously until autumn. In fact, most of them do well in moist, enriched soil; the species *P. fruticosa* is a native of Britain (and elsewhere) and grows in wet surroundings. Despite reservations mentioned last month, I have a warm spot in my heart for 'Vilmoriniana', which has been grown for as long as any.

RHODODENDRONS

Rhododendrons are now clamouring for attention as they bring up the rear of a distinguished and invaluable family. July sees the noble white 'Albatross' in flower and the various strains of the 'Angelo' hybrids. They are very large shrubs, like 'Bonito', and thrive best in thin woodland, where their large flowers and free scent are conspicuous. *Rhododendron griersonianum*, with its sharp colouring, has had a hand in

Rhododendron viscosum

'Azor', 'Fairy Light' and the great 'Aladdin'. To these should be added 'Arthur Osborn', a rich colour on a low bush. *R. elliottii* and *R. facetum* are two tree-like species for woodland conditions in our milder counties; both light up their surroundings with bell-shaped flowers of glowing red. (I am not sure that I want red in my woodland; cooler colours are more sympathetic.) In light maize-yellow is the great 'Bustard', a nobleman if ever there was one. And at the end of the month, or in August, we may expect 'Polar Bear' to flower. This is frequently some twenty feet (6.0 m) high with slightly glaucous foliage—a commanding sight with its great fragrant white flowers. It is almost the last to flower.

Among the smaller late azaleas, so valuable for extending the season in woodland gardens, *Rhododendron viscosum*—of which I prefer the forms with the most glaucous leaves, sometimes called 'Glaucum'—sheds a wonderful fragrance from its small, honeysuckle-like, white flowers, often touched with pink. A small creeping shrub for the rock garden on peat beds is *R. nakahari*; both it and the latest azalea of all, *R. prunifolium*, have flowers of rich brick-red; 'Summer Sunset' is a noted clone.

ROSES

The glory of July is really the roses—all roses, small, medium or large. They range from one foot (0.3 m) to forty feet (12.0 m). The latest arrivals in our gardens are the so-called ground-cover roses. I put it like that because up to the present very few are free of prickles, and if you have ever had to weed round prickly roses, you will know all about it. There are many charmers among them in a variety of colours. There are the once-flowering old French hybrids of the nineteenth century known today as old garden or old-fashioned roses. They have a special appeal to those who love a full, flat flower in white, pink, mauve, light crimson and murrey. The scent is proverbial and they embrace Gallicas, Damasks, Albas, Centifolias and Mosses. Since about 1939 a handful of us sought to bring back some of the hundreds of varieties which had been *the* roses of the nineteenth century. Such is their present popularity once again that every year or two conferences about them are held all over the world. With them came the Noisette and Tea roses, products of their hybridising with the newly introduced China roses, and in particular some soft yellows. These remain supreme for colour and exquisite scent—witness 'Gloire de Dijon',

LEFT: *Veronica teucrium*
'Shirley Blue' (enlarged)
BELOW: The Rose Garden at
Mottisfont Abbey, Hampshire

'Alister Stella Gray' and 'Desprez à fleurs jaunes'. Their like has never been surpassed any more than that of the old Gallicas. I think the time is not far distant when Hybrid Teas from the early 1900s, such as 'Mabel Morrison', 'Mrs Wemyss Quin', 'Rose Berkeley' and 'Christopher Stone', will also be collected and extolled.

Those who are so enthusiastic about the scent of the older roses should do as I do and walk past a hedge of 'Fragrant Cloud'. It was raised in 1963 as 'Duftwolka' and is as fragrant as any rose. There have always been certain roses which were wanting in fragrance. Increasing in size, in my little survey are such shrub roses as the invaluable Rugosa varieties, so prickly and floriferous. Invaluable, that is, so long as you garden on neutral or lime-free soil. Like so many Japanese plants, they do not tolerate excess lime. They were mostly raised around 1900. Since then many other species have been used for hybridising, some well-known results being 'Golden Wings' and 'Cerise Bouquet', from six to ten feet (2.0–3.0 m), and repeat-flowering, too. For this is what we have come to expect of a rose: that it shall flower from summer till autumn.

Then there are the climbers and ramblers. The older climbers, apart from outstanding varieties like 'Paul's Lemon Pillar', were mostly climbing sports from bush Hybrid Teas. Their faults were excessive vigour and often a rather long interval without flowers in late summer. 'Climbing Étoile de Holland' is the exception, and 'Climbing Shot Silk' is often the first rose to open. Many ramblers are lacking in fragrance but there are notable exceptions—'Goldfinch', 'Débutante' and 'Veilchenblau'. And now we have 'Crimson Showers', which brings the ramblers into August. With it for late and continuous flowers are 'Blushing Lucy', pink; 'Phyllis Bide', pale yellow shaded with pink; and 'Princess of Nassau', cream. I think it will not be long before these are joined by others; after all, *Rosa wichuraiana* itself is August-flowering, also *R. moschata*. The species roses belonging, as they do, to the Synstylae Section of the genus have a noted peculiarity: their often overpowering fragrance comes from the stamens, not from the petals. (This is why the early Noisettes were so sweetly scented.) There is a whole family of them from almost prostrate and evergreen *R. wichuraiana* to giants of thirty to forty feet (9.0–12.0 m) such as *R. filipes* and *R. rubus*. No shrubs shed so much rich aroma around as these and the earlier philadelphuses.

OPPOSITE: Rambler rose 'Débutante' in the garden at Mottisfont Abbey, Hampshire
TOP: *Rosa rugosa* 'Fru Dagmar Hastrup' and *Rosa rugosa* 'Roseraie de l'Haÿ'
BOTTOM: *Rosa* 'Fragrant Cloud'. All are very fragrant.

It is a long way from dwarf bedding roses of the late nineteenth century to these giants. In the early days the newest hybrids between the old French roses and the China roses were very weak in growth. Recourse was made to budding them not at ground level, which is usual, but onto stems of one or two feet, to raise them above their fellows and so make a bank of blossom. In this way were standard roses born, now to some three feet (0.9 m) or more, bringing the blooms to the nose, and incidentally adding some new styles in garden design. All too few modern bedding roses are of a suitable low growth to make standards—'Shot Silk' and 'Marlena' come to mind as exceptions.

We get good autumn colour and heps from *R. rugosa*, *R. virginiana* and *R. nitida*, and a wealth of resplendent heps from roses of the *R. moyesii* breed, such as *R. sweginzowii* and *R. webbiana*. The rose has much to offer us for furnishing our gardens, but, owing to the prickles on most of them, we must not grasp them too hard. Fortunately, there are several dozen without prickles, and I hope the breeders will produce more.

ABOVE: Rose 'Crimson Showers'

BELOW: *Rosa wichuraiana*

Salvia officinalis is the Common Sage so beloved by the cook, and it is usual to grow for the pot the English Broad Leaf kind which does not flower. But the most garden-worthy kind is 'Purpurascens', whose richly purple-tinted foliage makes a wonderful complement to the spikes of violet, hooded flowers. It can be, during July, the most striking plant in the garden. It will gradually build up into a large dome. Cuttings strike easily and when the plant gets too large can be used to replace it—"plant sage in May, 'twill grow all day". The two variegated forms do not flower much, but are valuable garden plants. 'Icterina' is yellow-flushed and variegated; 'Tricolor' is still a size smaller and noted for its purplish young shoots developing cream and pink variegation, without flowers.

Sambucus canadensis has very large plates of tiny cream flowers and can make an exceptional display, followed in autumn by masses of small murrey-coloured berries. It has no autumn colour to help it, but will thrive in any fertile soil. It responds nobly to hard spring pruning. Other elders, coarse and overbearing shrubs, are hardly worthy of a note in these pages.

Santolina chamaecyparissus is known, with other santolinas, by the misleading name of Cotton Lavender. All are of the Daisy Family and not related to lavenders. It thrives in dry positions in full sun as a sprawling low shrub with dense foliage if clipped over in spring. In fact, I feel it essential to clip this species when used in the best possible way—among flowers of soft blues and pinks for its incomparably fine grey foliage—we do not want the colour scheme upset by the santolina's little buttons of bright yellow. There are softer, paler flowers to be found in *S. pinnata* 'Edward Bowles', creamy white with extra grey-white, feathery foliage, and the green-leafed *S. rosmarinifolia* 'Primrose Gem'. But on the whole I think it best to forget the flowers and clip all of them over quite hard in spring for the sake of their lovely foliage. Each heeled shoot, pulled off in spring, will root in the open ground if planted deeply.

Scabiosa minoana (*Lomelosia* sp.) has the wit to produce lilac-pink flowers for many weeks over its mantle of grey leaves. It is a woody plant, rather like the growth of a sage, and it is perhaps well to call attention to those valuable shrubby plants here.

Tamarix ramosissima may be cut to the ground every spring, and the result will be a fountain of tiny greyish leaves and airy sprays of tiny pink flowers. It will, how-

Trachelospermum jasminoides
in a warm climate

ever, build up into a good shrub if not pruned, but the flowering period will be shorter. All tamarisks strike readily from hardwood cuttings simply stuck into sandy soil in late autumn.

Trachelospermum jasminoides, given a few vertical wires up which the shoots can twine, makes an excellent plant for a sunny warm wall. It is evergreen and densely bushy, every short shoot producing a little group of creamy, jasmine-like, very fragrant flowers. It can readily be distinguished from its less hardy relative *T. asiaticum* by the fact that in this species the calyx lobes are flush with the flower tube, whereas in *T. jasminoides* they jut out. It does not seem to be difficult to please in the way of soil, and roots from cuttings readily.

Yucca filamentosa and *Y. filifera* (*Y. flaccida*) are similar, their sword-like leafy rosettes making scarcely any stem. The leaves have sharp points and thread-like hairs to the edges (needle and thread, in fact). The stately stems bear pyramids of cream bells, fragrant of lemon in the evening, a

Yucca filamentosa

rosette of leaves taking about three years to produce a flowering stem. An especially good form is one known as 'Ivory', selected by Rowland Jackman for its floriferousness and outward facing flowers. Another that will frequently be in flower in July is 'Vittorio Emmanuele II', a big hybrid shrub with large stout leaves and massive spikes of cream bells, crimson-flushed in bud. A group of two or three plants can usually be relied upon to produce a flower spike every year, whereas *Y. recurvifolia*, although worthy, flowers with less regularity in our climate. *Y. filamentosa*, known as Adam's Needle, also has several variegated forms. The giant species *Y. gloriosa* is usually so late in opening that frost cripples it. There are other smaller species little known and, like *Y. gloriosa*, horribly prickly. But prickles or no, there are no hardy plants that can give such an air of tropical magnificence to the garden.

Perennials

We now come to the long list of July-flowering perennials. It is their heyday. A herbaceous border well graded for height is quite a work of art, but I like to see some taller plants among their shorter fellows, and this is best done with shrubs. They will still be effective even when out of flower, and are noteworthy for breaking the graded monotony and making something to look around or behind.

Acanthus spinosus has prickly whorls of flowers up the stems not unlike foxgloves—until you feel them. Its foliage is dark, shining and divided, produced abundantly from incursive roots. Lady Moore found in Ireland a form of it whose young foliage is so heavily dotted with white as to appear grey. It reverts to the usual dark green later in the season. Other species are *A. mollis* and *A. hungaricus*, but they may be left aside. *A. dioscoridis perringii* has bright pink flowers and is a dwarf grower; in my experience, it is not a runner like the others.

Achillea ptarmica, although offering invaluable pure white flowers in its double varieties 'The Pearl' and 'Perry's White', is an arrant runner, like couch grass, in any soil and best avoided. Likewise I should avoid the single and double varieties of *Houttuynia cordata* and its multi-coloured leaf-variant, 'Chameleon'; they are all invasive in cool moist soil.

Aconitum napellus, with its prettily divided, shining dark green leaves above which are held spikes of dark blue-purple hooded flowers, has, in one or another of its various forms, been for years one of the main ingredients of the summer border. Among popular varieties are the statuesque hybrid 'Bressingham Spire' and the branching 'Spark's Variety'. There are useful white- and flesh-coloured forms in 'Albidum' and 'Carneum'. *A. cammarum* 'Bicolor' is noted for its blue and white flowers. There is a welcome change for us in *A. lycoctonum*, in which the flowers are small, but of creamy ivory. They all have knobbly roots that are poisonous but which provide a ready means of increase. Planting should be done in autumn, not spring.

Alstroemeria ligtu hybrid

Alstroemeria aurantiaca, Peruvian Lily, is a creeping, tuberous-rooted plant not always easy to transplant unless you take up a big spadeful. The leafy stems support a head of light orange, lily-like flowers, beautifully marked but scentless. There is a more yellow form and a richer one called 'Dover Orange'. Long years ago they were the only Peruvian Lilies and then, between the wars, arrived *A. ligtu* and *A. haemantha*, pink and fiery tones respectively. They became hybridised and popular, and it is seldom that the separate species are seen. However, the mixed strain is a wonderful blend of sharp colours; a large bed of them at Oxford University Botanic Garden in flower at two to three feet (0.6–0.9 m) in height was a great July sight. Of late years hybrids of other species have been bred in Holland, England and elsewhere. They are known variously as 'Parigo' and Princess Lilies. They are well known in the cut-flower market and bid fair to become short or tall plants in a variety of tints, some parti-

coloured. As we have of late years been blessed with mild winters, I do not feel competent to pronounce on their hardiness.

Arisaema candidissimum, whose white hooded spathes, pink striped within, appear in July just when you had given up on them, is my favourite in a genus whose species have become much sought after in recent years. They undoubtedly have something that other plants haven't, but you can't make a garden with them. They are unobtrusive semi-woodlanders with intriguing flowers and beautiful three-lobed leaves, which they flaunt for several weeks.

Astilbe is for damp ground. Their ferny leaves are a delight in spring; some are deep red brown, denoting red and purplish plumes of flowers. The pink and the white ones have green leaves. I will leave you to select the colors you need. They make dense clumps sending aloft their flowers to two to four feet (0.6–1.2 m). Most have erect plumes, but there are several with graceful and drooping heads. All are beautiful and long lasting. They are easy to divide with a spade in the dormant season.

Astrantia major, at two feet (0.6 m) a little tall for the front row, still deserves a place well to the fore. There are darker, plum-coloured forms and hybrids for which I have not much use. One called 'Shaggy' (*A. major involucrata*) has extra long bracts. There is a good form, 'Sunningdale Variegated', whose leaves are marbled with yellow, turning to white, which captivates all. Another with good collars of rose-pink is *A. maxima*; this I find needs more moisture than *A. major*. In cool moist soil they are all easy from division in spring.

Campanula carpatica in its forms flowers now: quite short tumps of greenery over which are poised the wide cups of lilac-blue, purple or white. Some famous varieties are 'Bressingham White' and 'Blaue Clips', while its variety *C. carpatica turbinata* is noted for 'Karl Foerster' and 'Pallida'. They make admirable front line plants and can be divided in spring, or, if a general mixture is preferred, can be raised from seeds. *C. alliariifolia* is much taller; in fact, it can reach three feet (0.9 m), and its swaying stems hung thickly with nearly white bells overtop considerably the clumps of greyish leaves. They seed themselves freely in well-drained soils in sun. *C. trachelium* is a violet-purple species with a tuberous root. I only grow its double white form 'Alba Flore Pleno', which

TOP: *Campanula* 'Burghaltii'
BOTTOM: *Astrantia major*

is an heirloom of great charm. *C.* 'Burghaltii' is another treasure, with rather flopping stems strung with long tubes of strange, pale grey-lilac, beautifully shaped. If cut down after flowering and given a good feed and soak, it will usually produce a second crop in September.

Catananche caerulea, Blue Cupidone, is a sun-lover with grassy foliage and flowers rather like a cornflower held in papery bracts. Each flower is held singly on a good stalk. It can be propagated by seeds or root cuttings and is a long time in flower. It consorts well with astrantias, but plants of neither genus are noted for fragrance.

Chrysanthemum maximum, one of the stalwarts of the July–August garden, has suffered a fall: it is now to be called *Leucanthemum superbum*. It is the Shasta Daisy of our gardens, a good hearty plant for heavier soils, producing large white daisies for weeks over extra dark green leaves.

Cynara cardunculus has the most handsome grey leaves of the whole season.

Some are just bold and white, like 'T. Killin', some have fringed petals like 'Bishopstone', others have mossy centres like 'Wirral Supreme', and there are also full doubles which do away with the rather obtrusive yellow centres. They are easy enough to divide in autumn or spring.

Cimicifuga racemosa, Black Snakeroot, is a wonderful July flower with elegant divided foliage up the seven-foot (2.1 m), self-reliant stems, branching into long cream bottlebrushes. Some shorter species are mentioned in September.

Clematis recta 'Foliis Purpureis' is a fluff of creamy white over green or purplish leaves. It is a valuable fragrant summer flower and needs the support of pea-sticks. The following two are usually treated as climbers, though they die to the ground in winter: *C.* × *eriostemon* has small soft violet flowers, starry and recurved like those of *C. viticella* itself, which is one of the parents. It has a long period of bloom, as does the noble × *durandii*, whose splendid, wide, indigo-violet flowers are produced for weeks.

Cynara cardunculus, Cardoon, is a real giant of a plant, only suitable for large gardens. This is a close relative of the Globe Artichoke, but with even better and greyer leaves which reach great majesty by July. It requires full sun in well-drained soil. The great prickly blue thistle-heads take a bit of beating, reaching six to eight feet (1.8–2.4 m).   ·

Delphinium hybrids, the stalwart kinds that reach to six feet (1.8 m), are going over and are ready for pruning down to foliage level, at which height they make good support for Viticella clematises or the Perennial Pea. We are fortunate in that the shorter Belladonna delphiniums go on producing new flower spikes until autumn if in rich, good soil. Well-tried favourites are 'Lamartine' in dark blue; 'Cliveden Beauty', light

Dierama pulcherrimum

blue; and the closely related *D.* × *ruysii* 'Pink Sensation'. These seldom exceed four feet (1.2 m). One of the loveliest combinations I have known was a planting of good light blue delphiniums with the lemon-yellow *Thalictrum flavum glaucum*, whose fluffy plumes overtop the glaucous leaves; these remain in beauty for the whole of the summer when the flowers are over and, like the taller delphiniums, make a useful support for scrambling plants nearby.

Dierama pulcherrimum, best known of the lovely South African Wand Flowers, has four- to five-foot (1.2–1.5 m) wiry stems that move to the lightest breeze, causing the bell-like flowers to sway and nod. It is a member of the Iris Family and has all the elegance of leaf and purity of form we associate with these flowers. Although from a warm climate, it is reasonably hardy in the sunnier parts of Britain and prefers a loose soil in full sun. The slender bulbous roots can be divided in spring, but it is better to leave well alone and enjoy the yearly-increasing array of swaying stems. The flowers are normally some shade of lilac-pink, but dark wine-colour is not unknown. Another species, *D. dracomontanum*, is much shorter but has yielded good forms and hybrids for smaller gardens, though obviously they lack the exquisite grace of the taller species.

Echinops ritro is a good plant for the not-too-small garden; over dark leafy stems are poised spiky, spherical heads of blue. It is an easy plant to grow in any fertile soil in sun. *E. ritro ruthenicus* is not so easy but is smaller. The handsome jagged foliage is dark green but white beneath, the whole a lovely sight with the prickly blue knobs held aloft. Several of these Globe Thistles are coarse and overweening, but these two are choice and bring distinction to the border.

Erigeron speciosus has given us refined daisies of about two feet (0.6 m) occupying softer regions of the spectrum. They are good perennials for the front of the border, of easy division in spring and with no great preferences for soil or aspect, though they usually do best in full sun. There are many hybrids and varieties among which may be singled out the old 'Quakeress' and 'White Quakeress' in pale blue and white, respectively. But if you want more colour, I suggest 'Dunkelste Aller' ('Darkest of All') in rich violet. For desperately dry gardens, especially maritime, there is *Erigeron glaucus*, a lowly plant with spoon-shaped, dull greyish leaves and masses of short lilac daisies; a counterpart is found in 'Elstead Pink'. Both thrive and flower without drooping where few other plants would. All the kinds have neat, narrow petals and plenty of them.

Eryngium tripartitum, one of the thistle-like plants known as Sea-hollies, thrives in well-drained sunny spots, making a mass of blue starry flowers. *E.* × *zabelli* is the group name of several large-flowered hybrids such as 'Violetta'. As with Globe Thistle and Cardoon, Sea-holly can be propagated from root cuttings.

Galega orientalis, whose lavender blue pea-flowers do so much for us in the garden, is the shortest Goat's Rue. Most make a splendid July show of stems some six feet (1.8 m) tall and are easy from division of the several clones and hybrids. I have never had a garden big enough to accommodate them, but if I had just one, it would be *G. orientalis*—about one-third the size.

Galtonia candicans is a bulbous plant from South Africa whose stately spires support snow-white bells with dark eyes. It is a lovely thing for interplanting with a spring-flowering subject to prolong the effect. It seeds itself readily. Other species, *G. princeps* and *G. viridiflora*, flower rather later and are of a greenish white, but of the same elegance.

Geranium endressii will give you flowers for many weeks, sometimes until autumn. If the normal chalky pink is not to your liking, try 'Wargrave' in bright salmon-pink. It would be difficult to have a well-furnished July border or shrubbery without recourse to the hardy geraniums. Not only are they good flowering plants, but most are admirable for covering the ground, none more so than this one.

Galtonia candicans

GRASSES

I have hesitated over this introduction to the grasses and sedges, not because they are difficult or less ornamental, but because they represent a distinct group of plants best used as foils to the more flowery perennials. Today they seem to be returning to favour, so much so that we often see them assembled several kinds together— surely the least satisfactory way of showing their undoubted beauty. Grasses, in my opinion, need to mingle with other plants for full appreciation of their individuality. All the kinds I am listing seem to grow well in any fertile soil; if there is one thing to avoid, it is autumn planting. In my experience they are best planted—or divided—when spring is well advanced.

One of the most majestic species, *Stipa gigantea*, I mentioned with enthusiasm last month; I wish I could write persuasively about *S. calamagrostis* but this, while a beautiful plant, needs a lot of space unless you intend to stake it, which would destroy its beauty. It makes the same grassy tuft, but the stems spray outward, covering as much as six feet (1.8 m) in diameter. They are long plumes, at first green, then buff and later (by September) yellow. Unique is the word for *S. arundinacea*. Again the grassy leaves make a tuft which is smothered by a hairlike, drooping mass of purplish brown flowers perhaps three feet (0.9 m) long. It is best planted on a bank where it can reveal its tumbling beauty.

Among the rarest of plants in our gardens is *Cortaderia fulvida*, which may usually be seen in full beauty at Kiftsgate Court, Gloucestershire. At one time it was also at Chelsea Physic Garden, but I have not seen it elsewhere, and yet it is easy to raise from New Zealand seeds. It is as its name foretells one of the big group of Pampas grasses, but much earlier flowering, at its best in July. Instead of bearing upright plumes of flowers, they gracefully nod on stems of some five or six feet (1.5–1.8 m), and are of soft buff, rosy-tinted at first, but returning to buff with age. I hope some enterprising plantsman will get seeds from New Zealand and raise new stock. It is not completely hardy with us but is worth a deal of trouble with mulching and other protection.

Another grass which I should like to see planted more often is *Chionochloa conspicua*. I will not vouch for its hardiness; my experience with it has been in the soft climates of Northern Ireland and southwest Scotland. However there is no denying its beauty: it throws out from the central tuft airy inflorescences in creamy sprays.

Pennisetum orientale

The pennisetums give us several elegant species. For early July, there is the green-flowered *Pennisetum macrourum*, with long rat's tails of flowers, while *P. orientale* is a short plant with comparatively undistinguished grassy leaves but flower spikes like great hairy caterpillars, glistening and purplish at first but turning to snuff brown. Another good one, *P. alopecuroides*, we will look at later.

If you have some marshy ground, you could try *Glyceria maxima* 'Variegata', an especially pleasing, neatly striped variety with cream lines. But it is very invasive in the moister soils and not to be trusted.

One of the most elegant of grey grasses is *Helictotrichon sempervirens*, though it is not as completely evergreen as its name suggests. It makes attractive tufts of steely grey leaves overtopped at about three feet (0.9 m) by waving stems of steely grey flower heads of lasting beauty. I was given a plant of *Imperata cylindrica* 'Rubra', whose leaves are dark red, but what I offered it in the way of soil did not please it and it left me. I must try again in moister soil, perhaps, because it is a winner, from Japan. My last true grass shall be *Festuca glauca*, a neat tuft of wiry blue-grey leaves carrying at mid-

summer flower heads only a foot or so high of the same cooling colour. Unfortunately, families of ants seem to be as fond of it as I am.

We are left with three sedges, *Carex morrowii*, *C. riparia* and *C. stricta*. The first is a lovely plant in its white variegated form, and the same may be said of the second, but here the similarity ends, for the first is a neat clump-former and the second a wandering plant. I should have mentioned the last in May for its floral, dark brown beauty is then apparent in contrast to the form we all know as Bowles's Golden Sedge—the leaves forming a pretty clump longitudinally striped with yellow.

This list is a mere indication of the beauties of grasses in July. Further kinds will be recorded in August and September, but there is no doubt that they bring to the garden something very special in line and deportment.

GREY FOLIAGE

High summer is the time for silverlings—those plants whose foliage is so covered in white hairs that they appear to be what we call "silver foliage", as opposed to glaucous leaves, which are covered with a film of opaque wax. In my own garden these two grey tones are separated. My first borders are limited to flowers of white and yellow, blue and purple, with an occasional hint of orange. Here the yellow tones are echoed in the leaves of *Melissa officinalis* 'Allgold' and *Salvia officinalis* 'Icterina', while the invaluable purple-leafed Sage, *S. officinalis* 'Purpurascens', blends with all the plantings. The blue tones are abetted by glaucous foliage—the filigree of *Ruta graveolens* 'Jackman's Blue', the trails of *Euphorbia myrsinites* and the blue-green hostas.

The other borders, not visible from the first, are devoted to pink, mauve and white flowers with silvery foliage from *Santolina* (cut down in spring), *Artemisia canescens*, *A. stelleriana* and *A. ludoviciana*. With the aid of white-flowered plants, they give sparkle to an otherwise subdued assembly.

We should have to look hard at all silverlings to find anything better than *Stachys byzantina* (formerly *S. lanata*, *S. olympica*). All its relations make excellent ground cover with their velvety grey leaves. The normal species produces stout grey spikes of tiny pink flowers swathed in grey velvet, while 'Cotton Boll' is much the same without the actual flowers. 'Silver Carpet' does not flower but is valuable as its name suggests; 'Big Ears' is a much recommended larger version. They are all easy from spring division and planting and thrive in well-drained soils in full sun.

Hemerocallis hybrids in lemon yellow are ideal as a contrast to the many blue and bluish flowers in the July list. We looked at some earlies in June, but now is the time for the big hybrids. 'Dorothy McDade' and 'Marion Vaughn' remain two of the best, and, like most of the light yellows, are fragrant. There are many richer yellows and mixed shades to choose from, but those with the true lily shape are, I think, the best. One ancient Japanese double variety, 'Kwanso Flore Pleno', continues to lord it over all comers. It is rich in colour, tawny orange and long-lasting in flower. Unfortu-

Stachys byzantina 'Big Ears'

nately, it is of an invasive habit. The attractive white variegated form is a beautiful plant, but although called 'Kwanso Variegated', it is a separate plant with inferior flowers. 'Kwanso' is Japanese for Daylily. I am not going to start on the numerous debased colour forms that have been raised; I do not like them. They have lost the lily shape. Even so, I doubt whether 'Missenden' has been surpassed for size and colour (rich red) among new plants from breeders on either side of the Atlantic.

Hosta undulata erromena and the cultivar 'Tall Boy' are among the hostas most impressive for flowers. They make a great show with stems of four feet (1.2 m) and sheaves of hanging lilac trumpets. *H. ventricosa* winds up the *Hosta* season with particularly richly coloured, violet, wide bells. But, of course, we grow our hostas mainly for the foliage, of which there is such a bewildering range available today that I think it best to leave the choice to you. Fortunately, they can be planted from containers or the open ground at almost any season of the year. They all prefer cool conditions, with ample humus. Their only enemies are the garden molluscs, against which untiring diligence is essential.

Inula royleana is the first of the great army of yellow perennials to beset us in July. It makes a soft leafy mound and has rather sprawling leafy stems, each bearing a single, large, orange-yellow daisy of refined, narrow rays around a large orange disc. It is something quite out of the ordinary, and my experience tells me that it prefers a somewhat moist spot, when it will reach two feet (0.6 m).

Knautia macedonica is especially valuable for its pure rich crimson flowers—not a common colour among hardy plants. It used to be called *Scabiosa rumelica* and does indeed bear true scabious flowers over a long period. The plant makes a good clump, its stems spraying outwards, and should not in any circumstances be tied up. For all these many weeks since June, *Scabiosa caucasica* has been delighting us in cool or deep lavender, or white, and will go on until the frosts put an end to such matters. Not often seen, except perhaps on rock gardens, is *S. graminifolia*, a first-rate frontal plant with grassy leaves of silver-grey and a long display of lilac flowers in the scabious tradition.

Lavatera olbia (*L. thuringiaca*), of the Mallow Family, might have been included in the shrub paragraphs, but for all its size it is only half-woody and dies down considerably every winter; in a severe one it will go altogether. In the meantime you have a glorious feast of large pink blossoms from July till autumn. The plant may exceed eight feet (2.4 m) high and wide. In its well-known form 'Rosea', the flowers are warm pink, like hollyhocks. A sport, 'Barnsley', is nearly white with a rosy eye and is not quite so vigorous. *L. olbia* is a true herbaceous plant in pink or white, while

ABOVE: *Hemerocallis* 'Missenden'

BELOW: *Hosta minor*, an uncommon dwarf species from Japan

Lilium regale in the
Beth Chatto Gardens,
near Colchester, Essex

L. cachemiriana has more open flowers of cool lilac-pink. Some hybrids have recently been made in various tints, but until the botanists have finished arguing about their nomenclature, I think it best to leave them alone. All of these plants thrive in well-drained soil in full sun.

Liatris pycnostachya, the Kansas Gay Feather, is a strange plant. It has a bulbous root but is a member of the Daisy Family, with dense spikes of fluffy flowers which open first at the top of the spike. They have grassy basal leaves and are noted for the chalky pink of the flowers. Different colours are available in *L. spicata*—white, violet and magenta. It would be as well to keep them apart from the reddish orange lilies flowering this month.

Lilium candidum, the ancient white Madonna Lily, can be surpassed in beauty by no other when the flowers are opening, the lower ones wide open and the top ones still in bud. That is the supreme moment in a supremely beautiful flower that is also generous with its scent. My experience is that it is best grown in full sun in a sticky, limy soil, with the bulbs only just under the surface of the soil. And planting or transplanting should only be done during the few weeks of dormancy in August, or even late July. Much the same should be the rule for *L. × testaceum*, a hybrid of *L. candidum* with *L. chalcedonicum*. The flower colour has been given the descriptive name "isabelline", it is said, from Queen Isabella of France, who swore not to change her underclothes until the siege of Calais had been broken.

L. davidii is a reddish orange–flowered lily of the kind best kept away from *Liatris* (above). It can tower up to six feet (1.8 m) and enjoys abundant sunshine.

L. regale is a wonderful July flower and a more than satisfactory garden plant. Nothing could be easier from seed, which some gardeners simply scatter where lilies are wanted on soil in good tilth, and lightly cover them with sand, which also marks the site. Thereafter, they need only discourage weeds and moisten the soil when needed to enjoy substantial leafage in the second year, and flowers, perhaps, in the third. Once established, *L. regale* is capable of heads of six or more trumpet-shaped flowers on each four-foot (1.2 m) stem, white, slightly stained purple and deliciously scented.

In the days of the grand herbaceous borders, all the plants were over two feet (0.6 m) in height; many needed staking. Today we have a splendid assortment of smaller plants which I for one would not be without. They put the finishing touch to the foreground, acting often as useful ground cover and providing the link between the edge or verge of the border and the taller plants, whether they be perennials or shrubs. You just can't garden without them, and they are easy to increase. Many of them come between dwarf perennials and what we might call large rock plants. Take for instance that lover of the cool and somewhat shady places, *Viola cornuta*, available in rich lilac, pale lavender or white. They all come true from seed or are easy from rooted pieces pulled from the parent stalk. Few would gainsay the charm of the wide clumps so prettily spread with the little flowers, each on its separate stalk. And they keep up a long succession from early July onwards so long as the ground is moist. Or, in pink, there is *Calamintha grandiflora*, a dense little plant with small hooded flowers and fragrant foliage. Or, bigger, there is another pink plant in *Stachys macrantha*, of which 'Superba' is perhaps the best. This is a typical Labiate with square stems, good foliage in dense clumps and heads of hooded flowers galore. There is a comparatively new *Geranium*, 'Mavis Simpson', a hybrid that accrued spontaneously at Kew between, it is thought, *G. traversii* and *G. endressii*, with the silvery leaves of the former and the cool pink flowers of the latter. It is a non-stop flowerer like others of the same cross called *G.* × *riversleaianum*.

A special favourite of mine among the lowly plants, *Veronica incana*, has tufts of grey foliage from which arise neat spikes of blue; it has the one season of flower, but its seedling 'Wendy', though greener in leaf, has a longer and better flower display. Another good blue is the Japanese Balloon Flower, *Platycodon grandiflorus* (*P. mariesii*). A relative of the campanulas, it has buds just like balloons opening into wide cups of that soft bluish tint that is the campanulas' speciality. You can have it in blue, white or soft pink, on stems of about a foot. For a startling pure white to set off all these colours, I know of nothing better than *Malva moschata* 'Alba'. It is so purely white. Though not long-lived, it seeds itself about mildly and makes a good contrast to many of the penstemons, those doubtfully hardy but long-flowering shrubby delights. It is as well

Platycodon grandiflorus, some plants with blue, others with white flowers

Monarda 'Croftway Pink' to take soft cuttings before autumn closes down, for they are susceptible to cold winds and frosts. I am referring to the many large-flowered hybrid penstemons such as the gracious 'Alice Hindley' and hosts of others. *P.* 'Andenken an Friedrich Hahn' (which has long been known simply as 'Garnet') is hardier and seldom succumbs to frost in the south of Britain, or around the coasts. It is recurrent flowering, in a true garnet-red. There are innumerable other seedlings and hybrids all valuable for providing colour in the second half of the year.

Lysimachia ephemerum, a cool plant with greyish leaves and three-foot (0.9 m) spires of grey-white, small flowers, prefers moist soil and thus is a splendid companion for the species and varieties of *Lythrum*, or Loosestrife, whose main colour is madder-pink.

Lythrum virgatum 'Rose Queen' is an old favourite with small madder-pink flowers in long spikes on stout stems. Brighter are the forms of *L. salicaria*, which are also taller growing, ascending to four or five feet (1.2–1.5 m) in moist ground. In fact, they are admirable plants for the waterside. I ought to be rather careful about these plants, for apparently they are bad weeds in parts of the United States. They are all readily propagated from basal cuttings and easy to grow. Some of the most promising in both colour, rich rosy red, and stalwart growth are 'The Beacon' and 'Morden's Pink'.

Macleaya microcarpa is an old denizen of our gardens. It is a spreader underground and is to be avoided unless you choose the more colourful 'Kelway's Coral Plume'. Its descriptive common name is Plume Poppy, although you might not think of it as a poppy until you discover its orange sap. Its foliage is nothing short of magnificent, lobed and glaucous, borne all the way up as far as the flowering shoots on seven-foot (2.1 m) stems. But I would rather choose *M. cordata*, which is not a spreader and bears larger flowers of white in airy sprays like the former species. The roots form a ready means of increase.

Monarda didyma 'Cambridge Scarlet' is an old Bergamot hard to beat for a good red; 'Croftway Pink' is also a vintage variety. There are good mauves, too, bred from the lilac *M. fistulosa*; these will take a somewhat drier soil than the others. The bergamots are great treasures if you have a reasonably moist and fertile soil. They have invasive surface roots and deliciously fragrant leaves from which Oswego tea is made. The square leafy stems give a plenitude of hooded blossoms in long-lasting heads with coloured reddish purple bracts. They are, together, one of the stalwarts of the July garden (into August) and in spite of their three-foot (0.9 m) height do not usually require staking.

Morina longifolia, its prickly basal leaves redolent of cucumber, requires well-nurtured, cool soil. The flower stems stand bolt upright with prickly collars at every few inches, from which peep out tubular white flowers turning rich pink after fertilisation. It can be raised from seed, but is in some gardens not reliably hardy.

Persicaria (*Polygonum*) *amplexicaulis* is a spreading plant, leafy and rooty, whose every shoot ends in an upright pencil of crimson. These spikes continue to appear until autumn. But it is a big coarse plant suitable for large areas of cool, moist ground.

Phlomis russeliana, of the Sage Family, is another for a dryish spot. A statuesque plant if ever there was one, its broad velvety leaves make a weed-suppressing clump, and the square stems stand bolt upright through all weathers. At intervals up the

Morina longifolia

Phlox paniculata

stems are knobs of soft yellow hooded flowers. The stems and knobs remain far into the winter and are quite ornamental when brown. It is an easy plant for division or seed-raising.

Phlox paniculata, one of the great fragrant glories of the year, comes in July and extends through August. These tall phloxes give us just the colours that are lacking at the time—white, pink, crimson, scarlet, lilac and purple. They are wonderful palettes of paint for colour scheming. They also bring a note of sadness because theirs is the final touch of summer sunshine; in fact, one old and keen gardening friend used to say there was nothing to look forward to after the phloxes, except the daffodils. There are dozens of noble varieties and the great colour range is broadened at the centres of the flowers, which may be flushed with red or cooled with white. They will seed themselves if allowed to form pods, though the colours will not be maintained thereby, or may be divided in early spring. Best for them is a soil made retentive of moisture through being rich in old manure and leafmould. On some soils they suffer from eelworm, which causes distortion of the young shoots and is difficult to combat.

Primula florindae, the last of the primulas, whose handsome large leaves make a good clump a foot or more high and wide, throws stout stems above the foliage, carrying fragrant bells for many weeks. They are bright lemon-yellow, cooled by a powdering of white in the throat. It is a free seeder in wet ground and sometimes coppery orange hybrids arise. These are usually from plants mated with *P. waltonii*, but they are not nearly as beautiful as the type, and to prevent further mixing I should remove them directly they open the first flower.

SUNFLOWERS AND OTHER YELLOW DAISIES

Now, how should I approach the great tribe of yellow daisy flowers that enrich our summer gardens? *Coreopsis, Helenium, Helianthus, Heliopsis, Rudbeckia, Solidago* and all the rest? I may as well admit that my garden contains none of them, but nevertheless gives me satisfaction. *Coreopsis verticillata* is two feet (0.6 m) and has a cooler yellow counterpart in 'Moonbeam'. Heleniums give us good yellows as well as rich ma-

Rudbeckia 'Goldsturm'
with squash leaves

hogany browns. *Helianthus* has large flowers—they are the sunflowers of rich yellow and may ascend to six feet (1.8 m). *Heliopsis* includes valuable plants, some of them being double and very long-lasting; Rudbeckias may be equally tall or short with black eyes. Solidagos can be awful weeds, seeding everywhere, but not in the best short-growing hybrid 'Goldenmosa', which has the wit to colour its flower stalks and bracts light yellow and thus mitigates the indigestible green and yellow effect of all the others. None of these sunny daisies presents the least difficulty in any fertile soil except *Helianthus* 'Monarch', which needs a warm dry position. With them the gaillardias assort well. These are a bit fussy about soil; it must be warm, well-drained and in sun. *Gaillardia* × *grandiflora* is the group name for many splendid hybrids varying in the amount of yellow and maroon red in the central disc and widespread petals. There is something for everyone and almost every colour scheme in the rich array of tints. I am sorry, but this is the best I can do for all these "sunny" daisies. They are not even pleasingly fragrant.

Thalictrum delavayi, a Chinese plant of great daintiness and distinction, has long been known as *T. dipterocarpum*. With elegant foliage below the top of the five-foot (1.5 m) stem are hair-fine branches bearing at their extremities tiny rich lilac (or white) flowers, each one a-dangle with cream stamens. If you are thinking of cutting it for display, plant the crowns at least two feet (0.6 m) apart; otherwise the flowers will get entangled. It is easily raised from seeds.

Verbascum 'Vernale', an old and well-tried garden plant, brings yellow flowers on its stout stems to six feet (1.8 m) above a podium of large handsome leaves. In spite of its height, it is a foreground plant, being ornamental from ground level. It is propagated by means of root cuttings.

Verbena bonariensis is a fertile self-sower with heads of small violet flowers on tall naked stems. There is really no shortage of blue and bluish flowers for July.

Veronica longifolia and the superior, later flowering *V. virginiana* provide a succession of blue flowers in tapering spikes.

WATER PLANTS

I could well write a whole chapter on water plants, but it would extend the book unduly, so I will content myself with a few paragraphs calling attention to some very worthy and floriferous aquatics and bog plants. Their flowers are showy enough to enter into the garden furnishing. Pickerel Weed—to give its rather opprobrious name—is the lovely *Pontederia cordata*, a North American whose rich green blades stand well clear of the water and produce heads of small blue starry flowers for many

Water lilies and other water-loving plants in a pond at Chanticleer, Wayne, Pennsylvania

weeks. An equally long flowering season comes from the Flowering Rush, *Butomus umbellatus*. This has the appearance of some dainty Agapanthus with its rush-like leaves and rounded heads of subdued pink stars on tall stems. The Arrowhead gets its vernacular name from the shape of its glossy dark leaves; the flowers are white. *Sagittaria sagittifolia* is the single-flowered species, but more showy is the double form 'Flore Pleno'. A tall yellow Buttercup is *Ranunculus lingua*, and a plant to creep over both mud and water is the pleasing, rich green *Calla palustris*. It bears small white arum-like flowers, only a few inches all told. A white-variegated rush-like plant (in reality related to arums) is *Acorus calamus* 'Variegatus', which will grow in a few inches of water like *Iris laevigata*.

Of course, the most showy of all water plants are the Water Lilies, species and hybrids of *Nymphaea*. There is also the yellow Brandy Bottle, *Nuphar luteum*, but I warn you not to allow this in your garden pool or lake, for it is a terrible weed. Both *Nuphar* and *Nymphaea* have large round leaves that in young plants lie flat on the water, thus giving the perfect setting for the flowers. As they increase and become congested the leaves push each other up out of the water. Then is the time to consider thinning the clumps. The flowers, so prized in a small pool, arise in warm weather through the summer months. 'Escarboucle' is one of the favourites in rich crimson, and there are fine yellows and whites, but I fancy my readers may be more interested in some of the smaller species, such as *N. odorata* 'Sulphurea', which has prettily marbled leaves, the miniature *N.* 'Laydeckeri Hybrids' and *N. pygmaea*. There is a whole new world of gardening to be explored in these plants. I have only just touched the fringes of the subject. Before planting I recommend studying a specialist book long and

Nymphaea 'Escarboucle'

hard, for the actual work of immersion, the shape and structure of the pond and the selection of varieties. Above all, remember that water in the garden is meant to be seen and enjoyed, and not obscured by foliage.

AUGUST

It is still summer and we may expect the catalpas to be still in flower for the first two weeks of August. They are almost the last throw of flowering trees for the season. The limes or lindens have some late flowerers, particularly *Tilia oliveri*, which is so supremely beautiful in its spring growth. Its leaves are almost white beneath, and it is a tree rather large and spreading that in its various ways stands above all its scented fellows. It is now that two of the most majestic limes, *T. tomentosa* and its probable hybrid the renowned *T. petiolaris*, have pollen which is indigestible—even fatal—to bumblebees. They make immense trees, leaves grey-white beneath. *T. tomentosa* makes no bones about growing up into a grand tree, but *T. petiolaris* needs some coaxing. It is increased in nurseries by grafting, and because side shoots are used, the resulting trees do not readily make a single leader. The answer is to nip in the extremities of all side shoots as they grow, and after a few years a leader will emerge. These two lindens have a wonderful aroma of red clover. But here I am indulging my own fondness for these large trees; except for one or two limes of more moderate size mentioned in July, few of us have the space for them, and I should not detain you with personal enthusiasms, however appropriate to the season.

OPPOSITE: *Koelreuteria paniculata*
BELOW: *Celastrus scandens*,
a strong twiner grown
for its autumn berries

Trees

Eucryphia cordifolia, a tree-like relative of *E. glutinosa*, mentioned with the shrubs, is not so hardy, but in favoured places makes an imposing specimen, and it does not object to lime in the soil so long as it has humus. The hybrid between it and *E. glutinosa*, *E. × nymansensis*, is a columnar tree, evergreen (like *E. cordifolia*) and will put up with lime also. It can make a magnificent specimen and flowers all the way up the stem. My plants have both failed from cold in Surrey, but many fine specimens are to be found in warmer counties. They are, all of them, among the elite of shrubs and trees in August and will stand comparison with any others of the year's subjects.

Koelreuteria paniculata, a native of China supposedly immortalised in the willow-pattern plate design, is perhaps the most spectacular of August-flowering trees. It is a small and rather slow-growing tree with elegant, pinnate leaves that colour well in spring and autumn. When fully established, it may be expected to furnish large panicles of small yellow flowers this month. It is rarely seen, though hardy, reliable and a good sight in flower.

ABOVE AND BELOW:

Aesculus californica

Shrubs

Abelia × grandiflora begins a long season of flower this month. It is a rather tender shrub, and while in salubrious Cornwall its height and breadth may be six feet by ten (1.8 × 3.0 m), elsewhere it may only achieve four to five feet (1.2–1.5 m). But whatever size it attains—and it should be in full sun—it flowers freely, the little pinky-white lobed bells being produced in great profusion. It only needs a little thinning out now and again.

Aesculus californica and *A. parviflora* are two chestnuts leading us into the shrubs. The former makes a wide, high bush with typical leaves and superb spikes of pinky-white flowers with long projecting stamens. It needs all the sun it can get and takes several years to start flowering freely. I don't know why it is so seldom seen. *A. parviflora* is never more than a shrub, but a big thrusting suckering plant which in old gardens may exceed ten feet (3.0 m) through. The numerous vertical stems reach to about six feet (1.8 m), every shoot being clothed in typical foliage and carrying in this month stately spires of delicately scented, creamy white flowers well set with red-tipped stamens. It flowers from a young age.

Buddleja variabilis in wide variety, and also the more refined *B. fallowiana*, help demonstrate that, contrary to

the usual supposition, there are many good shrubs for August. The former species is the more popular with us and the butterflies. Careful selection over the years has brought many rich colours to augment the typical lilac shades. 'Royal Red' is the richest so far, a magnificent crimson-purple. 'Empire Blue' is about as far as we should go in the dark tones, and 'Fascinating' is a rattling good pink with extra long spikes of flowers. There are a few good whites such as 'Peace' and 'White Profusion', but I leave them severely alone. However beautiful they may be when they start to flower, the contrast between the white and the brown fading spikes is too much for me. The hybrid 'Nanho Blue' is a delight, with graceful slender arching spikes of blue-violet; its winter and spring young shoots are silvery grey. I have a soft spot for *B. fallowiana* in lavender-blue with, again, arching spikes, and both it and its white variety *alba* have long flowering periods extending into autumn. Against this must be levelled the criticism that they are less hardy than *B. variabilis* varieties and need the shelter of a wall in my district. A plea might be put in for *B. stenostachya*, which is reasonably hardy and has a long flowering period also. All buddlejas will thrive in poor soil in full sun and need severe cutting back in spring.

Buddleja 'Nanho Blue'

Calycanthus floridus, Allspice, is an unusual shrub. It has pointed green leaves, aromatic when handled, and bears intermittently strange double flowers of intense murrey-crimson and of an equally strange fragrance. If ever you have smelt a well-ripened ("bletted" is the term) Medlar, you will agree that these flowers resemble it closely. *C. occidentalis* has large leaves on a bigger bush but its fragrances are not so appealing. These two shrubs need a good sunny position but are not choosy about soils.

Ceanothus caeruleus (*C. azureus*) is a parent of many of the summer-flowering ceanothuses, and is deciduous. Although they may be trained on a sunny wall, they are hardier than the evergreen ceanothuses discussed in May, and do not really need cosseting; they are perfectly at home in an open bed or border, where they can be severely pruned in spring—like Hybrid Tea roses—to prolong the flowering period. Treated this way, as bedding plants, at Kew years ago they made a very fine display. Their colours range from soft pink in *C. delilianus* 'Perle Rose', to the best-known 'Gloire de Versailles' in powder blue, rich blue in 'Henri Desfosse' and the more delicate 'Indigo'. Another lovely source of true blue is found in *C.* 'Burkwoodii'; it is an evergreen into the bargain and needs the shelter of a wall with me. (How often it is in much-selected strains of plants that the darkest forms are the weakest grow-

ers.) A little later is the much hardier and stronger *C*. 'Autumnal Blue', a lighter colour, but the flowers are produced from late summer till autumn.

Clethra alnifolia, best known of the Sweet Peppers, is a vigorous suckering shrub for moist ground. Its best variety is 'Paniculata', and there are also forms with pinkish flowers. But I prefer *C. tomentosa*, whose leaves are grey beneath and whose flowers are produced a month later, into September. It is equally scented. There are also later-flowering, bigger, non-suckering shrubs such as *C. barbinervis* and *C. fargesii*, which need space to reveal their elegant tabular growths. All produce sprays of very fragrant small flowers, usually of a creamy colour, and as a general rule, yellow leaves later. Give them lime-free soil full of humus.

Cotinus coggygria in its green-leaf form tempts few of us, although a good plant of it in the full beauty of flowering is handsome indeed. It is well named the Smoke Bush or Wig Tree, for its fluffy heads in the best selections are of soft rosy brown, a hue only beaten by its leaves in autumn. It will be likely to flower well only after getting thoroughly established and may grow to six or seven feet (1.8–2.1 m) high and wide. It is more often seen in its astonishing murrey-coloured leaf forms such as 'Notcutt's Variety' and 'Royal Purple'—real heavyweights for contrasting colour schemes. They may be pruned down in spring to keep them compact and low and in good foliage, but are apt to resent this and die back. The species requires no pruning, and they all thrive in any fertile soil.

Deutzia setchuenensis corymbiflora, in dazzling snow-white flower, and *D. chunii* (white) and its pink form delay performance until the waning of their July brethren, but are worth the wait; they are the best of the late deutzias.

Dorycnium hirsutum is a dense, small, grey-leafed plant whose pea-flowers are white tinged with pink and are carried in small heads. But the real lasting joy of the plant is the red brown of the seed pods which mature and last into autumn. It prefers well-drained soil in full sun.

Escallonia 'Iveyi' is a wonderful, large, glossy-leafed shrub for warmer gardens. It does not start to flower until the earlier species and hybrids are over and is very popular with butterflies, which haunt also its parent *E. bifida*, which is more tender. Like all the larger-leafed kinds, the foliage is aromatic in warm weather. A cutback in spring will result in more of the white-flowered sprays.

Eucryphia glutinosa

Eucryphia glutinosa, from South America, is a large shrub as renowned for its long-lasting autumn colour as for its beautiful four-petalled flowers of white, crammed with red-tipped stamens. They are borne in abundance when established and is one of the outstanding shrubs of the whole year. The double forms, though equally floriferous, lack the beauty of stamens. It is a plant that thrives only in good humus-laden, lime-free soil such as you would prepare for a rhododendron.

Euonymus planipes (*E. sachalinensis*) becomes conspicuous with the lingering weeks of August; its rounded crimson fruits are usually the first of spindles to colour, and as the season advances the leaves start early to colour as well. It is a pleasing open-growing shrub, best on lime-free or neutral soils and achieves some eight feet (2.4 m) or so.

Genista aetnensis and the great *Spartium junceum*, among the brooms, retain lingering flowers; this is often a great feature as late as August. *S. junceum*, Spanish Broom, is not absolutely hardy and may take a severe knock in a hard winter. There is no gainsaying the beauty of its large, yellow, fragrant flowers. But I want to call attention to a short shrub, *Cytisus nigricans*, whose almost lemon-yellow flowers are carried on slender spires. It is a valuable late performer, happy in any fertile soil. Cutting back in early spring repays the gardener with longer spikes of flowers. Like the spartium it can be raised from seeds, and seedlings are best planted when quite young, as with all brooms.

Within the great family of heaths and heathers, garden forms are numerous in the extreme and should be left to individual choice. We in our small gardens may have space for only a few, but we may also admit that they look best in large assortments, not in tiny groups and patches. The heath season really starts in June and July with variants of the species *Erica ciliaris*, *E. cinerea* and *E. tetralix*. From them come varieties of many colours, with the middle one in brightest pinks and crimsons and the last in a grey-leafed, white-flowered 'Alba Mollis'. This variant and its relatives need a moist position and, of course, they all need lime-free soil with lots of humus. As do all heaths and heathers, they like wind to keep them compact and to blow away soggy, dead, tree leaves; they also benefit from a clip over in spring. Following them are the varieties of *E. vagans* and *E. terminalis*. This last is a shrub up to some four feet (1.2 m) and makes an excellent screen or hedge. It is not averse to somewhat limy soil. *E. vagans* and its varieties are some of the showiest late summer heaths. We will look at the heathers in September.

Holodiscus discolor, which used to be known as *Spiraea discolor*, is a pleasing shrub with arching branches, well set with leaves and bearing at every extremity a plume of minute cream flowers. One of the most pleasing flower decorations I ever saw was composed of this with the crimson flat heads of *Spiraea japonica* 'Anthony Waterer'. It would have been even better with the richer crimson of 'Wallufi'. They are two of the most richly coloured low shrubs, repaying, like the holodiscus, selective spring pruning.

Hydrangea macrophylla 'Lanarth White'

HYDRANGEAS

Without a doubt, the principal August shrubs are the species and forms of *Hydrangea*. They require adequate moisture to give of their best and most kinds demand a lime-free or neutral soil, with plenty of humus. The best known are the almost innumerable forms of *H. macrophylla*. This species is best grown in one or more of its typical forms, known as "lace-caps". Some favourites are 'Blue Wave', 'Veitchii' (white), the smaller 'Lanarth White' and 'Geoffrey Chadbund', usually pink. I say "usually" because only if the soil is rich in aluminium can we expect the pink ones to turn blue. The same applies to the great numbers of mop-head varieties. Usually the first to flower—and it can be a brilliant blue—is 'Générale Vicomtesse de Vibraye'. Rich reds and deep blues and purples can be found among the numerous varieties listed, and many of them last into autumn, especially the white 'Madame Emile Mouillère'. The sister species *H. serrata* is more refined and has a number of desirable lace-caps as well as a possible hybrid in 'Preziosa', whose reddish-pink tint is particularly rich and bold. All of the above are best served by leaving the dead flowers on the bushes until mid-May when severe frosts are unlikely to occur. When removing the flower heads, it is advisable to cut down to the first pair of big buds, which will in all probability produce flowers. Weak twiggy growths should be removed at the same time.

Although the above constitute the bulk of hydrangeas grown, they are not the end of the story. As mentioned in July, there are still the forms of *H. arborescens* in flower, and the first of the big velvety-leafed species, *H. sargentiana*, is coming into bloom. The leaves may be a foot across; the stems stout and hairy, and the flower heads, only lace-caps, are lilac in the middle (the fertile flowers) and near white in the surrounding large sterile flowers. It is a large grower of considerable impact. Then there is the climbing *H. petiolaris* that ascends a tree trunk or shady wall, attaching itself firmly to the support and then sending out horizontal shoots with white lace-caps at the extremities. Though spectacular in flower, it is soon over; for a much longer-lasting relative we must go to *Schizophragma integrifolium*, which has one large white bract to each flower as opposed to the four of *Hydrangea petiolaris*. It is a superlative plant worthy of the little extra care it needs in order to make it cling. A third relative, self-clinging, is *Pileostegia viburnoides*. This is an evergreen into the bargain and bears flat heads of small white flowers. It is vigorous and, like *Hydrangea petiolaris*, can easily reach twenty feet (6.0 m) or more. The leaves are hard, long and pointed. All of these climbers will thrive on a north or other cool wall.

ABOVE: *Hydrangea petiolaris*

LEFT: *Schizophragma integrifolium*, a most valuable climber with long-lasting flowers

Ligustrum japonicum is a mere Privet, but is an evergreen of some dignity with large dark glossy leaves and plenteous spikes of creamy white. It can easily reach eight feet (2.4 m) high and wide and requires no pruning. *L. sinense* is really a July flower, but we might as well keep all the privets together; the best form is 'Multiflorum', which can be a veritable fountain of creamy white spikes. My two other privets are very large growers: they are *L. confusum*, which can attain eighteen feet (5.4 m) or more and supports big sprays of creamy flowers, while the exquisite Chinese *L. quihoui* is nearly

as large. Thinking of old specimens in botanic gardens, I planted one but it got too large and had to be scrapped, after giving me extreme scented beauty for some twenty years from long elegant sprays of creamy white small flowers.

Meliosma cuneifolia is a beautiful thing in flower, for all the world like a spiraea, but the creamy flowers are disposed over a graceful, pointed, arching panicle. It is not particular about soil but pays well for a spring prune, thinning out the weak growths.

Microglossa albescens (*Aster albescens*), a good greyish-leafed plant for full sun, looks at flowering time like a Michaelmas Daisy. Is it my imagination or is it always a better colour in the cooler north?

Phygelius capensis, Cape Figwort, a subshrub native to South Africa, can be very effective when

trained up a warm wall, or perhaps just grown as a herbaceous plant in the open border. In any case the shoots that have flowered need cutting in spring to encourage good new shoots, which are hung along their whole length with scarlet tubular flowers. It is nothing if not spectacular and seems to thrive in any soil. 'Yellow Trumpet' provides a great contrast.

Rhododendron auriculatum is the rhododendron I promised for August. The snow-white, scented, lily-like, great flowers open to the accompaniment of red bracts and hold us spellbound. That we should have waited all these months for this queen of the tribe! The great leaves follow, and the woodland garden is enriched. The growth is large and broad and less tree-like than 'Polar Bear', which may still be in flower in this month.

I will avoid a long entry about roses; they have been covered fully in many other books, including my own, but I should like to mention here a few late-flowerers. Ramblers go over rather quickly in July, but 'Sander's White' is usually still in flower in August, followed by the admirable 'Crimson Showers'. This is not scented, but 'Sander's White' is, though not as penetratingly fragrant as the little-known 'Princess of Nassau', which is a very old variety. It always strikes me as very strange that the hybridists have not made more play with this, for it goes on flowering into the autumn, its silky cream double flowers no doubt descended from *Rosa moschata*. It has zig-zag shoots and small leaves and may attain as much as ten feet (3.0 m) on a support. *R. moschata* itself is semi-shrubby and begins flowering in late August, carrying on into the autumn likewise. It is single (or sometimes double) with recurved white petals. The scent is almost overpowering. Another August-flowering rambler is the Japanese species *R. wichuraiana*, nearly thornless and a very vigorous trailer for banks or arches. It has, of course, been much used for hybridising but is still full of latent possibilities. It is furthermore very fragrant, creamy white and partially evergreen.

August sees the beginning of the autumn crop of great flagon-shaped heps on *R. moyesii* and its relatives, particularly *R. sweginzowii*. They are all splendid contributors to red colouring which goes so well with murrey-coloured foliage. They all make large shrubs. On the other hand, *R. virginiana* is a wind-resistant, low shrub, with single pink flowers through July and August followed by red heps and gorgeous autumn colourings. A further delight is 'Rose d'Amour', probably a hybrid of *R. virginiana* or one of its American relatives. It can be used as a bush or a climber and for about eight weeks produces exquisite buds and blooms in warm rose pink and goes out in autumn with a flurry of bright foliage. It is a very old foundling always much admired though seldom planted. It is fragrant and almost thornless, and repays spring pruning.

TOP: *Rosa moyesii* heps ripening in a walled garden

BOTTOM: Rose 'Princess of Nassau'

Sorbaria assurgens and *S. arborea* were at one time classed as spiraeas. Most sorbarias are too large for the average garden. *S. assurgens* is the most compact, but even this spreads by suckers. *S. arborea* is one of the most magnificent of them, throwing out huge panicles of tiny cream flowers.

Spiraea henryi and the similar *S. canescens* head a valuable group of spiraeas. They flower rather earlier and might have been included elsewhere. If all weak twiggy growth is removed in winter or spring, the shrubs will be transformed into widespraying specimens with corymbs of white flowers along the branches and can be one of the most noted shrubs of the season.

S. japonica has yielded a great many garden forms, mostly pinks, but also crimsons and whites. I have no place in my garden for 'Goldflame'—I find the yellowish leaves unsympathetic with the soft pink flowers, though I admit the spring foliage has great merit. There are many forms of this species; 'Albiflora' is a useful dwarf white, needing selective spring pruning. An oddity quite on its own is 'Shiburi' ('Shirobana'), which has flower heads of pink and white at the same time all on the same bush. Two other cultivars are mentioned on page 178.

Tamarix ramosissima has tiny pink flowers made conspicuous by their quantity. We are used to thinking of the tamarisks as plants which will thrive in the sands of the seashore, but *T. ramosissima* prefers a good stiff soil where it may ascend to six feet (1.8 m) or more. It can also be treated to severe spring pruning, which will result in a longer display of finer flower sprays. Its minute foliage is grey green—a happy accompaniment.

The blush rose 'Cécile Brunner', an exquisite miniature which flowers on until autumn, and is sweetly scented

Climbers

Forms and varieties of *Clematis* are prominent in August, and for late summer, there is nothing to touch them. But much disappointment is met in the all-too-prevalent "wilt", which will attack without warning an apparently healthy plant. It is generally recommended to cut all the wilted portion to green leaves and hope for the best. The large-flowered varieties are the most prone. I prefer, however, the varieties of *C. viticella*, which have smaller flowers and are not susceptible to wilt in my experience. 'Abundance' is heather crimson; 'Kermesina' nearly crimson; 'Royal Velours' an incredibly rich, deep wine-purple, and there are many more, including little pink 'Pagoda'. *C. viticella* itself is, like the last, quite small-flowered, but of intriguing shape; it seeds itself, and ascends to some twelve feet (3.6 m).

Clematis tangutica, one of the several yellow-flowered species, of easy growth; the photograph shows the silvery seed heads as well as the flowers

There are several small-flowered yellow species with nodding bell-shaped blooms. The best known is *C. tangutica*, a pretty plant when hung with flowers accompanied by silvery seed heads. *C. orientalis* is even more striking if you can get the large-flowered form 'Bill Mackenzie'. *C. × jouiniana* is all on its own, usually seen scrambling up a shrub or wires on a wall (it does well on a north wall) hung with clusters of pearly blue small flowers. It is usually treated like a herbaceous plant and cut down to its woody base at the end of winter, but at Mount Stewart, in Northern Ireland, it has threaded its way through a large yew and has developed a woody trunk.

Also good on a north wall is *Berberidopsis corallina*. I think it prefers a cool moist climate where it can dangle its crimson, rounded flowers among its prickly evergreen leaves. It needs little pruning and is not scented but attracts attention always. *Eccremocarpus* can be woody if grown against a warm wall, but is more often treated as an annual. Its filigree leaves are a good setting for the sprays of tubular flowers in yellow, orange or red. It will in one season reach ten feet (3.0 m) and will sow itself true to colour. It is not scented nor particular about soil.

Perennials

Aconitum 'Spark's Variety', one of the stalwarts of late summer borders, is tall and branching, with hooded flowers of dark purple-blue. Another with equally branching, leaning heads of lavender blue is *A. japonicum*. The form I grow has light green leaves as opposed to the dark green of most others.

Agapanthus species and hybrids, African Lilies, are much to the fore these days mainly due to the Honourable Lewis Palmer, who raised a lot of good hybrids during the 1960s and 1970s. They are mostly hybrids of *A. campanulatus*, with noble heads

of small lily-like flowers borne well aloft over strap-shaped leaves. In addition to several good blues, there are some excellent whites. 'Loch Hope' (blue), raised at Windsor, is taller and later, while little 'Lilliput' in dark blue is seldom more than a foot high. They are all queenly plants of considerable merit (drought tolerant, weed-smothering) and are hardier than the old *A. umbellatus* of gardens with its broader, evergreen leaves. Even a handful of seeds will yield some good ones.

Anaphalis triplinervis does well only in reasonably moist soil and is almost alone in grey-leafed plants with this preference. If you want something white to go with *Aster × frikartii*, you could not do better than this. It grows to about one foot (0.3 m) and puts up branching heads of small, papery, "everlasting" flowers repeatedly until autumn. There are taller species of *Anaphalis* which do not appeal to me so much.

Anemone × hybrida 'Honorine Jobert', with its silky white petals, pale green central knob and circlet of yellow stamens, begins to flower now; nothing more beautiful has appeared during the whole year. It originated as a sport from the pink *A. × hy-*

TOP: *Anaphalis triplinervis*
BOTTOM: *Agapanthus* 'Loch Hope'

brida and was raised in 1858 in the Horticultural Society's (now Royal Horticultural Society's) garden at Chiswick and in my opinion has never been surpassed by the numerous semi-doubles raised since. The parents of the hybrid were *A. tomentosa* (then known as *A. vitifolia*) crossed with an ancient Japanese hybrid, *A. hupehensis japonica*. The former has single, rather lopsided flowers of soft light pink, whereas the latter is semi-double, of a dark crimson-pink. The origin of the latter is not known, but I gather it is a common wayside plant throughout Japan. *A. hupehensis* is a Chinese species somewhat shorter than the others that is well worth growing. It has lopsided flowers, usually dark pink, almost crimson, and the same good foliage and running roots. The only perfection that all these plants lack is fragrance. *A. tomentosa* has a prolific wandering rootstock, a feature that all have in some degree, making them questionable assets in small gardens (although I have them in mine). In fact, I wonder whether all of these admirable plants would not be better accommodated in a meadow where they could run at will. Some medium to large hostas, such as *Hosta ventricosa*, provide excellent contrast for these anemones, but in general they are better associated with shrubs than in the conventional herbaceous border. They can be propagated from thin root cuttings but often do not take kindly to division of old woody roots. There are many named forms, some double, some with merely an extra petal (sepal) or two, but my eyes always return to feast on the original singles. They thrive in sun or shade in any fertile soil, light or heavy.

Anthemis sancti-johannis supplies a need for orange, a rare colour in gardens. It has feathery foliage and pure orange daisies with a large central disc and short ray-florets—at least in its typical form. It has unfortunately become hybridised with *A. tinctoria*, resulting in plants with longer florets, but of a colour somewhat adulterated with yellow. It needs propagating from basal spring cuttings to keep it both healthy and pure. Any fertile soil suits it.

ABOVE: *Lathyrus nervosus*, Lord Anson's Blue Pea, a doubtful perennial but the contrast of colours and its delicious scent recommend it

BELOW: *Anemone* × *hybrida* 'Honorine Jobert'

RIGHT: *Aster × frikartii*

BELOW: A few August-flowering old clove pinks or carnations. At the top is 'Lord Chatham' and its striped sport 'Phyllis Marshall'; in centre is an Old Crimson Clove.

Aster × frikartii is a hybrid of *A. thomsonii* and *A. amellus* and can give a generous display for three months, lavender blue, wide flowers on a self-supporting stem—if you get the best and genuine form, 'Mönch'. There are, unfortunately, imposters about. The true plant is definitely rigidly upright, and the petals are in one plane. Others are not so self-reliant and tend to be ragged. This is not including 'Eiger' and 'Jungfrau', which are sister seedlings but nearer to *A. amellus*, nor the taller, darker 'Wunder von Stäfa'. I wish I knew where to get the genuine *A. thomsonii* from the Himalaya; it is usually represented in gardens by a form known as 'Nanus'—a good little plant with a long flowering period. All of these carry on flowering until about mid-October. I have been quoted as claiming that *A. × frikartii* is one of the six best hardy perennials, but I have never ventured to name the other five!

CARNATIONS

There is much romance, and not a little confusion, in the names of clove carnations. I wish some young enthusiast would take them in hand, collect them and sort them out. The task was begun by Oscar Moreton in his *Old Carnations and Pinks*, published in 1955. Unfortunately, so far as I can ascertain, nobody continued his good work. I have found a mere handful, mostly without names. I am not sure whether what I have known since boyhood as the Old Crimson Clove is the genuine article: two other claimants have cropped up in Northern Ireland. What makes these plants so precious is their rich scent of cloves. They all have good, strong, very glaucous leaves and make woody trunks in old age on limy drained soils, their flower stems ascending to eighteen inches (0.45 m) with support. They are not good perennials on acid soils. Whatever may be the names of the others I have found—embracing a stripe and a rich magenta purple—we can be sure now of what is known as the Old Salmon Clove. In reality, it is 'Lord Chatham', though also sometimes labelled erroneously 'Raby Castle'. Its date is prior to 1780. Its foliage is typically broad and glaucous. The colour salmon refers to the uncooked fish. Phyllis Marshall, the wife of the head gardener at Mount Stewart, Northern Ireland, found a beautiful form freely striped with white, and it is named in her honour.

Clematis × eriostemon,
a semi-climbing plant with
a long flowering period

Cautleya 'Robusta' is probably a hybrid or form of *C. spicata*. It is an unusual plant in many ways and is related to the hedychiums and roscoeas. Long before the flowers appear we have been arrested by the handsome sheaves of spear-shaped, blue green leaves on a stem rising from tuberous roots. The flowers are borne among the uppermost leaves, hooded, dark yellow with red-brown bracts. Later, black seeds are held in white cases. Altogether, this intriguing plant seems quite easy to please in moderately retentive soil and stands division in spring. I have not seen it much taller than two feet (0.6 m).

Clematis × eriostemon is small-flowered and makes a violet-blue bower of blossom. It is a hybrid of *C. viticella* and totally hardy; I cut mine down to a foot every late winter, and it ascends to eight feet (2.4 m) on an arch. *C. × durandii* has large flowers of indigo-blue and is in flower for an equally long period; it is woody at the base. Both have *C. integrifolia* as one parent—a comparatively dull little plant. On the other hand, *C. heracleifolia* is a fine plant, particularly in its variety 'Wyevale', which produces sheaves of nodding, wedgwood-blue, starry flowers like hyacinths, and sweetly scented, too. The two hybrids are herbaceous perennials and do not twine or cling but are beautiful when trained on supports.

Commelina coelestis is not reliably hardy with me. The three-petalled flowers are of clear, luminous, true sky blue and come and go among the leafy stems, not usually exceeding two feet (0.6 m), for many weeks. It can be increased by division of the tuberous root in spring.

Crinum × powellii is a large bulbous plant for warm gardens. It is usually seen growing against a south-facing wall, though in really warm districts it will thrive in sun in the open. A disadvantage is the long, floppy, dark green leaves, which get tattered and torn in windy places. The flowers are lovely, scented, lily-like and pink or pure white, carried at the top of stout stems. The parents of this popular hybrid are *C. moorei* and *C. bulbispermum*, both from South Africa. *C. moorei* is a dignified species whose leaves and flower stalks come off the top of a short stem; the flowers are large and pink and of superior quality. *C. bulbispermum* is a lesser plant; the white flowers have a dark pink median line along the outer segments. It also has somewhat glaucous leaves and may flower as early as June. Both, as well as others of the 130 or so species, have sweetly scented flowers that appear well above the drooping leaves from August onwards.

Crocosmia pottsii (upright, narrow red flowers) and *C. aurea* (drooping yellow flowers, wide open), crossed originally in France, gave rise to the well-known garden plant *C. × crocosmiiflora*. This was long known as Montbretia and has become something of a weed in many moist, west country gardens. Selections of *C. × crocosmiiflora* were made by sowing seed of the hybrid in gardens in our cold eastern counties early in this century. In that region, the necessary lifting in autumn and replanting again in spring to avoid damage by frost to their undoubtedly beautiful seedlings had an adverse effect on their popularity. But now that big collections are being made in the southwest and in Northern Ireland, perhaps we shall see a revival of interest in them, from the great 'Star of the East' in light apricot-yellow through many fiery and mixed shades to 'Mrs Geoffrey Howard' in rich mahogany-red. 'Nimbus', 'Lady Hamilton' and 'Citronella' are a few other distinctly good named varieties. But I hesitate to put forward more names until the collections of those early hybrids now being made by enthusiasts are assessed. There is also the plant long known as *Curtonus* that is now merged into *Crocosmia paniculata*. This is a stalwart plant of some three or four feet (0.9–1.2 m) with broad, pleated leaves and branching sprays of orange-red flowers. It is a variable plant and good forms should be sought. Hybrids between this and *C. masonorum* have been raised by Alan Bloom, and they are truly magnificent: 'Vulcan', 'Emberglow', 'Spitfire', 'Lucifer' and others.

Echinops nivalis (*E. niveus*), a possible hybrid of the rare spiny *E. tournefortii*, takes over

Crocosmia × crocosmiiflora 'Nimbus' (TOP), 'Mrs Geoffrey Howard' (LEFT) and 'Solfatare'. 'Star of the East' is depicted on page xviii.

LEFT: *Fuchsia* 'Mrs Popple'
BELOW: *Penstemon* 'Hidcote'
and *Fuchsia* 'Hidcote'

from the blue-flowered echinops of July. These are both greyish-leafed with conspicuous white knobs of flowers borne well aloft. They both require a warm corner in well-drained soil in full sun and can be increased by root cuttings. They may reach five feet (1.5 m), and are a great asset in the border.

Epilobium rosmarinifolium gives a feathery effect. The leaves are narrow and numerous, and the spires of flowers, in soft pink, attain some one or two feet and are long in beauty. The five-petalled flowers are guarded by reddish calyx lobes.

Fuchsia hybrids, where they thrive, in good moist soil, preferably in sun, will give you an incredibly long flowering season; in fact, only frost stops them. The smaller-flowered kinds are the most hardy, and the others are best treated as half-hardy in all but the most sheltered of districts, which is why they are such a success at the seaside. The smaller and shorter the cuttings, the more readily will they root, but are not ready for planting out until late spring. In maritime districts the most common is the old hybrid 'Riccartonii', crimson with a purple "skirt". Lesser plants in the same colours are *Fuchsia magellanica* 'Gracilis' (arching and elegant) and 'Thompsonii' (more upright). The former has a most pleasing form with greyish-mauve leaves named 'Versicolor'. These leaves elevate the plant to a positive winner for many purposes. Two favourites of mine are the tall 'Enfant Prodigue' and 'Mrs Popple' (with buds that explode between finger and thumb, could anyone invent a more appropriate name?). They are both rich red with purple skirts and quite hardy, likewise the noted 'Eva Boerg' and 'Lena', which have pink sepals and lilac skirts.

They both have droopy growth, just right for hanging over a low wall. Another quite hardy one is 'Sealand Prince', a fine plant of three feet (0.9 m) in rose-pink and rich lilac. We could go on picking out old garden favourites from the several hundred named forms in cultivation but there are so many. Try those I have mentioned while looking around for others.

Geranium wallichianum is one of those smaller plants that wait till August to display their charms. It is a real winner, delighting in a cool moist soil. The foliage, spreading from a compact central tuft, makes a mass of greenery tinted with bronze and purplish shades, against which the flowers show up well and go on appearing until the autumn puts an end to the effort. They are normally soft lilac, but 'Buxton's Variety' is limpid pale blue with a white centre and dark stamens—a great beauty. It will annually make a mass two feet (0.6 m) across and half as high, dying back in winter to the central crown. Of late years another star has appeared in the firmament: 'Syabru', in soft rich violaceous crimson and this goes on for weeks on end, too. Then there is the old 'Russell Prichard', again a tuft-former, but spreading its branches often to three feet (0.9 m) in all directions, smothered in greyish leaves and pink flowers with a hint of magenta. It is considered to be a hybrid between *G. traversii* from New Zealand and the well-known *G. endressii*, and is correctly placed under the name of *G.* × *riversleaianum*, commemorating the famous Riverslea nursery of Maurice Prichard & Sons in Hampshire. *G. traversii* is not without the suspicion of tenderness, and this also affects 'Russell Prichard' and another hybrid that cropped up at Kew a few years ago and is named 'Mavis Simpson'. This inherits good grey foliage from the New Zealand species and the clear pink flowers of the other parent, *G. endressii*. Altogether these few species and hybrids form a group that, with the tail end of the summer in prospect, we cannot afford to neglect.

Many geraniums have a comparatively short flowering season; not so *G. nodosum*, which started in July and will go on flowering into the autumn. Few plants will live, flower and flourish under Holm oaks and cedars, but this imperturbable plant is at home in such shade or in the sun. Its lobed leaves are glossy, which is unusual for a geranium, and the flowers are of light lilac. Truly a plant of great worth, it seeds itself gently. The others in the paragraph above are best increased in spring by basal cuttings or careful division.

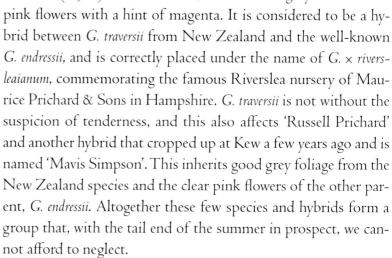

GRASSES

Hakonechloa macra 'Aureola'

I think gardens are incomplete without a few, at least, of these pleasing foils, so good a contrast are grasses with almost anything. Our British native *Deschampsia arvensis* is one of the most pleasing, and in August, above its clump of fine leaves stand aloft the upright stems covered in small, delicate, purple-tinged flowers, which turn to harvest tones later. It is a native, mainly, of acid, moist meadows and seeds itself about wildly. There is a curious form, 'Vivipara', whose flowers have turned into ready-made plantlets and this is to be avoided.

If you have a bank or a cool retaining wall, I suggest you plant *Stipa arundinacea*; it is nothing special in foliage but produces tumbling masses of purplish hair-fine flower stems. They hang down like girlish tresses and last long in beauty. It seeds itself but is seldom a nuisance. Adventurous gardeners may be tempted to plant *Elymus arenarius* for the sake of its long, steely bluish, glaucous foliage. I have been amused to find that Miss Jekyll used it to enforce her colour schemes; but beware, it has running roots like a giant couch grass and is not to be trusted. It binds sand dunes round our coasts effectively and its flower stems, also glaucous, attain four feet (1.2 m).

A much more modest plant is *Molinia caerulea* 'Variegata', forming a close tuft of arching leaves so clean and fresh in their neat striping of cream. Another lovely variegation is found in *Hakonechloa macra* 'Aureola'. I have seen this very gracefully clothing a cool shady bank with its down-pointing mat of leaves clearly striped with white and yellow. These two grasses are to be trusted in the most select company. The second spreads mildly underground.

The Ravenna Grass, *Erianthus ravennae*, is a tall plant to six feet (1.8 m) or so, and crowns its big rustling clump with dark purplish flower heads. It is not altogether hardy. Pampas grasses we must leave until September, but an early one is *Cortaderia richardii*, from New Zealand. It is quite hardy and thrives even in parts of Scotland, where the South American species do not prosper. It forms a large tuft of leaves above which the flower stems arch and sway, each carrying a large plume of silky white. In spite of its grace, it lasts in beauty for a long time, even though somewhat bedraggled through the winter.

Hieracium lanatum is an unusual daisy for any drained fertile soil in sun. The large, bright, sulphur yellow flowers are held above woolly grey leaves. It is long in flower and may be increased from seeds, or by careful spring division.

Iris fulva has flowers of strong terracotta with a hint of brown. It is not always free flowering. Its hybrid, *I. × fulvala*, is a better garden plant and owes its hybridity to *I. foliosa*; it is rich crimson-purple, murrey-tinted. These two irises have rich green leaves and are best divided after flowering, reaching to about two feet (0.6 m). It may seem neglectful to have left until this date a couple of irises, but, yes, they do flower in August. They are moisture lovers.

Kniphofia 'Royal Standard' is one of the best known among the many Red Hot Pokers, achieving four feet (1.2 m). Something of a change is 'Wrexham Buttercup', a stalwart plant of the same size but with wholly yellow flowers. I have had it next to *Solidago* 'Goldenmosa', making a harmony of colours and a contrast in form. About now Beth Chatto's ivory-white 'Little Maid' is most appealing with a much longer flowering season than most pokers.

Lilium auratum, the golden-rayed Lily of Japan, is one of the most outstanding plants of the whole year. Unfortunately, it is not always a good perennial, but one season of flowering from a bought bulb is an overwhelming reward for the trifling expenditure. We are all humbled by the majesty of the offering, which occurs from that single bulb planted in the dead of the year. In its original unadulterated form, *L. auratum platyphyllum*, I think you have all that could be desired with shape and colour. I am not so sure about the scent; I find it rather overpowering and heavy. But see those several great flowers widely expanded and showing the golden central rays and rich brown anthers—what more

Kniphofia 'Royal Standard'

Nepeta × *faassenii, Achillea*
'Coronation Gold',
Salvia × *superba,*
Campanula lactiflora
and phlox in a
well-planted border

save sweet fragrance and a long life could be desired? Both of these lilies, which like a cool spot in soil enriched by leafmould and bonemeal, delight in full sunshine aloft—a combination enjoyed, I believe, by most lilies. Seed-raised stock is the best. Nowadays much hybridisation and selection has been carried on until we can have this majesty in pink or almost crimson, but no amount of colour can make me turn from the unalloyed original species as I first grew it in my schoolboy garden.

Lilium 'Enchantment', one of the upright lilies with wide-open flowers in a cluster at the top of a leafy stem, provides some of the most vivid orange in any garden. Like all lilies, it needs good nourishment and division in autumn when the bulbs are congested and deteriorating. The same may be said of the beauteous *L. henryi*; this is of wayward arching growth, carrying lovely drooping flowers of soft orange. The Tiger Lily, formerly *L. tigrinum*, now *L. lancifolium*, is a splendid sight; *splendens* is good but I rate *fortunei* higher. They are both of a curious coral-orange spotted with black, a truly wonderful sight with their reflexed flowers. They produce ample bulbils in the axils of the leaves which can easily be detached and grown on for future use. They both suffer from botrytis disease against which the disease-carrying aphides can be sprayed.

Limonium latifolium, which used to be called *Statice*, is the ideal soft foil for pink or white flowers. From woody, thick roots the broad leaves grow up to a foot (0.3 m) or so and make a fine background to the clouds of tiny lavender blue flowers borne on wiry branching stems. They are semi-everlasting, though becoming grey with age. There are several good forms listed which should be increased by root cuttings.

Nepeta × faassenii (*N. mussinii* of gardens) is a well-known and invaluable Catmint for June that goes on flowering until the autumn; likewise, the much bigger and more hardy 'Six Hills Giant'. But these are both lavender blue. A totally different plant is *N. govaniana*, reaching to at least three feet (0.9 m) with cool, pale yellow, lipped flowers for weeks on end. It can be used as a foil for almost any colour. All of these revel in well-drained sunny places. Cats can be a nuisance, but a few prickly berberis or rose prunings among the plants will work wonders.

Oenothera macrantha has some of the largest flowers of any I have mentioned, and yet it is only a few inches high. The procumbent stems bear narrow leaves, and the huge flowers of lambent lemon yellow are like those of the common Evening Primrose to which it is closely related. It has a further attraction: as the flowers wane, they turn to orange wisps. After that the huge seed pods mature, from which the large seeds form a ready means of increase.

Persicaria affinis, one of the very best frontal plants, and a good carpeter, was for many years known as *Polygonum affine*. Though a runner, it keeps to the surface and does not spread underground. The narrow leaves make a rug of green from spring onwards but turn to rich chestnut brown for the winter. Meanwhile from late June onwards, it produces innumerable spikes of tiny pink flowers, making an excellent display. They seldom exceed one foot (0.3 m) in height. In the species as we originally knew it, the flowers were pink, but plants arriving more recently from its Himalaya home have revealed that some deepen to crimson in maturity. I think a good reliable plant and the most effective in all ways is the one known as 'Superba'. After a long cold winter and drying winds in spring, it may need lifting and the growing shoots replanting.

Phlox paniculata in a normal season for me comes into full glory in early August. I introduced them in July but mentioned no varieties, intending to give them proper treatment this month. They need good moist soil with plenty of humus. It is wise to propagate them from root cuttings or division, not from top cuttings, if you wish to avoid the dreaded

The well-known Catmint or *Nepeta* at Harlow Car, Yorkshire

eel worm. Among the whites, *P. paniculata* 'White Admiral' holds its own with the old 'Mia Ruys' with a creamy eye. 'Graf Zeppelin' has a crimson eye. There are many good pinks but the old 'Rijnstroom' holds its own. I regret the passing of the white-centred 'Antonin Mercier' and 'Evangeline', in lilac and pink, respectively. 'Border Gem' is about the best rich purple, with the old 'Le Mahdi' rather shorter. Among the reds, we have to be careful of the orange scarlets, 'Prince of Orange' and 'A. E. Amos'; they need different colour companions and are more at home with the yellow perennials of the season. But a visit to a nursery or garden with a good collection will reveal untold delights for colour schemes. These are not the end of the phloxes, however; there is the renowned white *P. carolina* 'Miss Lingard' and *P. maculata* 'Alpha' and 'Omega', which if well cultivated throw up successive spikes.

One of the light pink varieties of *Sidalcea malviflora*

Salvia virgata nemorosa, an ideal contrast to orange colours, has spikes of rich purple flowers reaching four feet (1.2 m) in good conditions. There are fortunately two shorter, newer varieties, 'Lubeca' and 'East Friesland', that have the same intense dark colouring but seldom exceed about half the height. If the spent flower spikes are removed promptly, subsidiary spikes usually carry on the flowering into September. 'Mainacht' is an earlier relative. They all have aromatic leaves, are easy to propagate from basal cuttings in spring, and thrive in any fertile soil.

Sanguisorba obtusa, a Japanese plant of some size and dignity, can be overwhelming but is valuable in cool colour associations. The pinnate leaves are greyish and make a good picture with the curving bottle-brushes of rose pink or white. It has a long flowering period and generally needs some support for its lanky stems. It is easy to divide in early spring.

Sidalcea malviflora, of the Mallow tribe, has a white form, but most are of some shade of pink, some pale, some approaching crimson. From a good basal tuft of rounded leaves, the straight stems ascend sometimes to four feet (1.2 m), with lovely cupped, silky flowers for several weeks. The old 'Sussex Beauty' and 'William Smith' are hard to beat, with 'Elsie Heugh' standing apart with fringed petals. Division in spring is a ready means of increase. I find the light pinks are the most useful in the garden, the darker ones tending to be rather dull. Sidalceas are good plants for any fertile soil that does not become too dry. A close relative is of course the great Tree Mal-

Lavatera olbia 'Barnsley'

low, *Lavatera olbia* (*L. thuringiaca*), of which the form known as 'Rosea' is the best known. In recent years this has been joined by 'Barnsley', a lovely blush with crimson eye, not quite so vigorous. But you must allow them plenty of room; 'Rosea' may easily achieve eight feet (2.4 m) high and wide and is a stout, woody plant, almost a shrub. Soft velvety leaves are lovely with the wide-open, small hollyhock flowers produced without stint for three months. Severe winters and old age will cripple them, and in any case they need their spent stems shortening in spring. 'Rosea' comes readily from seed, and 'Barnsley' must be increased from summer cuttings, with a heel. There are two related perennials, *L. olbia* and *L. cachemiriana*, which are smaller-flowered but no less effective up to about four feet (1.2 m), erect and soldierly. Of the former I have seen pure whites as well as pinks with shapely flowers; of the latter the flowers have intriguingly separated petals. Both may be raised from seeds.

Tritonia rosea is a pleasing pink-flowered plant closely related to crocosmias, and also a native of South Africa. It is not upstanding like them but throws its wire-fine stems out at an angle among the grassy foliage. The flowers come in long spikes of

Rodgersia pinnata 'Superba'. Its noble leaves are sometimes not markedly pinnate; it may be a hybrid. I first saw it at Rowallane, Northern Ireland.

warm rose with a touch of salmon. It increases freely and seems quite hardy, but should be planted or divided in spring.

Veratrum album and *V. nigrum*, strong-growing liliaceous plants, reach to six feet (1.8 m) high with noble, broad, pleated foliage. The flowers of all are small and star-like carried in great plumes well above the leaves. *V. album* is appealingly greenish-white (occasionally yellow), and *V. nigrum* is richly chocolate tinted. Much shorter is *V. viride* with stout spikes of green flowers—a study in green. They all take some years to get fully established, in rich moist soil if possible, and the foliage is all the better for some shade. They would take several years to flower from seeds but can be divided carefully with a sharp spade in early spring. They assort better with shrubs than in a traditional border.

WATERSIDE AND BOG PLANTS

It is useful, if you have a waterside, to include a few of the later-flowering species and varieties of *Astilbe*. There is not only *A. tacquetii* 'Superba' in rich magenta crimson but also a few hybrids of this and other species such as *A.* 'Lilli Goos', 'King

Albert' and 'Jo Ophorst', pink, white and lilac, respectively. They blend well with lythrums and *Lysimachia ephemerum* and present no difficulty in cultivation so long as the soil is moist or even wet. While we have moist soil in mind, it may be as well to look at a few orange-coloured bog plants, and few are more striking than the ligularias. They are much loved by garden molluscs, but are worth a lot of trouble with their handsome large leaves and magnificent heads of daisy flowers borne well above them. *Ligularia dentata* is one of the best known; it used to be called *Senecio clivorum*. There are two varieties with mahogany undersides to the leaves: 'Desdemona' and 'Othello'; the contrast is magnificent. Other excellent kinds are *L. × palmatiloba* with fine orange spikes over elegantly cut, large leaves, and the noted 'Gregynog Gold', which occurred as a self-sown seedling in a lovely Welsh garden. It has most handsome tall spires of blooms, a legacy from *L. veitchiana*, another good plant.

Some rodgersias flower rather earlier, even in June, but August usually sees others still in flower. They are, once again, moisture lovers, and have extremely handsome divided foliage two feet (0.6 m) or more in height, some chestnut-like (*Rodgersia aesculifolia*, *R. podophylla*), others pinnate (*R. pinnata*, *R. sambucifolia*). The flowers of all are tall and elegant, fluffy panicles in cream—or pink in the delectable *R. pinnata* 'Superba'. One species has been separated by botanists into a new genus and is now *Astilboides tabularis*. The flowering stems may top six feet (1.8 m) in good conditions, and the leaves are great discs of greenery—no divisions—and undeniably magnificent. It might be called the poor man's gunnera. Another large-leafed plant for damp soil, *Buphthalmum speciosum*, is apt to spread underground, but there is no denying the beauty of its fine-rayed daisies of rich yellow, displayed in a branching head. Quite different is the late-flowering *Trollius stenopetalus*, whose dark divided foliage goes well with the flaming orange "globe flowers" on their slender stalks up to four feet (1.2 m). It comes readily from seeds.

BELOW LEFT: Disc-like leaves of *Astilboides tabularis*, which may reach over two feet (0.6 m) across
BELOW RIGHT: Bronze divided leaves of *Rodgersia podophylla*, with those of *Lysichiton* at rear

SEPTEMBER

September cannot be other than colourful when we think of the several genera that started flowering in summer and will continue until autumn, such as potentillas, hebes, *Tamarix ramosissima*, fuchsias, *Hypericum × moserianum* and *Ceratostigma willmottianum*. This last is a sub-shrub with heads of pure ultramarine blue and leaves with rich autumn tints. It requires a warm, sunny position. The attraction of trees is at its lowest ebb in September; the leaves are tired from summer's work and it is too early for autumn colour and fruits. But there are two or three trees that brighten the garden landscape.

Trees

Aralia elata and *A. spinosa* are scarcely trees, being but gawky-stemmed giant shrubs. The former is known, appetisingly, as the Japanese Angelica Tree—for no reason that I know—and has a variegated form, 'Aureomarginata.' The second is called Hercules' Club. The prickly stems of either would make a formidable club. But we are concerned with flowers. The stems are all crowned with a palm-like array of much-divided leaves among which nestle the short sprays of small white flowers. *A. elata* has them in separate sprays, *A. spinosa* in a single-stemmed bunch, and both turn rap-

OPPOSITE: *Buddleja crispa* in the author's garden
BELOW: *Aralia elata* 'Aureomarginata' with matching daylilies

Abelia schumannii

idly into almost black berries, a fine sight among the yellowing leaves in early October.

Eucryphia × intermedia, a hybrid between *E. glutinosa* and *E. lucida*, makes a broadly columnar small tree covered with glittering small leaves of darkest green. Against them the numerous white flowers show up well. It needs lime-free soil.

Sophora japonica, Japanese Pagoda Tree, may burst into flower in August but I think it is usually at its best in early September. It is a tree of considerable size and majesty, rugged in shape and copiously covered in pinnate leaves like those of *Robinia*. And like that tree it bears dangling racemes of small pea-flowers, curiously greenish-white. They do, however, make a fine sight for a week or two. It is unfortunate that the weeping form, 'Pendula', which makes such a characterful head, does not flower, so far as I know.

Shrubs

Abelia schumannii, in lilac-pink, now joins *A. × grandiflora*, discussed in August. They both go on flowering into October. An interesting point with the hybrid is the variable number of calyx lobes, from two to five. This is because one parent, *A. chinensis*, has five lobes and the other, *A. uniflora*, only two; in all three species and the hybrid, the calyces become richly coloured with age and add very much to the display. *A. schumannii* looks particularly well with shrubs and plants with grey leaves; *A. × grandiflora* benefits from the contrast of coppery purple foliage.

Buddleja crispa is at its best on dry, warm days. If pruned hard back in late spring,

it can be a great sight, smothered in cool lilac flower heads over its velvety greyish leaves. *B. fallowiana*, particularly the white-flowered *alba*, continues to offer lovely scented spikes, but, like *B. crispa*, is only suited to our warmer counties.

Calluna vulgaris, Ling, in enclosed gardens will collect fallen leaves in autumn, a situation not to their liking. And I think all will agree that as it is a child of wide-open spaces, so should we look upon it in the garden if possible. But the collector's spirit among us may dictate otherwise. September brings it into prominence. There are innumerable varieties—over a thousand by some estimates—with flowers white, pink and mauve to rich lilac-crimson, in doubles and singles. Some are flat and dwarf, others tall. I will not attempt a selection, but leave the choice to you. They should be clipped over in spring to keep them compact (and thus help to free them of fallen leaves), and will not tolerate drought. Peat or leafmould should be added to the soil when planting to ensure acidity.

A handsome garden of heathers

Caryopteris incana (*C. tangutica*) is a good late flowerer, but the growths are drooping. In really warm gardens, it would make a pretty little weeping standard. It begins flowering just as its relative, *C. × clandonensis*, ends.

Clerodendrum trichotomum and its variety *fargesii* are two dignified shrubs for September with white, sweetly scented flowers borne in prolific sprays. There is not much to choose between the two. I think I prefer the species; the flowers are followed by the crimson tinting of the calyx lobes. Both kinds develop blue berries, but *fargesii* has less handsome foliage, although it is purplish when young. Both are inclined to sucker and are easy to grow in any fertile soil.

Clethra tomentosa now has its crop of sweetly fragrant spikes of small cream flowers and it scents the air around. Fortunately my soil is acid, which suits it well. But it is intolerant of drought, and spreads fairly freely from suckering shoots, but I much prefer it to the more usual *C. alnifolia*. Besides, it flowers much later. The name *tomentosa* indicates the grey undersides of the leaves.

Elsholtzia stauntonii associates well with heathers. Its erect stems, clad in opposite, nettle-like aromatic leaves, come to their climax of two to three feet (0.6–0.9 m) with spikes of heather-like tiny flowers of mauve. It is a good and stalwart late flowerer and can be increased by cuttings or division.

Eupatorium ligustrinum, an elegant daisy bush with a flowering season extending into late autumn, is for those who garden in the warmer districts. The small white tassels are produced over bushy plants well clad in small leaves, often prettily tinted.

Hibiscus syriacus and its many forms in early September have competition from no other shrubs but hydrangeas. In some seasons they are well in flower in late August, but usually September sees them at their best in Surrey. There are two significant facts about them that are worth noting. One is that the species is not native to Syria, as might be expected from the name. It hails from China and reached Europe and Western Asia long ago by sea, or via the Silk Route across Asia. The other is that the plants I mention here are worth growing only in our sunnier counties for their blooms to open well in the cooling air of September. They open their flowers best when the nights are still warm. And what flowers they are! The species is usually light lilac, but selection has resulted in a range of tints from white to pink and light crimson, lilac and blue. There are few truly blue-flowered shrubs and 'Oiseau Bleu' ('Blue Bird') is one of the best. All tints except the pure whites have crimson veins radiating from the centre. The flowers of some may be four

Hibiscus syriacus: 'Oiseau Bleu' ('Blue Bird') (TOP), 'Woodbridge' (MIDDLE) and 'Dorothy Crane' and (pink) 'Hamabo' (BOTTOM)

inches across, which allows them to compete in splendour with most shrubs of the summer season. 'Pink Giant' and 'Mauve Queen' need no words from me; 'Woodbridge' remains the nearest to crimson; 'Hamabo' pale pink; 'Dorothy Crane' and 'Red Heart' are white with conspicuous crimson veining; 'William R. Smith' and 'Diana' pure white. I have only picked out single-flowered varieties; they make the most effect in our rather too cool climate. For the doubles you should go to France, where all kinds are much in favour, heavily pruned in the spring to achieve long shoots studded with blooms. In fact, they need the same sort of treatment as a Hybrid Tea rose, and good feeding. They start into growth very late in spring; it may be June before the grey twigs reveal a return to life. *H. sinosyriacus* has three good colour forms for planting in warm, sheltered gardens. Its leaves are broader, the flowers larger, but they remain in trumpet shape. They all seem to have no particular preferences in the way of soil, but all need much sunshine.

Hydrangea villosa is undoubtedly the queen of the tribe, with its large velvety leaves and large growth—up to ten feet (3.0 m) in cool moist soil, acid or limy. The flowers are of the lace-cap form, rich lilac with conspicuous sterile florets. I think it surpasses in beauty its near relatives *H. sargentiana* and others of the *H. aspera* group to which they all belong. They are all large shrubs, but not so large as the species of the *H. heteromalla* group, to which *H.* 'Bretschneideri' and *H. xanthoneura* belong. These are big open shrubs, with variously flaking bark and wide heads of creamy white flowers which last into the autumn. *H. quercifolia* is totally distinct, as its name (oak-leaf) indicates. This comparatively lowly shrub has big jagged leaves and pyramids of cream flowers turning to warm tints with age, at which time the leaves may turn to rich plum colour. It always excites interest, as does the new double-flowered form of it, 'Snowflake'.

Hydrangea quercifolia 'Snowflake'

Itea ilicifolia, an evergreen with prickly leaves, almost holly-like, will by this time have developed its long, pale green, fragrant catkins a foot (0.3 m) or more in length. It is a free-growing, large shrub for warm gardens and prospers in any fertile soil in sun. I have it rather overhanging a pink hydrangea and the lovely, graceful, pale-leafed *Fuchsia magellanica* 'Versicolor', with the white variegated *Hedera helix* 'Little Diamond' below.

Solanum crispum is a large shrub often classed as a climber, which it is not; it is, however, often given the protection of a sunny wall both for support and warmth. There it becomes huge, with massive woody stems and a profusion of scented, light lilac-blue

potato-flowers held in clusters. *S. crispum* 'Glasnevin' is richer in colour, but not so effective in the garden landscape. On the other hand, it has a longer flowering period extending into autumn, which is my reason for mentioning them both in this month.

Syringa microphylla 'Superba', in addition to its summer crop of scented flowers looked at in June, produces a good second crop as the summer wanes.

Yucca gloriosa, another lover of warmth, only in exceptional summers produces its giant spikes of creamy bellflowers before the frosts stop it.

Several shrubs now show a foretaste of autumn in their fruits, even a tree or two, especially *Malus*. *Viburnum opulus* 'Compactum' is one of the first shrubs to show its translucent red berries, borne in clusters amongst the reddening leaves, and *Rosa moyesii*, *R. moyesii* 'Geranium' (the best of the lot), *R. sweginzowii* and others are carrying on the August display. Likewise, *Euonymus planipes* (*E. sachalinensis*) and *E.* 'Crimson Cascade' carry on for several weeks.

Climbers

Campsis radicans is the best-known Trumpet Vine, but is beaten into second place by 'Madame Galen', a hybrid, known under the name of *C. × tagliabuana*, between the above species and *C. grandiflora*. The flowers are of a glowing coppery orange, quite spectacular. Those of *C. grandiflora* are even larger and of a brighter, lighter tint. There is also a yellow variety, *C. radicans* 'Yellow Trumpet', but it has not been my

good fortune to see this in full flower. All are self-clinging to warm, sunny walls and have elegant Ash-like leaves. At the ends of the strong summer shoots bunches of fat buds open into startling trumpets with wide flanges. They can all be propagated by cuttings in summer or by layering and are not particular about soil.

Clematis orientalis, *C. rehderiana* and *C. veitchiana* are displaying their creamy yellow bells; the first is the brightest yellow and has an extra good form in 'Bill MacKenzie'. The other two are difficult to distinguish until you realise that the leaves are different, though similar. Those of *C. rehderiana* are pinnate, whereas those of *C. veitchiana* are doubly pinnate; both have the lovely scent of cowslips and are in flower for weeks. They are good hearty plants and are easily raised from seeds. 'Lady Betty Balfour' and a few others of the large-flowering hybrids will still be lingering in flower.

Polygonum baldschuanicum, now known as *Fallopia baldschuanica*, is far too vigorous for the average garden, but where there is room, few September (and October) pictures can equal its myriad pinky-white flowers.

Solanum jasminoides is of great value for those in sheltered districts. Its form 'Album' is perhaps even better than the bluish white species. It produces its bunches of pure white potato-flowers for weeks on end, but needs all the sun possible. It quickly scrambles through large shrubs and into trees and roots easily from cuttings.

Perennials

September sees the last big burst of flowering perennials. When we think that only in the last three hundred years or so have we been regaled by such a great influx of flowers from all over the world, it makes us realise how indebted we are to the enthusiasts who brought all these late-flowering treasures to our gardens. They not only enliven the September garden but carry on often into October, shortening the winter season in advance, so to speak. A few we have looked at already in August: the invaluable *Aster × frikartii* 'Mönch', for instance; the fuchsias, *Geranium × riversleaianum* and *G. wallichianum*; *Knautia*, *Aster thomsonii* 'Nanus', *Penstemon* and *Limonium*. These are just a few of the throng that can greet us in the garden. So many of these late flowers have a much longer season of blooming than earlier plants; it is as though they are all enjoying the cooler nights, dews and thinner sunshine which are peculiar to September. Then there are others that continue to push up flowers in spite of the late season: *Scabiosa caucasica*, *Acanthus*, *Crinum*, *Lobelia cardinalis*, *Pennisetum orientale* and other grasses, *Perovskia* and little *Astilbe* 'Sprite', always a charmer—and of course the Japanese anemones. One of my most lasting memories of the September garden is the blue *Hibiscus* 'Oiseau Bleu' surrounded by *Anemone × hybrida* 'Honorine Jobert', the blue and the white so amply complementing one another. An equally satisfying contrast would be achieved with *Anemone × hybrida* itself and a white *Hibiscus*. There would be few more satisfying groupings in the garden throughout the year. *Caryopteris × clandonensis* could well be added to the second example. There are many named forms of Japanese anemones, but nothing in my opinion equals the beauty of these two almost singles.

Actaea alba likes cool moist soil enriched with leafmould. It has deeply divided, elegant leaves but the flowers are mere spiky wisps of white stamens. But wait till early autumn and your expectations will be fulfilled, for it has a surprise ready: the flowers turn into white berries, and should this be insufficient attraction, the stalks thicken and become scarlet, while the leaves gradually turn to yellow. *A. rubra* has red berries, and *A. spicata* follows on with black. *A. rubra* is also known with white berries

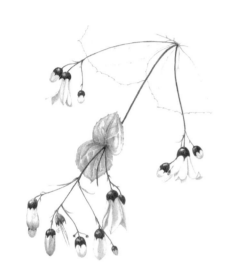

ABOVE: *Kirengeshoma palmata*
RIGHT: *Actaea rubra* with
Clematis × durandii and
allium seed heads

but without the red stalks. They may all ascend to three feet (0.9 m) when growing well, and the first two are from North America, where they are known as Baneberry on account of their poisonous nature. *A. spicata* is the Herb Christopher of Britain and elsewhere in Europe.

Agapanthus inapertus inapertus, another perennial from South Africa, needs a warm sheltered position in full sun. The flowers, in a head at the top of the vertical stem, hang straight down and are rather tubular, in dark blue or very rarely white.

Amaryllis belladonna in chilly Britain needs a hot spot, preferably against a warm wall. There it will throw up stout purple stems bearing at about two feet (0.6 m) the most ravishing lily-flowers of clear cool pink, darkening with age to near crimson. There are several cultivars with flowers of warmer or deeper pink, and a white. It is well worth the long summer wait for sight of these sumptuous flowers, which appear before the strap-like leaves; for this reason they have earned in the United States the quaint name "naked ladies." The bulbs are large and best left alone when thriving, but may need thinning and new positions when crowded.

Anaphalis triplinervis, at a foot (0.3 m) high, is one of the indispensable white-flowered border plants. Although it has greyish felted leaves and star-like "everlasting" flowers, it needs moisture. Most of the other species are taller and rather less attractive to my eyes; all are easy from division in spring.

Artemisia lactiflora has jagged green leaves and branching plumes of creamy flowers. I have written elsewhere of the danger of putting this among truly white flowers, which make it look dowdy. It is an easily grown and divided plant and lasts a long time in flower.

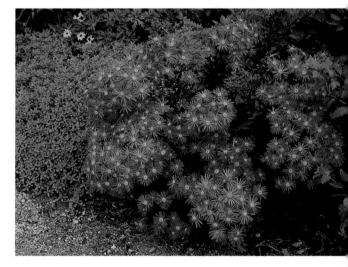

A. ludoviciana is an ardent sun lover, as are most plants with silvery-grey foliage. It is a lovely plant for cooling down rich mixtures of colours. It has invasive roots, like its derivatives *latiloba* and 'Silver Queen', which are both much shorter with jagged leaves. There are several sub-shrubby species of great charm with lacy silvery leaves, such as *A. canescens*, *A. pontica*, *A.* 'Powis Castle', *A. stelleriana* and *A. vallesiaca*, all of which are invaluable for frontal positions. It is sad that *A. absinthium* 'Lambrook Silver' and *A. arborescens* are not reliably hardy.

Aster amellus, in lavender or pink and only two feet (0.6 m) high with large long-rayed blooms, makes a stunning display. In lavender blue you can hardly do better than 'King George', and 'Sonia' for a pink. They are among the asters that precede

TOP: A richly coloured cultivar of *Amaryllis belladonna* growing in a warm climate
BOTTOM: *Aster amellus* 'King George'

the big show of Michaelmas daisies next month. For sheer mass of bloom, go for *A. acris*, especially its form 'Nanus', in bright lavender-blue. And for any odd corner, I suggest *A. divaricatus*. This has almost black stems and airy-fairy heads of near white stars over broad leaves, an admirable plant for almost any foreground position. None of these asters resents pulling apart in spring, when wise gardeners replant only the young shoots from the outer parts of the clump.

A. macrophyllus is not often seen. It is a flopping plant for wilder positions, and will even grow under trees. The big basal leaves give rise to branching heads of pale lavender daisies.

Astilbe 'Dunkellachs' can usually be counted on to be in flower in September given the moisture that any member of the tribe needs to flourish. Not much more than a foot in height, its airy pink sprays remind us of the past summer.

Buphthalmum salicifolium, a very good, long-lasting, compact dark yellow daisy, is a foot (0.3 m) high and wide, or a little more. The neat daisy flowers are produced for many weeks, and it is not particular about soil, nor division.

Calamintha nepetoides, one of the prettiest foils I know for small bulbous plants such as crocuses, is a sweetly aromatic little plant. Usually less than a foot in height, it presents for many weeks a cloud of tiny flowers of a cool blue-white, just right in size and colour to offset the comparatively large flowers of the bulbs. It does so often happen that the best contrasts are found not only in the colours of flowers, but in their size as well. The calamintha is easily settled in sun in any fertile soil and can be raised from seed or divided.

Cestrum parqui

Cestrum parqui is a shrubby plant that dies right down in cold winters but has sufficient strength to reach some five feet (1.5 m) by summer's end, when it will erupt with branching sprays of small tubular flowers of pale greeny cream, deliciously fragrant in the evening. It is a good mediator between the mauves, pinks and yellow shades, where pale off-yellow tones are invaluable softeners of contrasts.

Chelone obliqua, Shellflower, a stiff and handsome plant easily grown and propagated (from the root) where moisture is adequate, yields spikes of strange, rich pink flowers that shed pink caps before opening.

Clematis heracleifolia confuses the uninitiated. It has a woody base but produces a large clump of big dark leaves and lots of pale blue flowers just like those of hyacinths, but not as fragrant. There are several forms in the lists and I think I prefer

'Wyevale' to them all, for its richer colour. Equally unrecognisable as a clematis is *C. recta*, whose great bunches of creamy white stamens enliven the tall stems for weeks; if you can get hold of *C. recta* 'Foliis Purpureis', which has coppery purplish leaves, the contrast will be rewarding. They require propagation from short spring cuttings, or seeds for the ordinary white form, and thrive in most drained soils in sun.

Clematis × jouiniana 'Mrs Robert Brydon', when growing near to one of the late-flowering purple climbing clematises, illustrates well the contrast of flower colour and size I mention under *Calamintha*. 'Mrs Robert Brydon' has heads of milky white small flowers, resembling those of hyacinths, on stems (they need support) of about three feet (0.9 m). In the foreground I could well plant that superior Hyssop, *Hyssopus officinalis aristatus*. Its flowers, in dense spikes on a little bush, are of rich violet. It needs a warm, drained place and can be increased by cuttings, seeds, or merely lifting and pulling apart, like lavenders and heaths.

Colchicum speciosum 'Album', a so-called Autumn Crocus of magnificent size and proportions, is one of the most imposing flowers of the late year. It may well be likened to a tulip, and as do all the other autumn-flowering colchicums, it springs unheralded by any foliage from the bare ground. The great white goblets have a creamy perfection, subduing into second place all the pink-flowered species. The first to appear usually is *C. agrippinum*, whose small flowers, only a few inches from the ground, are pink and prettily chequered in a darker tint. My other favourite is *C. atropurpureum* in dark lilac-pink. There are many species and garden forms of great excellence: *C. speciosum* itself, *C. byzantinum* and 'Autumn Queen'. There are also doubles: *C. autumnale albo-plenum* and the big 'Waterlily'. I am not sure that I altogether approve of double lily-flowers, but when the pink 'Waterlily' is freshly opened, it is a paragon of beauty. There are several dozen other first-class forms and hybrids of goblet formation. Many gardeners admire colchicums when in flower but do not grow them because their leaves, which do not appear until spring, are so excessively overbearing. To my mind they come at a time when rich greenery is scarce, and I welcome them. Their clumps, of aspidistra-like form in the larger growers, can add much quality to an area given perhaps to daffodils. In the border the leaves can be removed as soon as they begin to turn yellow. Any fertile soil suits them, in the sun if possible.

ABOVE: *Clematis heracleifolia davidiana* 'Wyevale'

BELOW: *Colchicum* 'Waterlily'

ABOVE LEFT: *Cyclamen hederifolium* leaves
ABOVE RIGHT: *Cyclamen hederifolium*, available in soft pink or white

Crocosmia × crocosmiiflora 'Emily McKenzie' is another of those sturdy bulbous plants generally known as montbretias. It flowers later than those mentioned under *Crocosmia* in August; 'Vesuvius' is another. One of the ardent collectors of the many forms of the original cross is Mr Gary Dunlop in Northern Ireland. He has been fortunate in finding the red-eyed 'Prometheus', which I thought had been lost.

C. rosea is often called the pink montbretia, though it is quite separate in every way from all the others. A rather procumbent plant, its grassy leaves make a good background for the clear, almost salmon-pink flowers carried in spikes at the end of each stem. It seems quite hardy and easy to manage in any fertile moderately moist spot in sun.

Crocus speciosus and *C. kotschyanus* (*C. zonatus*) could find a place in every garden. They are quite easy to grow, preferably in thin turf or among the freer-growing rock plants in any well-drained fertile soil, preferably in sun. Like the colchicums, they do not produce their leaves until the turn of the year, and when they do come, they are only grass-like. (Colchicums are often called autumn crocuses, but they are really members of the Lily Family, whereas the true crocuses belong to the Iris Family.) *C. speciosus* has some selected forms in 'Oxonian', 'Artabir', 'Aitchisonii' and others; all are of great beauty, subtly shaded with violet on a violet-blue background and lit by fiery orange stigmata. *C. kotschyanus* is paler, but no less beautiful. Like the colchicums, they will produce flowers from a dry corm in a room; that is how I first got to know them.

Cyclamen hederifolium, which we used to know as *C. neapolitanum*, is a small plant that gives great satisfaction. Where it settles down, increasing by self-sown seed, it may often be seen in the hundreds—even thousands. While the flowers keep to two colours, pink and white, the leaves are indescribably different, marked and marbled with grey and grey-green on a dark green background. It is seldom possible to find two exactly alike. I have seen them in a variety of gardens, soils and positions in many counties, some in shady turf, others on hot sunny banks. Wherever they are this awakening to such beauty at the waning end of the year is positively stunning. They grow in my garden from corms which are thirty years old and very large, but they don't flower. Don't ask me why; I have given them every care and encouragement.

Deinanthe caerulea, one of the choice dignitaries of the shady border in September, thrives best in a cool moist spot. There it can develop its broad hairy leaves set at the top of a stout stem with its flowers held meekly among them on red stalks. They are four-petalled, emerging from round buds of an indefinable grey-lilac with grey central stamens. It needs to be seen to be believed and roused Reginald Farrer to claim that it must have "known sorrow both wisely but well". There is reported to be a white form of it but it has not come my way. There is also a species with larger leaves, cleft in two, with white flowers in small clusters: *D. bifida*.

Echinacea purpurea is a strange North American and not easy to place in colour scheming. Its big daisy-flowers stand up well, their usual colour a rich lilac-crimson in cultivars such as 'The King' and 'Magnus'. Paler colours, including 'White Lustre' and 'White Star', are offered, but they all have large reddish-orange centres disconcerting to my eye. They can be propagated by seeds with variable results, or from root cuttings. They thrive in good rich loam.

Epilobium canum (*Zauschneria californica*), California Fuchsia, is a leafy plant whose silvery foliage lights up the scarlet terminal flowers well. They enjoy warmth. (A really hot spot in well-drained soil is a suitable home for them.) Yet they defer their flowering until summer is almost past. The flowers are small, somewhat tubular, and apart from the red type, there is an appealing white and the comparatively new 'Solidarity Pink'—a good clear colour. The variety 'Dublin' is particularly free-

ABOVE: *Deinanthe caerulea*

LEFT: *Echinacea purpurea* 'White Star'

flowering and received the Award of Garden Merit from the Royal Horticultural Society—a well-deserved honour. They all have woody stems and wandering roots, are best planted or replanted in late spring, and are easy to root from summer cuttings.

Eupatorium ageratoides (*Ageratina altissima*), a tall, upright plant with nettle-like leaves and long lasting heads of fluffy truly white flowers, thrives best in part shade and is easy from division.

Gentiana asclepiadea, Willow Gentian, one of the great joys at this time of the year, is a good hearty plant with no tantrums so long as it is given a cool moist spot in a reasonably retentive soil. It will even sow itself when suited. I have known it to germinate in a shady moist lawn. The normal species will grow to at least two feet (0.6 m). It is a native of Europe on both limy and acid soils but makes deep thong-like roots and is not therefore suitable for division; it is best planted as a youngster. Flowers, usually of dark violet blue, are held in pairs along the arching leafy branches. There is a white-throated form known as 'Knightshayes', and delightsome pale blues and whites. All are beautiful. Another gentian for this month is *G. makinoi*, not usually more than one foot (0.3 m) or so, each stem crowned with a cluster of good dark blue trumpet-flowers. It delights in the same conditions as the above.

Hedera helix 'Buttercup', a mere ivy, represents the fraternity of climbing plants that is, apart from *Campsis*, poorly represented this month. It is, however, an ivy with flushed yellow foliage where exposed to the sun and light green where in shade. The flowering shoots are almost pure yellow in leaf, with yellow flower heads much loved by sleepy wasps and flies. The whole makes as brilliant a display as anything in the earlier months. But be ready with the secateurs; it is a vigorous grower and will thread its way over wall, fence, tree trunk and ground if not checked.

ABOVE: *Gentiana asclepiadea* 'Knightshayes' (TOP STEM) and other colour forms
BELOW: *Hedera helix* 'Buttercup', a cutting from the author's garden now growing in New York

Hedychium densiflorum 'Stephen', a fine form with spikes of intriguing orange flowers borne above the smooth leaves, is about three feet (0.9 m) high in all. *H. coccineum* 'Tara' is a giant of about six feet (1.8 m) with extremely handsome spikes of sweetly scented flowers no less intriguing in terracotta orange. The stout stems bear handsome large leaves. Both were brought back by Tony Schilling from northeast India and appear to be quite hardy with me. 'Tara' has a wandering rootstock; mine without branching has travelled a good yard, so make sure the rhizomes are pointing in the same direction when planting or dividing in spring.

Kirengeshoma palmata, an unlikely Japanese member of the Saxifrage Family, is the most dignified candidate imaginable for any really cool moist spot rich with leafmould. In really lush surroundings, it can top four feet (1.2 m), well clad in large vine-like leaves. The flowers on ebony stalks with ebony calyces are lemon-yellow, nodding from a long, spraying, drooping stem. The petals are peculiarly soft and spongy but make for attractive shuttlecock-like flowers. Another species, *K. koreana*, hails from that country and has more erect stems, giving greater effect but less charm.

Kniphofia caulescens I know not where to place. I have seen it in flower in September and October and also in June. On the whole I think it is a late flowerer. It thrives best in the cooler damper west and north, where its grey-green leaves are fresh and beautiful and not dried and wispy at the ends. The flowers are in good spikes of soft coral-red turning to creamy yellow. And when you are tidying up in early spring another delight awaits you, for the bases of the old leaves are shining amethyst. I will leave other pokers until October.

Lilium speciosum is a true September flower with a delicate perfume. Instead of carrying great, wide trumpet-flowers as did *L. auratum* in August, this species regales us with starry flowers with reflexed petals. They are of warm rose-pink heavily covered with crimson warts. This does not sound altogether nice, but it is nevertheless true and gives the flowers a great richness, accentuated by the curving filaments and rich brown stamens. There are few flowers in the outdoor garden with greater allure. Sometimes the plants seem settled and happy, even increasing, until along comes botrytis, spread by greenfly, and the game is lost. So be observant and careful with the insecticide. While a well grown *L. auratum* may reach six feet (1.8 m), *L. speciosum* is not usually more than half this height or a little over.

Ligularia × palmatiloba is a good hybrid between *L. dentata* and *L. japonica*. There is no doubt about the quality of this fine daisy whose orange-yellow flowers are borne in tall bunches over deeply cut leaves.

Liriope muscari is usually planted against sunny walls, but I doubt whether there is any reason for this favouritism. It seems equally at home in a sunny open place where its very dark green grassy tufts can produce the spikes of small, light violet flowers at the approach of autumn and keep them aloft through the early frosts. It is easy from division in spring. There are white varieties and a number of others, which though they may not flower, are popular as running ground cover called Lily Turf in the United States. *Liriope muscari* itself stays where it is planted.

ABOVE: *Hedera helix*. Even the common Ivy has a season of beauty late in the year.
BELOW: *Liriope muscari* 'Monroe White'

Lobelia fulgens in crimson, *L. syphilitica* in blue and *L. × vedrariensis* with its many progeny such as 'Tania' are all good for moist soil where they survive summer and winter happily and are a gladsome sight with their long spikes of flowers. *L. tupa* is hardy in moist climates also, though I should give it the protection of a warm wall. Nobody looking at the statuesque plant with its large velvety leaves and six-foot (1.8 m) spikes of curious flowers would take it for a relative of the blue bedding lobelias. It is one of the noblest plants of late summer and is best increased by careful division in spring.

Miscanthus sinensis 'Silberfeder', a grass for large spaces, excels itself in beauty, flinging up stems to ten feet (3.0 m) or more with silky sprays of flower at the top, warm beige in colour. It takes kindly to division, when necessary, in late spring.

Pennisetum alopecuroides, Fountain Grass, bears silky violet flower heads like hairy caterpillars with a white tuft at the end. At five feet (1.5 m) they overtop the leaves, which in selected plants are purple. The variety 'Woodside' has the reputation of being earlier in flower.

Persicaria affinis (*Polygonum affinis*), an invaluable member of the tribe, is a carpeter of the greatest merit, with creeping stems and greenery not more than six inches (15 cm) high and producing endlessly from July to October short spikes of pink flowers. Of the several selections available, I prefer 'Superba', whose nearly white flowers turn first to pink and then to crimson as they age, making a very pretty edging. Considerably taller are *P. campanulata* with flat heads of pink, and *P. amplexicaulis* with crimson rattails. Both of these are big invasive plants. Not so *P. paniculata*, whose stems are almost woody, making a good clump adorned with freely branching blush or creamy white tiny flowers in generous array. None of these has any preferences of soil or position so long as there is some moisture.

Phlox 'Fujiyama', which easily reaches five feet (1.5 m) or more, is a tremendous grower, increasing at the root very freely; every little piece of root will make a new plant. I find that if some of the foremost shoots are pinched out when about two feet (0.6 m) high, the season for its pure white flowers is lengthened. Meanwhile the varieties of *Phlox maculata* are throwing up fresh spikes. Can we ever have too many phloxes?

Physostegia virginiana is a tall flower of pink, but I think the most popular is *P. virginiana* 'Vivid', which seldom exceeds eighteen inches (0.45 m). The spikes of small, somewhat tubular flowers carry on for many weeks if adequate moisture is available. Propagation is easy from division of its running roots. There are other cultivars, including some with white flowers; all are known as Obedient Plant from the strange ability of keeping flowers pointing at whatever angle they are turned.

Ratibida pinnata (*Lepachys pinnata*), Drooping Coneflower, earns high marks as another providing cool yellow for the border. It is an erect four-foot (1.2 m) plant that inherits the style of *Rudbeckia* in that the petals of the big daisy-flowers droop round their central cone. The foliage is elegant and divided. I have found it a bit intolerant of winter wet, but otherwise an amiable plant that may be divided in spring.

Rudbeckia 'Goldquelle' and *R. subtomentosa* are rather strident in their yellows, as are most of the tribe. But I will put in a special word for *R. maxima*, whose big basal leaves are glaucous grey and upstanding, while the good yellow daisies are borne well aloft and have big nearly black central cones. It is a plant all on its own and suitable for spring division.

Sanguisorba canadensis is a somewhat unruly plant usually needing support, but there is no denying its beauty. The tall stems bear copious pinnate leaves and branch freely, each branch finishing with a long white catkin.

Schizostylis coccinea, Kaffir Lily, bears silky six-petalled flowers all up the erect stem in Gladiolus style amid grassy leaves. Its flowers are gorgeous deep red—best found in the larger-flowered form 'Major', and there are good pinks, among which my favourite is the silky-petalled 'Sunrise', and a rather small white. They are for a moist position in full sunshine.

Scutellaria canescens, whose little skull-cap flowers throng the spikes in palest lavender-blue, is a good companion in the border for *Veronica exaltata*. Both can be divided or raised from seeds and like open sunny positions in any fertile soil.

Sedum maximum, one of the largest sedums, has flowers of pale yellow. In the more popular form 'Atropurpureum', they are coppery brown with leaves and stems of rich beetroot colour. It will achieve over two feet (0.6 m) in good conditions. *S. spectabile* is a well-known old garden favourite with fleshy glaucous leaves all up the stems which terminate when a foot or so in height with wide flat heads of tiny pink stars. They are as much beloved by butterflies as are the buddlejas. (Considering that butterflies of browny-orange such as commas and tortoiseshells predominate on them, I often wonder whether they have any colour-sense.) Good forms of *S. spectabile* are 'Brilliant' and 'Meteor'. Considerably smaller are 'Vera Jameson', 'Sunset Cloud' and 'Ruby Glow'. The runner-up is *S. populifolium*, a procumbent woody plant with characteristic leaves and heads of pinky cream stars. All thrive on limy soils.

Tricyrtis species, Toad Lilies, derive their name from the spotted flowers, not because they squat on the ground. They are all natives of Japan and the Far East. Some are tall and erect with small flowers of pinky-mauve with dark brown or purple spotting, such as *T. formosana* and *T. hirta*, or yellowish in *T. latifolia*, while a real gem is *T. ohsumiensis*, with large flowers of yellow borne along arching stems. They all help to show that even in late September, nature has yet surprises in store. They can be raised from seed or can be divided, carefully, in spring. Leafmould in the soil is an essential for them.

Veronica exaltata is a close relative of *V. longifolia*, which we looked at earlier, with greyish leaves all up the stem and branching spikes of tiny light blue flowers. It makes a good companion for *Scutellaria*.

Colchicum speciosum 'Album' (TOP),
Colchicum 'Waterlily' (LEFT),
Colchicum autumnale tenori (RIGHT)
and *Colchicum agrippinum* (BOTTOM LEFT)

AUTUMN

OCTOBER

This is above all a month of fruition. Apples and pears are mostly ready for gathering and some of the first flowers of the season are with us. Roses of the Hybrid Tea and Floribunda groups put forth a new crop, as if to make the most of the waning sun. There is even a Snowdrop to greet us—*Galanthus reginae-olgae*—whose flowers precede the leaves; it thrives best in sharply drained soil in full sun. Mostly we are fed with leftovers from September but there are also quite a few October specials. Sometimes even in September, at the time of the Autumnal Equinox, there is danger of a slight frost, and of course, as the days shorten a frost will often occur in October. The abelias are still in flower, their reddening calyces adding to the display. And the yellow bells and silvery seed heads of *Clematis tangutica* remain to enliven the waning year.

Shrubs

Arbutus × *andrachnoides* is a stout hybrid of *A. andrachne*; the bark in winter sunlight is not far short of red. All arbutuses should be planted in spring from containers; those with beautiful bark need thinning while young. Arbutuses belong to the Heather Family and thrive on sandy soils.

OPPOSITE: Autumnal colours beside the lake at The Dingle, Welshpool, Wales
BELOW: *Aesculus californica* leaves and fruits at the Cambridge University Botanic Garden

A. menziesii is tree-like, and although it hails from California, where it is called Madrona, it is hardy in Surrey. It has large leaves and large bunches of creamy bells followed by small red fruits. Perhaps its greatest attraction is the red brown bark which annually peels to reveal pale green young bark.

A. unedo is one of the finest of evergreens for all but the coldest of districts, and alone among arbutuses it thrives in limy soils. Known as the Strawberry Tree, it is a native of Western Europe, including southwest Ireland. Dark green leaves tend to hide the nodding trusses of small, pitcher-shaped, waxy, creamy bells. The fruits take a full year to mature, and it is a great sight to see a specimen hung with both flowers and orange-red fruits, whose likeness to strawberries in appearance and flavour demands great imagination. *A. unedo* 'Rubra', with pink flowers, is a form of the Strawberry Tree that so far I have not had the good fortune to see in fruit.

Caryopteris incana (*C. mastacantha*) is a lowly shrub in violet-blue; like the ceanothus below, it needs full sun and is improved by spring pruning.

Ceanothus 'Autumnal Blue', a good contrast with hypericums, is a vigorous hardy hybrid of eight feet (2.4 m) or so. It gets its hardiness from *C. thyrsiflorus*.

Elaeagnus × ebbingei 'Gilt Edge' is a beautiful variegated form and one of the few that seldom reverts to green. *E. × ebbingei* is a hybrid between *E. macrophylla* (a rampageous shrub only for the largest gardens) and *E. pungens*. I have not noticed the latter flowering so well as the former, but it was the flowers on 'Gilt Edge' that prompted these notes. October usually has only just arrived when a sweet whiff greets us as we pass an elaeagnus. The scent comes from tiny crystalline bells produced on last year's wood, flowers that might pass unnoticed but for their fragrance. A few twigs will scent a room. Though the several variegated forms of the different species are sold in quantity yearly on sight, they will usually outgrow their positions quite soon. In common with other variegated shrubs, those with the variegation in the middle of the blade are more prone to revert to green after cutting back than those with marginal variegation.

Hypericum acmosepalum's summer display is usually extended into autumn. The flowers are of good size and rich yellow, and it adds to its attractions with reddish seed capsules from the earlier flowers and very often brightens November with scarlet leaves. It is easily grown and may be expected to reach four feet (1.2 m).

Hypericum 'Rowallane' throws up its late stems with sumptuous dark yellow goblets. This is a July flowerer in mild districts but continues to produce for months; in cooler conditions it frequently dies down in winter but gives a good crop of late flowers. 'Rowallane' may achieve six feet (1.8 m) or more in mild districts.

Lespedeza thunbergii (*Desmodium penduliflorum*), a wide-spraying sub-shrub that tends to die to the ground in winter, has multitudes of rich red-purple pea-flowers catching the eye in late sunshine. It is best planted on a bank or on top of a retaining wall so that its cascades of blossom have space to display their beauty.

Osmanthus heterophyllus (*O. ilicifolius*), with garden value similar to that of elaeagnus, is a holly-like evergreen with prickly leaves. But there the resemblance stops, for the leaves are borne in pairs, opposite to one another, whereas in hollies they are borne alternately. In the fullness of time, as with the elaeagnuses, flowers emerge from last year's wood. They are in small bunches, tiny and white, with a delicious fragrance.

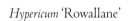

Hypericum 'Rowallane'

Perennials

Many of the most prominent and popular of September perennials continue into October; their long-lasting displays are characterful of the period. Whereas in spring each plant comes forward, makes its bow, and declines rapidly to make way for the next performer, the autumn flowers have a life only terminated by frost. Judging by the last dozen or so years, the autumns are getting softer and the springs long drawn out with dry cold winds. But we must take them as they come and rejoice in the mild Octobers—a blessing for the spiders. (I have watched those crab-like, white

An autumn border arranged regardless of colour scheming but showing plenty of late flowers from physostegia, *Rudbeckia fulgida deamii*, *Sedum spectabile*, asters, solidago, helianthus and *Rudbeckia* 'Goldquelle'

spiders that lurk in the white bases of colchicum flowers, ready to jump and catch hover flies. They leave uneaten just the legs and wings.) It would be churlish to head the list with anything other than that queen of flowers, *Aster × frikartii*. The penstemons continue to put up a brave show, likewise many geraniums, particularly *Geranium endressii*, which is seldom without a flower, and those persistent charmers *G. wallichianum* and *G. × riversleaianum* in their several named forms. Then there is the great group of Japanese anemones, still keeping the flag flying over the yellowing leaves. *Liriope* and *Nerine bowdenii* 'Fenwick's Variety', *Tricyrtis*, various persicarias (*Polygonum*) and the splendid scarlet zauschnerias. I am never quite sure where to include fuchsias; in my district they die to the ground in winter, and so I look upon them as perennials; in warmer districts they may be classed as shrubs. In any case, they are among early October's prime delights.

Aconitum carmichaelii, whose stout stems from poisonous tubers end in an array of hooded wedgwood blue flowers, is one of the season's great joys. It grows to about four feet (1.2 m), but *A. carmichaelii* 'Barker's Variety' achieves six feet with flowers in violet-blue. They are plants of great nobility, stand erect without staking, and are especially fine when seen with *Cimicifuga simplex*. They are best moved in autumn.

Aster cordifolius is similar to *A. ericoides*, but plants usually need some support. Among the best are the varieties 'Silver Spray', 'Ideal' and 'Photograph', all in pale colours. They are easily distinguished by having broad basal leaves.

A. ericoides yields innumerable small flowers on wiry stems, mostly in pale colours. In October these are a huge attraction for all manner of insects. Some famous varieties are 'Pink Cloud', 'White Heather' and 'Brimstone', all compact, floriferous and easily grown.

Aster ericoides 'Pink Cloud'

A. lateriflorus horizontalis has the wit to give its lilac flowers rosy stamens, not yellow. As its name suggests, the growths are erect from the ground but branching into flat sprays, the better to display the countless little flowers. It is an attractive plant through the summer and the foliage becomes dark purplish before flowering time.

A. novae-angliae, from the eastern United States where it is known as the New England Aster, is slightly earlier than other popular asters. It numbers among its variants some good pinks: 'Harrington's Pink' has rather superseded the older 'Barr's Pink', and 'Alma Potschke' and 'Herbstschnee' are two striking forms in almost crimson and pure white. They are all highly thrifty plants reaching five or six feet (1.5–1.8 m) at their best but able to do well even in dryish soils, and do not increase so freely at the root as the true Michaelmas daisies.

Aster novi-belgii, the true Michaelmas Daisy, must often accept impostors as Michaelmas Day, September 29, ushers in asters of many kinds. *Aster novi-belgii*, a native of the eastern United States, has been a prolific seeder in this country, too, and may be seen decorating railway embankments and other waste land. The breeders and selectors were busy on these plants throughout most of the twentieth century. The variety 'Climax' was raised at Aldenham, Hertfordshire, prior to 1900, and in my opinion has never been surpassed. Many varieties have been raised since with larger semi-double flowers and shorter bushy growth, but they lack the grace and elegance so evident in 'Climax'. The way to grow this and other original varieties is to select single large-rooted offsets in spring and plant them in good soil at least two feet (60 cm) apart. The result will be great pyramids of blossom in a lovely soft

lavender-blue. They sometimes need staking. I leave you to appraise the many modern sorts after having tried my recipe for success. There is a 'White Climax' and a later-flowering close relative named 'Blue Gown'.

A. turbinellus, superb, dark-stemmed and wiry, comes when all those above are over and reaches up to about four feet (1.2 m). The flowers are of rich lilac-blue and perfect in shape. It is seldom seen, more's the pity. There is a freshness as of springtime in all the above plants, and they not only put some of the finishing touches to the flower borders, but also assort well with shrubs. And of course, they come at a time when silvery-leafed plants, their perfect companions, are at their best: *Stachys* 'Silver Carpet', *Centaurea*, *Santolina* and many of the bedding plant fraternity.

A. umbellatus is a good but little-known plant whose small white flowers are followed by attractive fluffy seed heads.

Boltonia latisquama flowers towards the end of the month, producing great masses of small whitish daisies; to keep their bulk aloft, the plants need stout stakes. It is perhaps superior to the better-known *B. asteroides* and has a more definite lilac tint.

Ceratostigma willmottianum, in mild districts, may make a bush some four feet (1.2 m) high and wide, but in my area it usually dies to the ground in winter. The resulting wiry stems, well-clothed in bristly leaves, reach about two feet (60 cm) and produce a seemingly endless succession of flowers of pure cobalt blue from bristly dark heads. Few flowers of the whole year produce such unadulterated blue and, planted at the foot of a hot sunny wall with *Senecio pulcher*, might well cause surprise even in full summer.

Chrysanthemum rubellum has flowers in a range of colours, and the many varieties bred from it are at their best this month.

Cimicifuga simplex is a great beauty. From dense clumps of finely divided foliage, it sends up arching stems bearing creamy white bottlebrushes. There is a form called 'Elstead Variety' whose lilac calyces give a noted hue to the flowers. Like other cimicifugas they thrive best in cool moist soils and take kindly to division.

Cortaderia argentea 'Monstrosa', whose great, graceful plumes will top six feet (1.8 m), is perhaps the best of the great pampas grasses. 'Sunningdale Silver' is almost equally good, but it holds its plumes erect and they seem rather congested, as against the widely arching inflorescences of 'Monstrosa'. There is a further large variety, 'Rendatleri', which may reach nine feet (2.7 m) and whose plumes are tinted with lilac pink while young. In some climates, in parts of New Zealand and the western United States for example, pampas grass has escaped from gardens and become a severe pest; I urge gardeners to check locally for information on plants that threaten the native flora. So often we see these plants trying to bring grace to small plots, where the great clumps are out of scale. They are best admired at a distance in wider landscapes, as at Sheffield Park, Sussex, where contact with the arching, rasping-sharp leaves is easily avoided. Fortunately there is a well-known form called 'Pumila' which has shorter leaves and flower spikes of five to six feet (1.5–1.8 m). It is the most appropriate for constricted sites. All pampas grasses are best divided and moved in moist weather in late spring; I have known heavy losses to occur from dry roots and dry weather.

Eupatorium purpureum, Joe Pye Weed in its native United States, is a giant with wide heads of rich mauve flowers on six-foot (1.8 m) stems. *E. maculatum* 'Atropurpureum' is similarly tall and handsome.

Chrysanthemum rubellum 'Clara Curtis', a good, clear pink flower

Leucanthemella serotina, formerly known as *Chrysanthemum uliginosum*, has plentiful large white daisies borne well aloft on six-foot (1.8 m) stems. They have the disconcerting habit of turning to face the sun, which will determine their placing in the garden.

Miscanthus sinensis has a useful variant in 'Zebrinus', a grass that has not only the attraction of yellow cross-banded leaves but also the merit of producing silvery brown, elegant flowers in October. It will reach six feet (1.8 m) in most seasons and is an easy Japanese plant.

Pennisetum alopecuroides, a grass whose dark purplish blue spikes have a tuft of white at the end, is much smaller than the miscanthus. A reliable flowering form is 'Woodside', but it needs a warm sunny exposure to flower well.

Poterium canadense is a six-foot (1.8 m) pretty bearer of white catkins.

RED HOT (AND OTHER) POKERS

Another great group of flowering plants for late September and October, the red hot pokers, includes species and varieties of *Kniphofia*. These are natives of South Africa and appreciate maximum sunshine, but they also demand adequate moisture. We were all brought up on *K. uvaria*, which is a coarse plant with flopping leaves but with handsome spikes of orange-red, perhaps six feet tall (1.8 m). It is better left for larger, wilder gardens, but its form 'Nobilis' is well worth a place.

Although I am writing about October flowers in this chapter, I must mention that the poker season starts in June with the popular hybrid plant known as 'Atlanta'. Nobody knows its origin, but it is a likeable plant of about three feet (0.9 m) with bright red spikes. It is succeeded in July by the handsome 'Royal Standard' in red and yellow, and later by the pure yellow 'Wrexham Buttercup'. These are all good plants and reliable.

Kniphofia triangularis, a gem among the smaller pokers with neat grassy leaves and dainty spikes of brilliant red flowers, seldom exceeds three feet (0.9 m) in height. There is a good yellow called 'Brimstone', and Beth Chatto's noted 'Little Maid' in ivory. During the last several decades, innumerable varieties have been raised embracing a wide range of tints—green, coral and amber among them. The old names, *nelsonii* and *macowanii*, are now forgotten and obscured by these lovely generous, neat plants, all characters being in proportion. They take kindly to spring division and planting and need to be well fed if they are to give of their resplendent best at the end of the season.

K. rooperi, once called 'C. M. Prichard', is the last poker to flower. It has big, almost ovoid heads of orange-red flowers. It is a splendid plant to finish the series, though 'Underway' sometimes outlasts it into November. This is a hybrid with good spikes of apricot-orange blooms, raised by Norman Hadden in Somerset, between a garden poker and the apricot form of *K. triangularis*, which used to be known as *K. galpinii*.

Eucryphia × nymansensis 'Nymansay' and *Fuchsia* 'Mount Stewart', a fine hardy double raised in Northern Ireland

Salvia blepharophylla, S. confertiflora, S. involucrata, S. leucantha and *S. rutilans* are among the many blue-flowered, half-hardy salvias that do much to enliven sunny autumnal borders. They are all highly desirable but unreliable except in warm districts. The same may be said of the perennial *S. patens* in true vivid blue, and the lighter variant *S. patens* 'Cambridge Blue'. I have wintered them in Surrey for a few seasons, but eventually they disappear. Except for grasses, salvias will, however, finish the season.

Salvia caerulea, one of the most spectacular of true bright blue flowers of the whole season, is a tall plant (of some five feet [1.5 m]) which usually needs support. It flaunts its sky blue flowers for several weeks in the late sunshine.

S. guaranitica is as tall as *S. caerulea* but with dark, almost navy blue flowers. They are fitting plants to close October.

Sedum 'Herbstfeuer' ('Autumn Fire') is a most handsome end-of-the-season plant, with the usual fleshy leaves and large flat heads of tiny flowers, like those of the earlier *S. spectabile*, but of a warm coppery pink. They are much loved by late butterflies. Speedily making large clumps they tend to flop, but this can be cured by judicious division into smaller clumps in spring.

Senecio pulcher carries several big daisy-flowers on each two-foot (0.6 m), dark-leafed stem. They are of a startling, vivid magenta-crimson with clear yellow centres. I fancy it needs adequate moisture at flowering time. While this plant is a native of Uruguay, the *Ceratostigma* that I propose as its companion hails from western China and immortalises the name of Willmott, a famous and extravagant gardener in Essex and the French Riviera in the early part of this century.

S. tanguticus we are now told to call *Sinacalia*; the heads of small yellow flowers are giving way to fluffy seed heads that last a long time on the four-foot-high (1.2 m) stems from wandering roots.

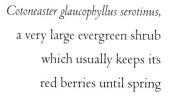

Cotoneaster glaucophyllus serotinus, a very large evergreen shrub which usually keeps its red berries until spring

Autumn Colour

There comes a time in late October when there is little profit in looking for fresh flowers. The tender exotics that have enlivened our borders during the last three weeks or more are coming to an end, and with the shortening days and cooler nights even the hardy perennials are getting scarce. Although this is a book about flowers, I feel it cannot appear complete without some reference to autumn colour and berries, and so I am including in October a few notes on the former and leaving berries to November. Already in early October, we have seen that regular performer *Prunus sargentii* change from dark green to crimson. It is indeed, though fleeting, one of the most noted among all the exotic trees that grace our gardens. How fortunate we are to have all the hundreds of trees and shrubs which have been brought from other countries to supplement so lavishly our few natives in the display of autumn colour. Nothing outweighs *P. sargentii*. I suppose as a plant raised from seeds it would have originally developed into a very large bush; because it makes no leading shoot the nurseries have resorted to top-grafting

LEFT: *Acer palmatum* 'Dissectum'
in autumn colour with the hardy
fern *Arachniodes simplicior* beneath
BELOW: *Gentiana farreri*, a lovely
autumnal for the cool rock garden

it on stems of the common Gean, with the rather incongruous bushy top to a stout stem. Few of the Japanese cherries have this trait; their growth is more individual. Their leaves contribute delicate peach tones, and orange rather later in the season. One of the earliest of yellow-colouring trees is the majestic Tulip Tree, *Liriodendron tulipifera*, the American Whitewood of the timber trade. Its large leaves are a wondrous sight, but it is too large for the average garden. We must look among smaller foreign trees in our quest—the stewartias for instance, certain maples of the snakebark kind, *Sorbus*, too, though they are more noted for berries. *Sorbus sargentiana* is noted for its foliar colour as well as its berries. On the whole though I think it is autumn colour from shrubs that fills our need best; there is no shortage of them.

Acer japonicum, one of a large group of maples from the Far East and especially Japan, is found in gardens most often in the form 'Aconitifolium', a small tree with rich crimson autumn colour in its deeply lobed leaves.

A. palmatum, the best known of Japanese maples, has given rise to numberless forms, from the lacy 'Linearilobum', 'Dissectum' and others, to the noted Heptalobum group with its most famous form, 'Ozaka Zuki', turning without fail each year to brilliant scarlet. Many of the forms raised in Japan and elsewhere have leaves of coppery purple; these tend to turn into the darkest reds. A glade devoted to Japanese maples goes a long way in satisfying our craving for brilliant colour at the fall of the year. They are, some of them, slow growing, especially the Dissectum group, but many of the others, free growing, may easily attain twenty feet (6.0 m) on soils away from chalk.

Amelanchier lamarckii, a noted large shrub almost unbeatable for autumn colour, is almost as noticed for leaf tints in spring. It enjoys the common name Snowy Mespilus that belongs strictly only to *A. ovalis*. *A. ovalis*, the true Snowy Mespilus, is more shrub-like and has similar colouring in spring and autumn.

Berberis × *carminea* contains some especially good hybrids, as noted for their foliage colour as for their well-coloured berries borne in lavish bunches; they are such as 'Bountiful', 'Sparkler' and 'Pirate King'. *Berberis dictyophylla*'s leaves turn to scarlet and then drop, leaving the pink berries and white twigs to last well into the winter. Few autumn sights can equal it.

B. thunbergii is one of the most brilliant of shrubs with scarlet tones for lime-free soils and forms with purplish-copper leaves are equally good. *B. sieboldii* is a medley of long-lasting tints.

CHERRIES

Several ornamental cherries put on a good show at the beginning of the winter season. None in my opinion is the equal of *Prunus incisa*. Although often seen as a small tree, it can be grown as a large bush. In addition to the complete smother of small blush single flowers in spring, it goes out in late October in a flush of murrey crimson. Its noted hybrid 'Okame' can also be relied on for this late feast, while its early spring display in warm, dusky pink is scarcely equalled by any other tree. These cherries—not by any means the only autumn joys in the genus—bring to mind other small suckering cherries: *Prunus besseyi* has no outstanding floral attraction but develops apricot autumn colour, and when the leaves have gone they reveal bunches of almost black fruits, like small sloes, and in fact they make a piquant jelly. *P. tenella* is another dwarf cherry that lights the garden with pink in spring and lingers long in its fiery autumn tints—though it was not for these that its best variant was named 'Fire Hill'.

CLIMBERS

Ampelopsis megalophylla has a magnificent array of colours in its doubly pinnate leaves, a display equalled only by the great rounded plates of *Vitis coignetiae*, both natives of the Far East. I have seen the latter used to decorate fully grown trees, and also to cover banks too steep to mow. In each case one comes away stunned by the beauty. *Vitis davidii* is another splendid colourer, while *V. vinifera*, the common Grape, has a noted form in 'Purpurea' in which all summer long the leaves are dark green, gradually turning to beetroot; finally they go out in crimsons and scarlets at which time

Vitis vinifera 'Purpurea' in the author's garden

there is little to touch it. Allied to the vines are the *Parthenocissus* species. We all know the so-called Boston Ivy that covers so many great buildings with a curtain of scarlet in late October. Less known are *P. henryana* and *P. quinquefolia*; this last is the true Virginia Creeper, which, unlike the closely allied *P. inserta* (*P. vitacea*), is capable of clinging to its supports. All three are noted for their brilliant colouring; *P. henryana* adds a sort of velvety touch to its pale-ribbed leaves which enriches them beyond compare. And if we want a touch of yellow by way of contrast what better than *Celastrus orbiculatus* (*C. articulatus*)? Like all of these climbers, it is very vigorous and will ascend to the tops of trees. If you are able to get a hermaphrodite plant, so much the better. Then will the orange seeds in their creamy capsules delight you, for they are relatives of the spindle trees.

Parthenocissus henryana

Cornus florida, a lovely shrub or small tree usually modestly white when in flower, has a free-flowering pink clone, and if you can find a plant of it you will be doubly rewarded, for it is very good again in autumn colour.

C. *kousa* has the most elegant tabular growth, and it is fascinating to watch it changing colour week by week accompanied by the luscious-looking red fruits.

C. *nuttallii*, the tallest of this group of large cornels for autumn colour, is not easily satisfied. One of the best trees I have seen—for it is tree-like—is on hungry gravel, and I think that the failures one hears about are the result of hastening growth with too much rich feeding.

Cotinus coggygria is a regular performer in a genus that provides us with some of the most brilliant colours; its named forms with coppery purple leaves seem to outreach the species itself. *C. obovatus* is a larger shrub of special brilliance. At one time classed as *Rhus* these shrubs still have noted relatives in that genus, such as *R. typhina*, *R. glabra* and *R. trichocarpa*, all distinguished from *Cotinus* by their pinnate leaves. They are brilliant, but for a short spell.

Cotoneaster bullatus is a forthright splendid shrub as good in berry as it is in leaf colour. Rather smaller are two neat-leafed species, *C. divaricatus* and *C. dielsianus*, both of which may be relied on for strong red colouring. *C. horizontalis* likewise, but this has a pretty variegated form whose leaves turn to pink.

TOP: *Enkianthus campanulatus*

ABOVE: *Hamamelis* 'Jelena'. All witch hazels colour well in autumn—mostly yellow.

LEFT: *Hydrangea quercifolia* has unusual large leaves which reveal rich colours in autumn.

Enkianthus campanulatus is a worthy example of a two-season shrub, but *E. perulatus* is much smaller and excels in a smother of snow-white flowers in spring and is fierce blood-red in autumn.

Euonymus europaeus, our native Spindle, is usually purplish red in autumn, but also has pink capsules that show orange seeds while opening. *E. oxyphyllus* colours richly in autumn with a fiery display of leaves and fruits. *E. planipes* is a little more subdued, but rich in colours that appear early in the season.

Fothergilla major and *F. gardenii* are also noted shrubs for two-season display. Their fluffy white spring flowers from the bare branches are equalled by a long-lasting flurry of red, orange, yellow and purple in autumn.

Hamamelis × intermedia, a hybrid Witch Hazel in its many named forms, also contributes nobly to our theme, while *H. mollis* turns to yellow. For lime-free soils there are also *Gaylussacia* and *Vaccinium*.

Hydrangea quercifolia is a dignified hydrangea with large, coarse, indented leaves which assume rich colours while the pyramids of flowers are still lasting in muted white. There is a fascinating new form of this called 'Snowflake' in which the flowers are double, with a consequence of longer lasting display and equal beauty from the leaves.

Hypericum acmosepalum, one of two St. John's Worts listed here, is among the lesser lights in both colour and size. Their sprinkling of scarlet leaves and ruddy seed capsules (often accompanied by a few late flowers) appeal very strongly to me. *Hypericum forrestii* is the other St. John's Wort that pleases me at this season.

Pistacia chinensis, the Chinese Pistachio, provides a brilliant scarlet panoply of pinnate leaves in autumn that is hardly to be equalled.

Rhododendron luteum (*Azalea pontica*) is one of the commonest, and hard to beat for bronzy leaves in autumn (and for perfume when in flower). *R. vaseyi* is noted for its autumn brilliance and is very lovely in May if you get a good pink form; its curving stamens put the finishing touch to a flower of rare beauty.

Sorbus fruticosa, a suckering shrub about eighteen inches (0.45 m) high, provides rich leaf colour contrasted with white berries. *S. poteriifolia*, a name often ascribed to a spurious tree of small stature noted for its pinky-white berries, refers in truth to a suckering bush only a foot or two (0.3–0.6 m) high with crimson berries and good autumn colour. *S. reducta* is again of similar habit but with pink berries. All three sorbuses are to be treasured.

Spiraea prunifolia is a graceful shrub with arching sprays of scarlet leaves.

Hypericum × moserianum, in flower from July till autumn

RIGHT: *Euonymus alatus*

BELOW: *Viburnum lentago*

Stephanandra incisa has a variety 'Crispa' which makes a dense rounded hummock of interlacing branches and twigs, completely covered with cut leaves of sober warm colouring.

Viburnum dilatatum, a free-flowering and too seldom seen shrub from Japan, may be relied upon for good autumn colour, and for scarlet berries if other plants of the species are nearby. *V. lentago*, a large shrub, also seen as a small tree, has flowers in flat heads. In autumn the long, pointed leaves color excellently. *V. opulus*, a British native, is outstanding in the reds of its foliage and its scarlet berries. It is wise to keep most viburnums far from the nose, for they have an objectionable smell on damp, mild days.

V. plicatum is one of the most popular of a great garden group that seldom fails to gladden us whether it be for foliage, flower or berry. Its flowers are sterile and gathered into balls in the manner of the mophead hydrangeas. *V. plicatum tomentosum* holds its flowers, some of which are fertile, in flattened heads. Both this and the mophead above are noted not only for their floral excellence—like white tablecloths spread over the horizontal stems—but they also go out in a glory of plum-crimson and red, and not infrequently those with fertile flowers add a benison of scarlet berries. *V. setigerum* has metallic tints in the leaves in spring giving way to orange and red in autumn.

I find too much red rather boring, and the obvious contrast is yellow, which we find in most of the clethras. There is also *Aronia melanocarpa*. This contrasts its yellow leaves with black berries—unlike *A. arbutifolia*, resplendent in red. But even yellow is not the only contrast to be searched for. I have in mind a grouping, using the pink of *Cotoneaster horizontalis* 'Variegata' with the ivory white of *Orixa japonica*. To add to our "different" group is *Euonymus alatus* in pure crimson (not scarlet), and if you can add *Callicarpa bodinieri* for the sake of its purplish leaves and violet berries you will have a unique group. *Euonymus verrucosus* will add a pink tone to this little assembly.

Viburnum farreri (*V. fragrans*),
in flower from autumn till spring
in mild spells, and sweetly scented

NOVEMBER

While December brings us the joy of Christmas, the usual feeling is that poor November has little to recommend it, even for us gardeners. It is a time of sweeping away not only leaves, but also all the last vestiges of summer. But the truth is not so dismal. With the leaves all fallen and carted away, or swept on to the borders under shrubs to provide mulch and increase humus, the light now falls more easily on the ground showing up fresh vistas and good greenery. In searching for diversion we shall discover flowers that we never thought to find in "drear November". Trees, shrubs and perennials are all there to welcome us. There are even trees flowering.

Trees

Alnus nitida—although Alders as a group are far from showy trees in flower—produces its catkins at this time of the year. Considering they are wind-pollinated, it is rather surprising that an Alder should select what is usually a damp period of the year to bring forth its flowers. They are of little account in the garden or woodland but serve as just another species that braves the weather. And brave it must be, for

the last Buchan Cold Spell of the year occurs usually in about the second week of the month. A cold spell in November is sometimes valued: witness the old saying "If November ice will hold a duck, we shall have but slush and muck". Being interpreted, this intimates that if winter gets a good start before the end of the year, it often proves that the early months of the new year will not be severe. But who can predict the fickle British weather? Even Dr Buchan, who kept records for some seventy years for Scotland, would be the first to admit the difficulty.

Prunus subhirtella 'Autumnalis' will, before its leaves have all fallen, be opening its pinky-white flowers. This is a reliable tree of medium size and never fails to flower in autumn, winter and indeed spring in some years, whenever the weather is reasonably mild. When the leaves have fallen, it presents a cloud of blossom best seen against a dark background with the southern rays of sun shining upon it. Launched by Daisy Hill Nursery in County Down at the beginning of the twentieth century, it has never failed to astonish us gardeners. There is a pink variety 'Rosea' which some may prefer; they are both admirable for cut sprays to open indoors.

Shrubs

Camellia sasanqua, a November-flowering shrub for lime-free soils, is a Japanese species that does best in Devon and Cornwall in full sun. There its buds will be encouraged to form, and the shelter of a west or south-facing wall is sometimes recommended, though I have yet to see a plant damaged by cold in Surrey. There are a dozen or more varieties listed, mostly of pale colours, white or pink or flushed with pink, and I believe all such have a rarefied and delicious fragrance. One with grey white variegated leaves flowers well for me. It is unfortunate that one of the most

OPPOSITE: The pink winter bark of *Acer pensylvanicum* 'Erythrocladum'
ABOVE: *Camellia sasanqua* 'Crimson King'
LEFT: *Camellia sasanqua* 'Kanjiro'

RIGHT: *Jasminum nudiflorum*

BELOW: *Fatsia japonica*

showy and floriferous, 'Crimson King', is not fragrant. But there are many others and compared with *C. japonica*, they are less ponderous shrubs, with wiry branches and smaller leaves, and in warm climates reach a great size.

Choisya ternata, Mexican Orange, often has a late crop of white flowers, and they show up well against the dark polished leaves.

Fatsia japonica has perhaps the grandest fingered foliage among reasonably hardy shrubs, but much as I love it, it is not much use in my district, where its flowers are nearly always spoiled by frost. We have to go to the Southwest to see it in full beauty. It is a close relative of the Ivy, but the round heads of flowers are ivory-white and borne on equally white stems. Judging by the fine crops of blackish berries that mature in the spring in the environs of London (it is a good town plant) and in the Southwest, it must be a great sight in flower. It develops into a large impressive shrub, with stout stems, and seems to thrive in any soil.

Jasminum nudiflorum is the Winter Jasmine; even if it did not flower its dark green stems would cheer us in winter, while the starry yellow flowers come and go in mild spells throughout the dark months. When established it makes very strong, long shoots whose side branches produce the best flowers in the following season. But you can cut this long-suffering plant about in spring as much as you like; it will always rebound with an ever more prolific display of flowers, which last well indoors. It is usually seen trained up a wall or fence; its subsequent drooping growth proves how suitable it would be flowing down a bank with red-berried *Cotoneaster horizontalis*. They are both much at home on shady banks and walls.

Mahonia × media embraces offspring from a number of crosses between the late autumn-flowering *M. lomariifolia*, tall, gaunt and not very hardy, and the low-branching *M. japonica*, whose sweetly fragrant blossom does not reach its best till early spring. Both have magnificent evergreen, pinnate leaves. It was probably with the desire of giving some hardiness coupled with delicious fragrance that prompted Leslie Slinger of the Slieve Donard Nursery in Northern Ireland to cross-pollinate these two species. The first result was called 'Charity', which earned the Award of Merit from the Royal Horticultural Society in 1959, and the Award of Garden Merit ten years later. It has become the forerunner of several others. Lionel Fortescue and Norman Hadden, both West Country gardeners, made the same cross and several fine plants resulted, two of which are 'Lionel Fortescue', which takes after *M. lomariifolia* in its upright growth and dark yellow flowers; and 'Underway', a bushy plant with, I find, a rather later display of cool creamy greeny-yellow flowers. They are both excellent; 'Underway' has more scent. There are several more hybrids about; Slinger also raised 'Winter Sun', which inclines towards *M. japonica*. In all, *M. × media* is a magnificent gift for our autumn gardens and all plants under this banner appear hardy and quite happy in shade in almost any soil. In sun the foliage often becomes yellowish.

Rhododendron 'Yellow Hammer', a pretty little upright shrub with small fragrant leaves and small tubular creamy yellow flowers, is a regular out-of-season performer. And in some seasons we may expect to see the first blooms on *R. nobleanum*, of which I favour most the pink form, 'Venustum'. It is a hearty grower and usually flowers in mild spells from autumn onwards.

ABOVE: *Mahonia × media* 'Lionel Fortescue'
LEFT: *Mahonia × media* 'Underway' in the author's garden

RIGHT: *Viburnum tinus* in
winter at the Cambridge
Botanic Garden
BELOW: *Viburnum foetidum*

VIBURNUMS

Concluding this section are some of the best of shrubs: viburnums. Directly the leaves fall on *Viburnum farreri* (*V. fragrans*) we may expect to see the heads of sweetly scented flowers beginning to open. The last few autumns have seen a wonderful display of the palest pink small flowers smothering the bushes and casting their Heliotrope-like scent around. Unfortunately they speedily drop in the warmth of our rooms. It is a shrub that prefers a suitably moist soil where it will become large and—a blessing for our friends—every twig that arches to ground level will tend to take root. *V. grandiflorum* is a rather more open shrub with similar, though longer flowers, but not quite so sweet a scent. The hybrid between the two, *V. × bodnantense*, is an excellent tall shrub with big bunches of sweet flowers which I find last better indoors. But it is a mighty grower to some ten feet (3.0 m) or so and not for small gardens. The same might be said of the others, which all get large in time.

We cannot close our notes on these invaluable shrubs without mentioning one of the oldest foreign shrubs, cultivated in our gardens since the late sixteenth century: *Viburnum tinus*, Laurustinus, so called because evergreens were so much prized in those early days. Of the several named forms in cultivation, I give the prize to 'Gwenllian', whose rich pink buds open to blush white flowers in flat heads. It is not unusual to find last season's flowers have matured into blue-black berries at the same time, with a lovely contrast of colours amongst the deep green leaves. It is a comparatively compact form which has much to recommend it, but, as I have mentioned elsewhere, in some mild spells, especially after frost, it puts forth a disagreeable smell and is best kept away from doors and windows. There is a pleasing, compact variegated form for those who hanker after such things, but its flowers are not so colourful as those of 'Gwenllian'.

Perennials

Chrysanthemum cultivated varieties, now flowers for every season, were once essentially flowers of the autumn only. Methods of growing under glass, excluding light to shorten daylight hours artificially, disbudding and propagating brought about the change. For many decades I had been growing a tough old variety—a sound perennial blooming in mild Novembers. Its flowers were deep pink when unfolding, opening to rayed flowers with tubular petals. These gave way as the days or even weeks passed to spoon-shaped rays of light pink, while the centres, as yet unfolded, remained a dusky crimson. At the time of flowering, the uppermost leaves turned to the same dusky crimson. I did not know its name, but idly turning the pages of Jekyll's *Flower Decoration* one day, I recognised its portrait in a good black-and-white photograph. Moreover, in William Robinson's *The English Flower Garden*, there was an excellent engraving of the same thing. Both writers stressed the leaves turning dark red. It was named 'Old Cottage Pink', or 'Emperor of China'. There seemed to be no doubt about its authenticity; the red leaves were confirmation. The Robinson book was the edition of 1893, and I think it likely that it is a genuine old Chinese variety, for its flowers resemble chrysanthemums in old Chinese paintings. While hundreds of named garden varieties have long since been lost, this variety, not subject to disease, is soundly perennial. And what a luxury it is to go out so late in the year to pick armfuls of the beautiful blooms! I have given roots away and many nurseries, some in America, now list it.

Equally perennial is the group of pompon-style dwarfs, achieving about two feet (0.6 m). The first I grew, 'Anastasia', was given to me by Frank Galsworthy. The little double blooms are borne freely and are a dark murrey tint on opening, becoming old-rose purple with age. Its lovely sport in brownish maroon is called 'Dr Tom Parr', and in the hands of Messrs. Ingwersen, sports of this and the closely allied 'Mei Kyo' have arisen in buff and even yellow. They are all resilient little perennials and require no staking. It is likely that these, too, are ancient cultivars from the Far East. They are, however, caviar to slugs.

Cimicifuga racemosa, a tall plant for a cool, moist position, has bottlebrush flowers of white ascending to seven feet (2.1 m). You may admire the imposing stance

Chrysanthemum 'Mei Kyo'

of the plant displaying its tiers of divided leaves. At its foot *Liriope muscari*, with evergreen iris-like leaves, mentioned in September, might be grown.

Crocus banaticus used to be called *C. iridiflorus* on account of its short, upright inner segments; the whole flower is of warm violet, enhanced by yellow stigmata. I find this species seems to prefer shade, whereas my other treasure for these darker days, *C. laevigatus fontenayi*, thrives in sun. A gleam of sunshine and they are open, the buff purple-striped outer segments folded back, revealing the rich lilac inner surfaces and segments, the whole set off by orange yellow stigmata. It is a diminutive plant, needing a carpet of some dwarf plant to poke through and to protect its flowers from rain splashes. But I really grow it for its scent. Just three to four little flowers in a wine glass will scent a small room. It is quite easy to grow in any friable soil.

Saxifraga fortunei, one of the most exquisite things at this time of the year, is a shade-demanding plant needing the sort of soil you would provide for rhododendrons. Handsome scalloped leaves, hairy and glistening and reddish on the reverse, make a handsome podium for the airy sprays of small white flowers, each with the lowest petal much longer than the others. 'Wada's Variety' is noted for its dark reddish leaves; this, or the big white 'Windsor', should be sought. Though the plants are hardy, they turn brown at a touch of frost.

Crataegus × *lavallei* 'Carrierei' and *Iris foetidissima* 'Citrina'

Fruits and Berries

Some intriguing questions emerge when we think about the colours of autumn. Why for instance do our most brilliant colouring trees and shrubs come from the other side of the world, to whit Eastern Asia and the United States? Again, why are so many berries of some shade of red when they are ripe? Admitted that red is opposite green on the colour wheel, and so might more easily catch the eye of a bird, but the berries of some species of viburnum are first red, but not ripe until they turn black. And why are some other berries white, pink, violet or blue? I see no explanation in evolutionary terms and must leave the questions unanswered. To our eyes a red berry is traditional; it suits the eye against the green or yellow of foliage as no other colour does. As early as mid-October some trees and shrubs start to show their autumn crops and will continue to brighten the scene through the winter if the weather allows and birds dine elsewhere.

Among trees there is hardly anything to excel the great rosy cones—splitting to reveal vermilion seeds—of *Magnolia obovata*. And it drops its great paddle-shaped leaves at the same time, falling to the ground in dusky brown. Otherwise the Rose Family is well to the fore, with *Crataegus, Malus* and *Sorbus*. The various crab apples are among the first, *Malus* 'John Downie' showing its pointed orange red crabs as early as the first weeks of October, at which time the rounded, crimson 'Dartmouth' is an even greater showpiece, and more toothsome too; while 'John Downie' is a rather erect grower, 'Dartmouth' is a graceful grower. Both were praised in April for their flowering. They are followed by 'Golden Hornet' in bright yellow. It is a rather ungainly grower when young and needs a little shaping from time to time but in maturity makes an excellent head of branches laden with fruits.
'Red Sentinel' is another spectacular small tree, while 'Red Jade' is a noted weeping tree. They both descend from the common Crab, and their fruits last well into the winter. All of them are suitable for making jelly.

Malus 'Red Jade'

The species of *Sorbus* are varied in both growth and berries. As early as August, the native *S. aucuparia*, Rowan or Mountain Ash, will be showing red berries that are usually quickly stripped by the birds. It has two compact selections, 'Sheerwater Seedling', a rapid, erect tree admirable for close quarters, and the strange 'Fastigiata' which has been known as 'Decora Nana', 'Americana Nana' and also as 'Scopulina'; it is a slow-growing, columnar, small tree with extra dark green leaves and bunches of scarlet berries. This is a plant for small gardens.

S. *commixta* is the name now given to the tree long known as *S. discolor*. It is one of the most reliable for autumn colour and berries; 'Embley' is closely related. Another noted tree, long grown as *S. pohuashanensis*, is *S. × kewensis*. *S.* 'Joseph Rock' heads the list of yellow-fruited rowans, and it has the wit to turn its leaves to a rich mahogany tint at the same time. In some districts it is wretchedly prone to fire blight. *S. scalaris*, a wide-spreading tree, has fine foliage, and the broad heads of red berries are as good as any. A smaller tree with equally striking foliage is *S. esserteauiana*; the late-maturing berries are red, but yellow in the variety 'Flava'. 'Winter Cheer' is a splendid late-maturing hybrid of this species. A totally different tree, sometimes merely

a large shrub, is *S. vilmorinii*, in which the small leaves give a ferny effect, and the berries in small clusters are deep rose-red to start with, fading to nearly white as the leaves take on dusky tones.

Crataegus species and varieties, Thorn Trees, can be spectacular this month. In addition to the rich colours the leaves assume, *C. prunifolia* produces a large crop of rich red fruits in bunches. It is a tree of horizontal branching habit, useful and not too tall. *C. mollis* is noted for the same characters of foliage and berry colours, but the leaves are larger, the growth more upright and the fruits are large and of bright crimson. Carrying the flag well into December is *C.* × *lavallei* 'Carrierei', whose leaves stay dark, dark green and glossy, and are lit by large orange fruits that turn to red as the leaves drop. It makes a nice bushy head.

SHRUBS

Ampelopsis brevipedunculata, a climber, may, in mild autumns when luck is with us, yield a crop of blue berries, but it really needs greater warmth than my Surrey climate provides.

Callicarpa bodinieri (*C. giraldiana*) is especially noted for its violet-tinted leaves and clusters of small lilac berries. 'Profusion' is a renowned cultivar which makes a delightful contrast with *Colchicum speciosum* 'Album' in the September sunshine. The callicarpas are somewhat attractive to birds but usually last through November.

Celastrus orbiculatus is one of a tribe of climbing plants related to *Euonymus* and with fruits of the same shape—orange seeds enclosed in yellow husks. All are vigorous scramblers, and the several species are all good, but because their sexes are on separate plants, it is best to choose the species mentioned, a hermaphrodite that thrives

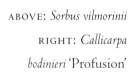

ABOVE: *Sorbus vilmorinii*
RIGHT: *Callicarpa bodinieri* 'Profusion'

in almost any soil. I have seen them decorating high hollies and contrasting gaily with the red holly berries.

Chaenomeles japonica, which used to be known as *Cydonia maulei*, is a low bush producing a lavish display of orange red, stemless flowers before any leaves have emerged and then in late autumn scents the air with its small, hard, round yellow quinces. A bowl of them will perfume a room. It prefers a lime-free or neutral soil and makes a dense little thicket up to a couple of feet high. *C. cathayensis* is a big rangy shrub with pink-tinted, white flowers which give rise to very large green quinces. Unfortunately, they are not noticeably fragrant and the shrub is armed with big prickles.

Citrus trifoliatus (*Aegle sepiaria*), Hardy Orange, is a prickly brute but glorious in its white spring flower; in warm districts and sunny seasons, it produces small oranges, often the size of tangerines, green turning to yellowish-orange. It would make a burglar-proof hedge on well-drained soil.

Clerodendrum trichotomum has blue berries and its calyx lobes turn to crimson at the same time. The leaves are handsome, and the flowers are deliciously scented.

Cornus kousa is seen as a tall shrub or, especially in the variety *chinensis*, small tree to about twenty-three feet (7.0 m). It is pleasing for the lovely effect of its flat-branched habit, displaying so well the white flowers which later turn into strawberry-like crimson fruits. The hybrid 'Norman Hadden' is equally noteworthy and to come across either at flowering or fruiting time is a great experience, especially because the leaf colour contributes to the later display. They are best on lime-free soils.

Cotoneaster frigidus, the biggest of the genus, is an arching shrub of some eighteen feet (5.4 m). Smothered in bunches of red berries, it is a grand autumn sight, but too large for the average garden. Some hybrids with species of the *C. salicifolius* group are more suitable for small gardens; these are found under the name *C.* × *watereri*. Best known of these are 'John Waterer' and 'Cornubia'. They make large graceful shrubs usually well hung with large bunches of scarlet berries. The birds usually leave these alone until well after the New Year; in fact, I have seen them still in beauty as late as February. *C. salicifolius* has given rise to other hybrids, possibly with *C. frigidus*, two of the most appealing of which are the yellow-berried forms 'Rothschildianus' and 'Exburyensis'—magnificent arching shrubs. I find that these plants do not cast dense shade, but make suitable high canopies for shade-loving plants beneath them, such as hellebores, False Solomon's Seal, Lily of the Valley and epimediums. *C. salicifolius* itself is usually red-berried and is a graceful shrub of medium to large size. Its name means "willow-leaved" and there is more than just a

Cotoneaster conspicuus

RIGHT: *Cornus kousa*
in flower in June, and
(BELOW) in fruit in autumn

leaf resemblance to a small weeping willow. This is obviously the place to extol the merits of *C.* 'Gnom' ('Gnome'); it is admirable as a rapid ground cover or may be trained up walls or fences. The narrow, small, glittering, dark leaves are the ideal background for its scarlet berries. The birds are fond of them and easily get at those near the ground but seem to find it difficult to perch on the slender drooping twigs on shoots trained upwards. I have known such specimens still displaying berries until spring. There is no doubt that this is a highly desirable selection.

Cotoneasters and berberises were in vogue during the second quarter of the past century when so many species of both genera reached berrying age from Asiatic introductions. The cotoneasters hold their own as popular denizens of our gardens, but the deciduous species of *Berberis*, which I spoke of in October, are less popular now than they once were. While they may hold their berries well into the New Year, they are soft, and frosts destroy them, whereas those of cotoneasters are less vulnerable at those temperatures. And they are terribly prickly!

Decaisnea fargesii, an unusually gaunt, open shrub with long straight branches, is well set with elegant pinnate leaves. As these drop, the fruits are revealed—pods like broad beans of an unusual tint—clear, cold cobalt blue. There is nothing like it, and it seems at home in any fertile soil in a reasonably sunny spot. The flowers are star-like in branching spikes of pale green, but not conspicuous.

Euonymus europaeus 'Red Cascade', launched by Rowland Jackman, is about the best of several large handsome shrubs in this genus, with its bright crimson-pink capsules showing orange seeds. But *E. oxyphyllus* and *E. planipes* are also noteworthy and of richer colouring. The foliage of all these glows with color.

Hippophaë rhamnoides, Sea Buckthorn, is somewhat awkward for us gardeners as it is essential to have a male plant with a female in order to secure berries. It is a rather prickly shrub, and prone to suckering, but the charm of the narrow greyish leaves is enlivened by copious orange berries. After frost it has a repellent smell. *H. salicifolia* is less thorny and has yellow berries. They thrive in any soil, notably in maritime and sandy conditions, and will reach well over your head. There is no autumn leaf colour.

PEAT LOVERS Peat lovers, plants that require acid, or in some cases at least neutral soil, include *Gaultheria*, *Pernettya* and *Vaccinium*. Anyone who has the right conditions will find them irresistible. They have so many varied attractions. Evergreen or deciduous shrubs, they are vigorous or gently suckering, with small white- or pink-tinted flowers and fleshy berries of white, pink, blue, purple and near black. The *Pernettya* genus is one of the more uniform with tiny, evergreen, prickly leaves and abundant fruits, from white to pink or lilac and dark red. But only the 'Davis Hybrids' and 'Bell's Seedling' are self-fertile, and I believe even these are more prone to produce their fruits if a male is present.

You need a lifetime to get to know all the possibilities of *Gaultheria* species. There is a wide range of beautiful foliage shrubs of small to medium stature, the best known being an arrant spreader where it is suited: *G. shallon*. It is not to be trusted in gardens, but where partridges abound, it is invaluable. *G. procumbens* is also a spreader, but since it seldom exceeds a foot (0.3 m) in height, it is not a nuisance; indeed, as a ground cover it has great value in a woodland position. The leaves are glossy and rounded and, when crushed, smell freshly of wintergreen; the pinky-white little bell-flowers nestle among them in clusters and are followed by luscious-looking rich crimson berries, long-lasting. It is a first-rate carpeter for any semi-woodland area on lime-free soil—which is of course what they all require, with plenty of humus. There are many desirable small gaultherias that need careful appraising—neat evergreens, usually under three feet (0.9 m) in height, with small waxy white- or pink-touched flowers followed from early autumn onwards by attractive berries in white, blue or pink. They are principally the realm of collectors, and if you venture into it a fascinating task of selecting species for your particular conditions awaits, remembering always the soil requirements of these captivating plants.

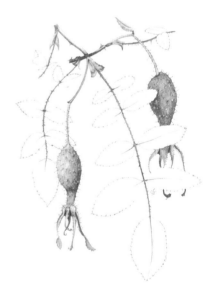

TOP: *Pernettya mucronata* hybrids
ABOVE: *Rosa setipoda*

Vaccinium corymbosum, a large shrub of six feet (1.8 m) or more, is one of the star performers in the genus. Few shrubs have so many assets: prettily tinted young foliage, small white flowers in abundance, gorgeous autumn leaves and a good display of blue-black, luscious berries—it is in fact the Blueberry, in its cultivated forms, of commerce. From my brief description, it will be understood that it is deciduous, but I think the evergreen *V. glauco-album* stands almost equally high in garden value. Its special moment is autumn, when the blue-black berries, so covered in "bloom" that they appear almost white, match the undersides of the leaves. I have seen this as much as three feet (0.9 m) high covered with berries. My other special selection of the numerous small species shall be *V. vitis-idaea*, the native Cowberry, for a selection has been made in Holland with conspicuous bunches of red berries, named 'Koralle'. This and others need neighbouring bushes to ensure pollination, and when you get a crop of berries on any of them, be sure that the birds will see them too, and be prepared.

Skimmias have a special point in their favour: they seem to repel birds. Even so you have to grow a female form and there must be a male nearby to help. For this we fortunately have the excellent *Skimmia japonica* 'Rubella', already referred to, and its ruddy buds enliven the winter scene. 'Nymans' and 'Scarlet Queen' are two good females with extra bright red berries. There are many other low suckering forms, and also the dwarf, regular-berrying *S. japonica reevesiana*, popular for city window-boxes. All skimmias require at least partial shade, and they grow best in neutral or lime-free soil.

Photinia davidiana (*Stransvaesia*), closely allied to cotoneasters, is a large shrub, almost evergreen, but in autumn bushes are decorated with the odd scarlet leaf. The real attraction is the clusters of red berries. These are almost unique in not being shiny; their matte finish is rich and satisfying. There is a good yellow-fruiting form, 'Fructu Luteo', and a form misleadingly known as 'Prostrata' which can easily reach four feet (1.2 m) in height.

Pyracantha atalantioides (*P. gibbsii*), showy, upright and broad-leafed, with red berries, and *P. angustifolia*, a compact grower with greyish, narrow leaves and orange berries, are the two of their tribe giving the longest display. The latter makes an excellent hedge, and the birds generally leave the berries until the turn of the year. My special favourites for the sake of their lacy, cream, sweetly scented flowers—which are not found in others—are *P. rogersiana* with red berries, and its variety 'Flava', with yellow. But the berries do not usually remain on the bushes for

Pyracantha rogersiana

long; seemingly the birds find them toothsome, or perhaps I should write "beak-some"; there are several new hybrids of great quality which may prove more bird-resistant. Pyracanthas are most usually trained on walls. I am unable to suggest why except that they will stand pruning and shaping.

Rosa moyesii is famous for the magnificent flagon-shaped, orange-red heps borne in early autumn, but it is a giant of a shrub, sometimes achieving eighteen feet (5.4 m); the form 'Geranium', selected at Wisley by Brian Mulligan, is more compact and has better foliage as well as fruits of equal magnificence. Many other roses compete for a place here, *R. sweginzowii* and *R. setipoda* having shining flagon-shaped fruits also. Then there are the Japanese Ramanas roses, *R. rugosa*; I like the white single-flowered 'Alba' above most others, for the scarlet heps are a better contrast to the white flowers than they are to the purplish pink of other varieties—except the clear, light pink of 'Fru Dagmar Hastrup', who carefully colours her heps in dark red.

Symphoricarpos albus, Snowberry, is a native of North America and in the form *S. albus laevigatus* is well worth a place in our gardens, though it is apt to spread by suckers. It thrives on good soils, preferably limy, and if given a little attention in thinning out weak twiggy growths will produce long, whippy, slender grey shoots carrying the white berries that are the reason for its name. On a good shoot there may be as many as two or three dozen berries weighting the shoot into a graceful

ABOVE: *Rosa rugosa* heps

LEFT: Rose 'Nymphenburg' (TOP),
Rosa moyesii (TOP RIGHT), Rose 'Penelope'
(LEFT), *Rosa filipes* 'Kiftsgate' (LOWER
RIGHT), *Rosa rugosa* (BOTTOM LEFT)
and Rose 'Ormiston Roy' (BOTTOM)

arch. They last well into December. 'Constance Spry' is a noted large-berried form, while 'White Hedge' is more compact and upright but has smaller berries. There are several hybrids, such as 'Mother of Pearl', with pink berries that have great attraction, especially when growing near to *Callicarpa bodinieri*.

Symplocos paniculatus has bright blue berries, and as birds are fond of them, it is as well to lace the bushes with black cotton, which defeats the marauders. The flowers are small and white.

Viburnum opulus comes to the fore at berry time and among the welter of Far Eastern shrubs, it is pleasant to find this native species. One other native, *V. lantana*, also takes a high place to start with, but its scarlet berries turn black before ripening. This always seems to me one of Dame Nature's mistakes: if the berries are to distribute the species, surely they would have more chance of getting eaten and carried away if they remained red? *V. opulus* has also been extolled in October for its crimson leaves, but its particularly translucent berries are a more lasting beauty. The only snag is their disagreeable odour. It makes a large shrub on any well-drained soil, preferably in sun, and there is a form called 'Compactum', but in time it becomes almost as large as the type. Another excellent shiny-berried species is *V. setigerum*, coupling its splendid fruits to good leaf colour. Anyone who remembers the great vases of *V. betulifolium* exhibited by Exbury Gardens at the Royal Horticultural Shows will realise there was possibly something in the maritime air near Southampton that contributed generously to those lavish bunches of scarlet fruits.

Vitis vinifera 'Purpurea' has magnificent beetroot-purple leaves that turn to scarlet and on dropping reveal handsome bunches of dark wine-coloured, bloomy, small grapes. It is thus known as the 'Claret Vine', but the grapes are sharply acid in our climate. It is a vigorous grower but can be kept under control by pruning in late autumn or winter, not in spring, when cutting allows copious bleeding of the sap.

Viburnum opulus
'Compactum' fruits

Ferns

It may seem strange in a book almost wholly devoted to flowers to give some pages to ferns, which do not flower in the accepted sense of the word. But I have included them for two reasons. One is that there is nothing like them; the other is that in my opinion no garden is complete without them. They are noted shade lovers, but many will grow in full sun. Even so they are so much part of woodland and bosky spinney that their presence in a garden fosters thoughts of such places even though shade comes only from house or fence or a single apple tree.

There are ferns of all sizes and almost without exception their usually delicate tracery of leaves lends enchantment to the view. If we go to the damper warmer West Country—Cornwall, for instance—we may stand under great tree-ferns and find their spores germinating in moist, mossy banks at our feet. At the other extreme, little saxatile species such as *Ceterach officinarum* and *Asplenium trichomanes* may be seen in old walls in much cooler, but also damp, parts of the west and north of these islands. They are only a few inches high but nothing gives so definitely the touch of the wild to a rock garden, peat bed or even the rocky edge of a border.

With the exception of *Blechnum* species all ferns grow well in limy soils, as well as those on the acid side. Blechnums demand an acid soil. They all need a loose crumbly medium with ample humus; given these and adequate moisture and shade, they are among the most tolerant of hardy plants. I intend in the following paragraphs to review some hardy evergreen ferns which come into their full beauty late in the summer and only succumb to a heavy fall of snow. Their unfurling fronds are of great beauty, no less than the fully developed greenery. While most are green there are several with other tints.

Blechnum chilense is one of the most magnificent with the pinnae (the sections of the leaves) being as wide as your fingers, smooth and dark green, and borne on large arching stems. The roots wander over the soil and in severe winters may be harmed. It has been known erroneously as *B. tabulare* and *Lomaria magellanica*. Down the scale we come to our native species *B. spicant* with much smaller leaves also only divided into fingers. It will thrive in dry or wet soil. *B. penna-marina* is an invasive carpeter just right for edging a bed of dwarf rhododendrons. As with the other two species, the fertile fronds are borne separately.

Blechnum spicant

Polystichum setiferum
'Divisilobum' with
Daphne laureola philippi

The Hart's Tongue Fern, *Asplenium scolopendrium (Scolopendrium vulgare)*, has no divisions to the leaves; they are simply long, narrow, shining and dark green, making handsome rosettes where grown singly. The spores are borne in straight brown stripes on the backs of the frond. There are many forms with abnormal leaves that may amuse the curious, but I leave them aside except for 'Crispum', which is frilled and goffered along the edges most appealingly. There is a rare variant known as 'Golden Queen', which is bright yellow throughout so long as it is not in dense shade. It is a unique fern and worth a lot of seeking.

I wish *Cyrtomium falcatum*, the Japanese Holly Fern, were a little hardier. It will not take winters in Surrey but is hardy in the South and West. Few ferns are so splendid; the pinnae are broad and with a little imagination may be described as holly-like, of shining dark green. In good conditions it may reach three feet (0.9 m). *C. fortunei* is less glossy with narrower, smaller pinnae; in fact, were it not a fairly hardy cyrtomium, only collectors would grow it. Neither presents any difficulty in cultivation.

The various plants we used to know as forms of *Polypodium vulgare* are now grouped, often, as separate species. Apart from *P. vulgare*, itself with many variations, there are also *P. glycyrrhiza*, *P. interjectum* and *P. cambricum*. I am going to limit myself to just a few distinct kinds. Everyone wants *P. interjectum* 'Cornubiense' with its doubly or trebly divided pinnae, creating a very lacy effect. There is also *P. vulgare* 'Longicaudatum', which has its ultimate portion elongated into a sort of tail. There are various crested types, which I shall leave severely alone, but we must award all of them a prize for thriving in dry shade, even surviving on mossy tree branches. The creeping rootstocks should not be buried. Their great attraction is the fresh green fronds which arise in midsummer; bearing this in mind it is wise to remove old fronds at the end of May. None will normally exceed a foot (0.3 m) in height.

While the polypodies have numerous named forms, they are nothing when compared with the several dozen odd forms of *Polystichum setiferum*, most of whose crestings and frillings add little if anything to their beauty. The species itself, however, is distinguished by the pale grey-brown of the scales on the stems, and by the dainty divisions of the pinnae and their dull dark green. Above all they are ferns that will thrive on dry banks, even in sun, and still produce fronds three feet (0.9 m) or more long. They are among the most elegant of all hardy ferns. First I must pay tribute to

Polystichum setiferum
'Acutilobum'

a well-known form named 'Acutilobum', whose fronds are extra finely cut and often bear on the stems amongst the lower pinnae little bulbils which form a ready means of increase if pegged down on a nice humusy bed. Due to its ease of increase, it is one of our commonest ferns. In the 'Divisilobum' group, the pinnae are divided and divided again and again, making a handsome pile of greenery which is a brighter, fresher green than those mentioned. They are worth a lot and were much prized in Victorian times when one wonderful specimen scored against all others with its array of names—*P. setiferum* 'Divisilobum Plumosum Densum Erectum Perry's No. 1'. Amos Perry was not only a famous nurseryman, but also a great fern enthusiast. *P. setiferum* is treasured also on the Continent, and recently two varieties have reached us which are well up to the standard set in Victorian times: 'Herrenhausen', a strong-growing traditional form achieving three feet (0.9 m) or more, and 'Dahlem', rather smaller and of 'Divisilobum' persuasion. Both of these are easily propagated by stem buds. But it will not do to think only of forms of *P. setiferum*; there are other excellent species, and all will put up with dry shade.

Two very distinct species are the Sword Ferns from North America. My acquaintance has been mainly with *P. munitum* from the Western States, but *P. acrostichoides* from the Eastern States is possibly more entitled to the vernacular name. This is because its evergreen fronds with simple pinnae end in a point, bearing the spores, whereas fronds of *P. munitum* do not end in a point but bear serried rows of pinnae. Both are true evergreens of darkest hue and have reached nearly three feet (0.9 m) in my garden. Their greatest beauty is from a single crown. *P. polyblepharum* has fronds of similar size and beauty and is exceptionally elegant when unfolding, the ends of the fronds are so beautifully curved. *P. aculeatum*, a British native, is also of great

beauty and is fairly common, but I hand the palm to *P. discretum* for its hard, glossy pinnae. The so-called Holly Fern, *P. lonchitis*, may be easy to grow in the cooler West, but I have never been able to satisfy it in Surrey for more than one season. *P. squarrosum* is another highly desirable species in dark shining green, and to finish I will call attention to the charm of dark, shining, miniature *P. tsussimense*, which with me declines to achieve more than a few inches. Taking them all together, the polystichums (with the stress on the second syllable) represent much that is best in ferns and, apart from *P. lonchitis*, present no difficulties in any shady garden in friable soil.

The species of *Dryopteris* are not so evergreen, and it is for this reason I omit what is possibly the most handsome species of all—*D. wallichiana*. But *D. pseudomas* (which used to be known as *D. borreri*) runs it pretty close for beauty and is nearly evergreen. In spring its young fronds topping four feet (1.2 m) are bright yellowish-green and show up notably along our western shores, relapsing into soft dark green later in the season. *D. aemula* is worth acquiring also, as is the colourful *D. erythrosora*. The young fronds are prettily tinted in coppery tones, and the caps of spores in late summer, on the leaf's undersurface, are bright red. It appears to grow to about two feet (0.6 m) only.

There are two rare Japanese species of *Arachniodes*, *A. simplicior* and *A. standishii*. The former is not likely to be confused with any other on account of the yellowish stripe down each side of the midrib of the small fronds, while the latter is noted for its daintily divided, shining dark green fronds. *Athyrium nipponicum* 'Pictum' is another unusual fern; its fronds are small, purplish-grey on unfolding, becoming almost glaucous later in the year.

ABOVE: *Jasminum nudiflorum*

RIGHT: *Arachniodes simplicior* 'Variegata'

Conifers

The terms "golden" and "silver" become somewhat overworn when it comes to describing conifers. There is no doubt that however bright the "gold" is, yellow at its best outshines it. And yet the term "golden yellow" is used so often. Likewise it is a special tint of glaucous grey that can outshine "silver". I shall accordingly use gold and silver sparingly in the following paragraphs.

It is no extravagant flight of words to say that certain conifers joined with the most brilliantly coloured foliage of callunas (heathers) can hold their own in winter brilliance against anything provided by the summer months, especially if accompanied by *Mahonia × wagneri* 'Moseri' and a few other shrubs. Such a grouping has great character far from the gloomy dark green tones of many cypresses and other conifers. While it is just this darkness that elevates the pine to great contrast in Japanese gardens, we are here looking for conifers in November to remind us that all need not be dark and drear. And my remarks are not solely concerned with yellow, red and blue, but with contrasts from plum colour as well. The effect is quite different from that of summer flowers and foliage, and I hope the following paragraphs may lead you to think in different terms when adding winter colour to your garden.

Pinus mugo 'Wintergold'

YELLOW-FLUSHED FOLIAGE

When I was a student at the University Botanic Garden at Cambridge many long years ago—in the late 1920s to be exact—an old pine on the rock garden used to intrigue me. It was obviously old and gnarled, about five feet (1.5 m) high and wide. It was green during the growing months but became suffused with yellow at the approach of winter. It was then called *Pinus laricio* 'Pygmaea', but this has been altered to *P. sylvestris* 'Moseri'. I know of no other big old specimen; there was one at Nymans, Sussex, but this was destroyed in the great storm of 1987. The change of colour shown by that old pine is just what we should be seeking for our gardens; a shrub or tree that remains yellow or yellowish throughout the year can be troublesome and dictates the colour scheme the whole time. There are two or three other pines that change colour from soft green to brilliant yellow by December. One is the really brilliant *P. sylvestris* 'Gold Coin'; another is 'Gold Medal'. These are both bushy plants.

P. silvestris 'Aurea' will very slowly make a tall tree and is conspicuous from youth onwards, bright yellow in winter. There is another, comparatively dwarf, *P. mugo* 'Ophir', which becomes suffused with yellow in winter, as does *P. mugo* 'Wintergold'. One striking, yellowish, flat-growing plant is *Abies nordmanniana* 'Golden Spreader'; it is brilliant in winter. There is also the amazing *Podocarpus* 'County Park Fire', which caps its spring pink tints with exceptional orange-yellow in winter, green meanwhile.

YELLOW VARIEGATION

This little list about exhausts those conifers that turn their summer greenery to winter yellow. There are other bright yellow variants which keep their colour throughout the year: the feathery, quick-growing *Cupressus macrocarpa* 'Goldcrest', the slim *C. sempervirens* 'Swane's Gold' (for warmer gardens) and the slow-growing, creamy yellow, tapering spire of *Juniperus chinensis* 'Aurea'. *Abies koreana* 'Aurea' is also slow growing and becomes orange in winter. The various chamaecyparises are not wanting in yellow variants. There is the time-honoured *Chamaecyparis obtusa* 'Crippsii' with its feathery sprays of brilliant colour and the old *C. obtusa* 'Tetragona Aurea', also 'Fernspray Gold' and *C. obtusa* 'Nana Aurea', a congested bun of a plant suitable for very small gardens. *C. pisifera* 'Filifera Aurea' is one of the most brilliant; its shoots are threadlike and drooping and it is usually described as a dwarf but I have seen quite tall specimens that it would be hard to better. While they cannot be called yellow or golden, two forms of the Lawson's Cypress may be mentioned here; the first is *C. lawsoniana* 'Summer Snow', a light creamy green, feathery plant that slowly makes a column if clipped over in spring, and *C. lawsoniana* 'Pygmaea Argentea', whose dark green rounded mounds are tipped with palest yellow, looking as if a bowl of cream has been spilled over them. It does not revert to green and is a long-standing joy in winter. There is a yellow form of the plumose *Juniperus* × *media* 'Pfitzeriana' named 'Aurea' which is less vigorous than 'Pfitzeriana' itself. Completely prostrate is a form of *J. horizontalis* from the United States, called very appropriately 'Mother Lode'. It is slow growing, for full sun, turning bronzy in winter. Finally, a *Thuja*, *T. orientalis* 'Nana Aurea', has shoots erect from a small, warm yellow-flushed, little bush. This list by no means completes the many forms of "golden" cypresses and others, but will do as a starter.

Chamaecyparis lawsoniana
'Pygmaea Argentea'

BLUE-GREY

The glaucous blue-grey conifers are headed by forms of *Picea pungens*, two of the finest forms, apart from 'Koster', being 'Moerheim' and 'Spek'. These all make comparatively tall trees with horizontal branches and branchlets, and their short, prickly needles are arranged on the upper side of the shoots. In good, open, sunny gardens they are very conspicuous. Less formal—for the piceas are of formal outline—is the Japanese *Pinus parviflora*; good forms are of glaucous tone and, while usually seen as somewhat windswept specimens, they assume slightly more formality as tall trees. One of their many attractions is the freely borne dark cones. An attractive dwarf form, to be measured in inches rather than feet, is 'Adcock's Dwarf', and it is a good glaucous colour also. Two really slow-growing firs are *Picea glauca* 'Alberta Blue' and *Abies lasiocarpa* 'Compacta', both of good glaucous colouring. *Abies procera* is a great and glorious tree in its best glaucous forms, and *A. procera* 'Glauca Prostrata' is a procumbent form with notably prostrate fanlike branches.

Among the cypresses, I think the bluest is *Chamaecyparis lawsoniana* 'Pembury Blue', a fairly wide-growing cultivar, while *C. lawsoniana* 'Columnaris Glauca' is only a little less blue and comparatively narrow. Though it is often lauded, I should avoid

Chamaecyparis pisifera
'Filifera Aurea'

'Boulevard': while beautiful in youth, it becomes congested with dead brown foliage after a few years.

Juniperus squamata 'Meyeri' is a tree of some distinction. It is slow-growing but may achieve fifteen feet (4.5 m) and become nearly as wide in time. It is wonderfully glaucous blue, but is best kept for gardens where the air is moist; in dry districts it seems to attract caterpillars. A much dwarfer bush of rounded habit is *J. squamata* 'Blue Star'; there is also the flat, spreading 'Blue Carpet'. Among junipers, *Juniperus horizontalis* is outstanding; several forms make superb rug-like effects with notably blue-green, closely appressed twigs. *J. horizontalis* 'Glauca', brilliant grey-blue in summer, is one of the best, but there are many good glaucous blue forms.

PURPLISH HUES

Now we come to darker tones, even murrey-coloured verging on purple. The most noted is a little plant that for many years was known as *Juniperus sanderi* but now is, I believe, correctly known as *Thuja orientalis* 'Sanderi'. Unfortunately, it is only hardy in sheltered conditions and is frequently seen in alpine houses. It is a small bush that in the winter becomes almost purple. Something of the same deep colouring is found in the larger, hardier *T. orientalis* 'Meldensis', and in *Chamaecyparis pisifera* 'Lombart's', *C. thyoides* 'Purple Heather' and *Cryptomeria japonica* 'Vilmorinii'.

Rhododendron ponticum
'Foliis-pupureis'

There is a rhododendron with something of these dark tints: the remarkable *Rhododendron ponticum* 'Foliis-pupureis' has leaves of a wonderful beetroot purple in normal winters. The flowers, in June, are nothing out of the way and fortunately it is a compact, slow grower. My plant, about thirty years old, is only approximately six feet (1.8 m) in each direction. I find that in normal seasons, and wet ones, the foliage colour is good and strong, but in the recent drought years it has been rather green. My plant was propagated from a large plant in the Rhododendron Dell at Kew. The original has been growing in the Dell since 1895, when it was given by William Paul, the famous rose grower. It has received a First Class Certificate from the Royal Horticultural Society. It is probably the best of all backgrounds for light-coloured forms of *Hamamelis*.

There are two noted forms of *Juniperus horizontalis*, 'Bar Harbour' and 'Douglasii', whose summer tint of glaucous grey turns to violet on the approach of winter.

I have been at pains in the above paragraphs to call attention to slow or prostrate conifers, bearing in mind the smaller gardens of today. Even so it must be remembered that a so-called dwarf conifer may get large in time. There is no stopping them. They do not respond well to cutting back, and pruning only makes them grow stronger. A spruce or fir is simply not suitable for reduction. Therefore always choose slow- or dwarf-growing cultivars, place them with regard to their full potential size, and bring every ounce of true gardeners' patience to bear.

There is another point which is confusing: prostrate forms of *Abies* and *Picea* are of this shape because they have been propagated from horizontal branches whose leading shoots have one terminal bud with another on either side of it, making three in all. So long as this total is not exceeded, the branches will remain flat. But sometimes a shoot will develop with four or even five side buds and will immediately grow upright like the parent tree. This is most noticeable in *Abies concolor* 'Wattesii' which, being propagated from side shoots, is loth to make a leader. You may stake it for years, leading it upright, but still only three buds will be present. If you can harden your heart sufficiently, it is best to cut it down; one of the resulting shoots may have the required number of buds. It is particularly galling to have this gloriously tinted glaucous form without a leader.

Another case in point is *Sequoia sempervirens* 'Prostrata'. This broad, glaucous-leafed form originated on the great tree at the south end of the Order Beds in the University Botanic Garden at Cambridge. A side branch had developed these wide glaucous leaves, and I was the first person to strike it from cuttings. Plants were duly distributed to various gardens, and after a number of years several have produced vertical shoots. To distinguish these from the prostrate original form, these are known as 'Cantab'. From all appearances these are superior to the wild species from California which does not take kindly to our winters, turning to brown.

All these colourful variants of conifers thrive best in sandy soils and in full exposure to light. While they are very different from other foliage and flowers, they are with us throughout the year, though it must be admitted that by the spring the yellow forms look a bit tawdry and tired. And they go on growing inexorably and eventually have to be removed if the borders or garden are small. Then is the time to assess their value in the garden landscape and decide whether to repeat them or to return with relief to winter greens, such as *Juniperus conferta* and *Hebe rakaiensis*.

Richly coloured cones of *Abies koreana*, a slow-growing tree of great beauty

DECEMBER

The weather is so fickle at this time of the year that it is difficult to say what may be in bloom during its milder days. Few plants are opening their first blossom this month, but pleasure for the gardener is promised by those that defy the weather and continue flowering until the year's end. Probably we shall have with us still the Autumn Cherry, the hybrid *Mahonia × media* varieties, several viburnums, *Camellia sasanqua* and Winter Jasmine. Often the first blooms will open on *Lonicera × purpusii*, a hybrid of excellence between *L. fragrantissima* and *L. standishii*. There is also a selected form of the hybrid called 'Winter Beauty', but there is little to choose between them. They are all medium-sized shrubs, mostly leafless in winter, but displaying on every twig small creamy white flowers with an unforgettable, sweet fragrance. As a contrast to them we may choose *Skimmia japonica reevesiana* 'Rubella'. Throughout the winter months it cheers us with bunches of flower buds of warm red-brown among the evergreen leaves, ready to burst into pinky-white stars in April, when it will flood the garden with sweet scent. It is an asset for garden and house, whereas the loniceras tend to drop their flowers when cut.

Most leaves are off the trees by the end of November, but those of *Crataegus × lavallei* 'Carrierei' often linger until well into December. When they fade, the bright orange-red haws, of good size, present a lively spectacle in the winter sunshine;

OPPOSITE: Winter leaves cut from the garden: *Bergenia purpurascens* (plum), *Elaeagnus pungens* 'Dicksonii' (golden), *Hedera canariensis* 'Gloire de Marengo' (creamy grey-green), *Iris foetidissima* 'Variegata' (striped), *Arum italicum* 'Marmoratum' (marbled) and *Mahonia* 'Heterophylla' (red-brown)

267

remember to place it so that the light shines on it. It is a small- to medium-sized tree and will grow almost anywhere.

Jasminum nudiflorum, Winter Jasmine, is a wonderful plant for the dark months, enlivening every aspect with its clear yellow, starry flowers, shown up by its masses of dark green twigs. Except in very dry ground, it is a success wherever it is planted. So far as I know it has never set seed in this country, which makes me wonder whether it is a drooping clone of some upright species. At any rate it is usually trained up fence or wall and hangs down elegantly. I should dearly love to have a large bank covered with it, perhaps with a red-berried *Cotoneaster* for company.

Iris foetidissima fruit

Heather

December sees the beginning of the winter-flowering heather display. Many gardeners are unaware of the long-lasting enjoyment they give: they will be with us until early May. *Erica carnea* spans this period with early and late varieties; two of the earliest are the old favourites 'King George' and 'Queen Mary', both of good clear pink. They need neutral or lime-free soil with ample humus, and do best where the wind can blow away fallen tree leaves and keep them compact. A hybrid cropped up in Darley Dale, Derbyshire, between *E. carnea* and *E. erigena* (*E. mediterranea*); it is known as *E. × darleyensis* and is a thoroughly good garden plant. It lasts in flower from midwinter till late April, is a good drought resister (much better than *E. carnea*) and in its best form, 'Arthur Johnson', produces really fine spikes of pink blooms up to two feet (0.6 m) or more. There is a much-lauded white form named 'Silberschmelze', but I find it a dull grey white, and much prefer 'White Profusion', which is a strong creamy white and very telling in the garden landscape.

Another plant which continues from November is *Liriope muscari*, and scarlet seeds in buff pods gladden the eye on *Iris foetidissima*. This is a splendid plant in its 'Citrina' form, the pods larger and the leaves of lustrous dark green; its admirable form 'Variegata' I mention later in this chapter. Occasionally one comes across a seedling of the Christmas Rose, *Helleborus niger*, which will flower at the right time, but usually they do not produce blooms until well into the New Year. They thrive best in heavy limy soils, whereas the Lenten Hellebores (*H. orientalis* and hybrids) are happy and thrive in almost any fertile soil. Here again one may light on early-flowering seedlings, but they are usually at their best in spring.

Little Bulbs

There are many small bulbs that delight us where there is some protection from the vagaries of the weather, such as an unheated greenhouse of the kind often used for alpine plants. There, without heat, they will open their flowers in the least glimmer of sunshine. There are several species of hardy cyclamens that would gladden our eyes and nose in the darkest days. Outside, *Cyclamen coum* is a reliable plant in crimson, pink or white, only a few inches high. They thrive in well-drained soils at the foot of shrubs and trees, and will seed themselves. *C. ibericum* follows closely. We are not really looking for daffodils in the depths of winter, but the little 'Cedric Morris', only six inches (15 cm) high, is a charmer that flowers regularly before Christmas for me. It was discovered in the wilds of Spain before the Second World War, and stocks were built up in England and at last released. As to snowdrops, we have looked at the autumn-flowering *Galanthus reginae-olgae*, which is a good plant for sunny, well-drained spots; it is closely followed by *G. caucasicus hiemalis*, which seems to enjoy the same conditions.

BELOW: *Crocus laevigatus fontenayi*
BOTTOM: *Crocus imperati*

With them I like to grow the reliable winter-flowering *Crocus laevigatus fontenayi*. It is a good perennial, increases well in sandy soil and produces flowers over a long period, generally being at its best in December. The little goblet blooms are buff outside, with very dark stripes, but with a ray of sunshine display their lilac interiors. Moreover, they have a delicious aroma, and a few flowers in a wine glass will perfume a small room. Rather larger and later in appearing is *C. imperati*, with equally beautifully coloured flowers and fragrance, but I have not found it so generous of increase.

The shortage of outdoor flowers in winter turns us inevitably to foliage for diversion. It is manifest that this must come from variegation. We have to bear in mind two important points: will variegated evergreens be an asset and a refreshment to the eyes in winter, and, being evergreens, will they appear to be overbearing and garish during the flowery months? We have to settle both these doubts before using the spade. There is no doubt that green foliage makes the best background for flowers, and variegation can easily be overdone. Yet even one variegated shrub can make a tremendous difference to a grouping of dark evergreens, though they may also be lightened by choosing some with glossy leaves, such as hollies, and *Mahonia* × *wagneri* 'Undulata'.

Variegated Foliage

The most successful gardens are those where due regard has been given to the value of foliage. Whereas flowers come and go with only a short stay, leaves are evident through the whole year if evergreen and for six months or so if deciduous. You cannot overdo the planting of shrubs and plants with good foliage. Among them is an ever-increasing number with variegated leaves, or shall we say leaves that are other than green. It is these that can easily be overdone, resulting in a bizarre effect, whereas they should be used circumspectly to add point to an assembly of flowers and foliage.

When the dark days arrive in late autumn and winter, then is the time to assess the value of evergreens with variegation. On a bright sunny day, they add life and lightness to any planting, and if you can arrange for the Holly 'Golden Queen' to be planted so that your exterior light shines upon it, the colour will be doubled. Yellow variegation is the most telling in a garden, and we must always bear in mind the salutation it will have during the lighter months of the year. Will it shame or war with seasonal flowers? Will it sicken us with its continual brightness? I am writing these paragraphs entirely with evergreens in mind, for they are part of the garden's attraction during the dark days.

There are a few yellow variegated evergreens which we may look at before the well-known hollies. There is a majestic Privet, *Ligustrum lucidum* 'Excelsum Superbum', with fine, bold, shiny leaves and markedly yellow variegation. Even as late as November, it may still be showing its pyramids of small cream flowers, lighting a bush which may well exceed twelve feet (3.6 m) and half as wide. The ordinary Golden Privet (*Ligustrum ovalifolium* 'Aureum') is a much smaller plant, but a very popular one for hedges and colour grouping. Today the aucubas are not looked upon with much favour, mainly because they are usually seen in what used to be sooty back yards, and they were usually of an ineffective spotty leaf type. But I have noticed a few other varieties appearing in new plantings in my district: partly the gay, heavily spotted *Aucuba japonica* 'Crotonifolia', which is so useful for adding variety to an otherwise sober vaseful of evergreens, but also the form with yellow middles to the leaves, 'Picturata', and the cream-edged 'Sulphurea'. These are all useful plants for dry rooty places under trees, or shaded by walls.

Elaeagnus varieties are popular plants, but many are too large for the average garden. I was led astray by the popular *E. pungens* 'Maculata' when I started my present garden. There was a plant some seven feet (2.1 m) high and wide, and I fondly

Aucuba japonica 'Picturata'

thought I could keep it to approximately those measurements by occasional pruning. This would have been possible, of course, but I was not aware that, with the variegation in the middle of the blade, reversion to dark green would be prevalent. Reversion to green is not so usual with varieties whose variegation is marginal, as in *E. pungens* 'Dicksonii' and 'Fredericii'. These are both moderate growers while *E. × ebbingei* 'Gilt Edge' is strong growing and really brilliant.

HOLLY

Let us now look at the hollies—wonderful shrubs, or even trees, that light up many a dark spot. Besides their glossiness, the leaves have prickles turned this way and that, enabling them to catch all the light. In our gardens the hollies are usually seen as shrubs, but if trained to a single leader, they make trees of thirty or forty feet (9.0–12.0 m) or more. As in the old Christmas carol, "of all the trees that are in the wood the holly bears the crown", but this of course dates from days long before other evergreens from abroad became so numerous and popular. The Common Holly (*Ilex aquifolium*) is normally grown from seeds—which need stratifying for a year before sowing—and the resulting plants are each different in leaf and habit one from another. Cultivars, on the other hand, are usually grown from cuttings, or layers, or by budding onto seedling hollies, so that the individuals are all the same. Apart from budding, in which case a strong initial shoot is made, these methods of propagation result in plants of wayward shape until a leader occurs. Careful pruning of side shoots and staking a possible leader will hasten the tree-like shape, which is desirable if tall plants are wanted.

Hollies have a serious disadvantage to us gardeners. They drop their old leaves at the approach of summer just when the borders are beginning to look presentable; moreover, clearing up or working among prickly leaves is not a desirable pastime. They have yet another disadvantage: the birds seem to discover the tastiness of the berries by about the second week of December—just when we were thinking there would be good berried sprays for Christmas decorations. The fieldfares and blackbirds are some of the most hungry, apparently, but when we remember the four months of delight the blackbird's song gives us in the earlier part of the year, I suppose the reward of the berries to them is just.

Ilex aquifolium
'Handsworth New Silver'

Evergreens were scarce in the earliest British gardens, and especially fine variegated and other forms were being segregated as early as the seventeenth century; any fleck of variegation was cherished. Today, with several dozen variegated and abnormal forms being known and grown, the selection is wider. The different cultivars are either male or female (with a few exceptions) and it is therefore perhaps fortunate that, despite its cultivar name, *Ilex* 'Golden Queen' is male, for it is a highly conspicuous plant with broad margins of bright yellow and thus fulfills its mission as a pollinator as well as being a bright and colourful specimen. 'Madame Briot' (female) is of rather darker tone, while 'Golden van Tol' is not only brilliant but self-fertile, too. 'Golden Milkboy' has the yellow in the middle of the leaf blades and is thus prone to reversion to green. Glorious though these can be in the winter sunshine, they are apt to be obtrusive in summer, at which time the white variegated forms are more acceptable. And in winter, before birds get at the berries, there are few more lovely sights than 'Argentea Marginata'. Once again contrariwise, 'Silver Queen' is male, but 'Handsworth New Silver' is a splendid female, and 'Silver van Tol', a sport from 'J. C. van Tol', has the qualities of its handsome forebear, with the addition of fine variegation. There are many hollies noted for their berries, mostly red, but there are orange- and yellow-fruited forms of *I. aquifolium*; the yellow is particularly pleasing.

Euonymus fortunei
'Emerald Gaiety'

This is a mere sketch of the many forms of *I. aquifolium*, Common Holly; *I. × altaclerense* has also some excellent forms. Very compact and prone to reversion is the female (yes!) 'Golden King'. 'Belgica Aurea' and 'Camelliifolia Variegata' are two good forms of this hybrid holly with broad leaves.

We have long been used to forms of *Euonymus japonicus* in our gardens; they might even be relics of Victorian times. *E. japonicus* 'Pictus' is not reliably hardy in Surrey, but the broader-leafed forms *E. japonicus*, 'Ovatus Albus', variegated white, and 'Ovatus Aureus', yellow, are much hardier. Even so, they are not much planted today, though 'Ovatus Aureus' frequently throws shoots with wholly yellow leaves, in which condition it can easily be the brightest note in the garden. Another species, *E. fortunei*, has of recent years been a prolific bearer of abnormal leaves: witness 'Emerald Gaiety' and 'Emerald 'n' Gold'. 'Silver Queen' remains the most conspicuous cream variegated form, but is less vigorous than 'Emerald Gaiety'. There is also the old white

variegated *E. fortunei* 'Variegatus', and all forms of this species perform equally well as self-clinging climbers and as ground cover.

A plant for really large gardens (it can be overpowering in small ones) is *Phormium tenax*, New Zealand Flax, so-called because its long, upright leaves, up to six feet (1.8 m), yield excellent cordage. The yellow-striped form, *P. tenax* 'Variegatum', has long been a conspicuous landscape plant, but recently a number of forms and hybrids have been raised in New Zealand with brilliant leaves embracing stripes of yellow, pink and orange. These are only for sheltered conditions. On the other hand, 'Cream Delight' and 'Tricolor' are forms of the hardier *P. cookianum*, which obligingly seldom exceeds three feet (0.9 m).

Something of the same style is found in two yuccas. First, there is the handsome *Yucca gloriosa* 'Variegata', with creamy yellow-margined leaves. It will achieve some five feet (1.5 m) after a long time but is not a pleasant companion on account of its sharp leaf-points. *Y. filamentosa* 'Golden Sword' is a much more amenable plant with strik-

ing yellow leaf-margins. Its rosettes of leaves do not usually achieve more than about two feet (0.6 m), and the flower stems, hung with scented cream bells, reach twice that.

Before we pass on to lower plants, I must pay tribute to what is probably the most spectacular of all hardy variegated climbers—the large-leafed Ivy, *Hedera colchica* 'Dentata Variegata'. Even those who deplore the use of variegated plants in our gardens must admire this magnificent plant, so redolent of lemons when crushed. It can be grown from cuttings off flowering branches and will then make handsome

Hedera helix 'Goldheart'

bushes up to four feet (1.2 m) or so, but otherwise is a rank grower, shoots achieving six feet (1.8 m) or more in one season being quite common. The cool primrose yellow and grey green of the leaves is only surpassed when a leaf appears (frequently) wholly without green. These leaves I treasure for picking with the lavender blooms of the Algerian Iris (*Iris unguicularis*). Much smaller in leaf is *H. helix* 'Goldheart', a variety of the Common Ivy; it is a bright and rapid climber but is prone to revert to plain green, for its leaves are yellow in the middle, not at the safer perimeter.

Myrtus luma 'Glanleam Gold' is a useful plant for mild localities, beautiful in its cinnamon-coloured peeling bark and also for its yellow-edged leaves. It makes a large shrub or small tree in very favoured localities.

For sun-loving ground cover on poor dry soils, we do not have to look beyond the sages: *Salvia officinalis* 'Icterina' makes a dense high carpet of light green leaves edged with creamy yellow. It is first-rate with lavenders. Another lowly plant with dark green, grassy leaves streaked with yellow is a rush, *Carex morrowii* 'Variegata'. It seldom exceeds ten inches (25 cm) or so and prefers a moist spot.

Periwinkles are a rather mixed bag, as although somewhat woody and with stems hardy through the winter, they are scarcely shrubby. The largest is *Vinca major* 'Variegata'. Though very beautiful through the year, it is a rapacious spreader, making trails several feet long, which root where they touch the ground. It is however a wonderfully bright sight for the darkest corner. Much the same may be said for varieties of *V. minor* in yellow or cream, but these are of a better ground-covering nature when established in almost any soil in shade or sun.

LEAVES FLUSHED YELLOW

Before we move on to cream and white variegated plants, I want to spare a thought for evergreens flushed, not variegated, with yellow. Like yellow variegated plants, they are best in full sun. They are headed by the Sweet Bay, *Laurus nobilis* 'Aurea'. This may be killed to the ground in a severe winter but usually survives to grow up again, if well established. The leaves are bright yellow on the sunny side of the bush, which may achieve twenty feet (6.0 m). There is an even brighter yellow bush of much smaller stature, *Choisya ternata* 'Sundance'—only a few feet high and wide. Where the sun strikes it, it is really brilliant, but green in the shade. The clusters of white flowers, like orange blossom, appear in spring, and the foliage, if bruised, gives off a pleasant aroma. It is a dominant plant wherever it is grown, but the question remains whether we want such a blatant bush of yellow throughout the four seasons. It seems to me that it would be best kept in a container and planted in the border when the days begin to get dark. The useful Privet, *Ligustrum* 'Vicaryi', is a good colour if in full sun and makes a big healthy bush, as also does *Lonicera nitida* 'Baggesen's Gold'. Among climbers, there are two ivies, *Hedera helix* 'Buttercup' and *H. helix* 'Angularis Aurea'. But perhaps the latter should have been included with the yellow variegated plants for its leaves are often only partially yellow. 'Buttercup', on the other hand, is reliably bright yellow whenever the sun strikes it and it can be like a ray of sunshine on a dark winter's day. Both these ivies are strong growers.

There is a whole palette awaiting us among the callunas or heathers. In lime-free soils and full light, a grouping of yellow-leafed kinds such as 'Serlei Aurea' and red ones like 'Robert Chapman' can create a winter brilliance not excelled by any summer schemes. There are many more colourful varieties, and they all need not only leafy soil but also sufficient moisture during the summer. The one thing they cannot stand is being invaded by fallen tree leaves amongst their growths. A good clipping in late spring helps to prevent this by keeping them compact.

WHITE VARIEGATION

On the whole, I find white and cream variegated shrubs easier to place in the garden than the yellow ones. They are certainly easier on the eyes during the growing months and blend, I think, more happily with the floral delights of the year. And they are not dependent upon sunshine to bring forth their tints, being very often most conspicuously marked in shade.

Iris histrioides 'Major', a dwarf bulb whose lavender-blue flowers appear in the New Year

Ligustrum lucidum 'Tricolor' heads the list for size; it may well achieve ten feet (3.0 m) and its leaves are not only creamy-marked but grey as well, and pink-tinted when young. One has to go to the warmer West to see several beauties: *Pittosporum*, for instance—*P. eugenioides* 'Variegatum' is one of the prettiest sights in Cornish gardens when the hydrangeas are blue. There are several varieties or hybrids of *P. tenuifolium*—'Garnettii' and 'Irene Paterson' come to mind, either of which will slowly achieve ten feet (3.0 m) or more, but survive only mild winters up country.

Another tender plant is the beautiful white variegated form of *Azara microphylla* 'Variegata', whose bright spring foliage challenges the delicious vanilla scent of the tiny yellow flowers for pride of place. Also for favoured localities is *Cleyera japonica* 'Tricolor' (formerly *C. fortunei* 'Variegata'), a lowly dense shrub with beautiful variegation and some pink tinting in spring. There is also the rather tender variegated Myrtle, *Myrtus communis* 'Variegata'. The large-leafed hebes offer some tantalising forms: they are only hardy in maritime districts. Among them are *Hebe* × *andersonii*

Pieris japonica 'Flaming Silver'

and *H.* × *franciscana*, both with variegated forms and conspicuously lighted up by the pink or blue flower spikes that are apt to be produced in spells of mild weather.

There is no shortage of good hardy evergreens with white or cream variegation. I wish I could place the variegated Portuguese Laurel, *Prunus lusitanica* 'Variegata', at the head of the list, but its creamy edge to the leaves is rather indistinct. It is a pity because the green type is such a fine thing, especially in its Azores form, *P. lusitanica azorica*. So we come down in scale to Box, Pieris, and Rhamnus. Of these the Box, *Buxus sempervirens* 'Argentea', is a pleasing bush for hedge or general planting, prettily cream-margined, while its sister 'Elegantissima' is a dwarf grower, even more distinctly variegated. There are several good forms of *Pieris*, all for lime-free soils and semi-woodland conditions. Among them are 'Flaming Silver', a sport from *P.* 'Forest Flame' already well known as Lily-of-the-Valley Bush for its early white bellflowers. It also has brilliant red young shoots. 'Flaming Silver' has all these good points plus the variegation. Long before 'Flaming Silver' occurred, we had to be content with *P. japonica* 'Variegata', a dumpy, slow-growing, dense bush of creamy colouring and pinkish young shoots. There is also 'Little Heath' which is even more compact than 'Variegata'. But the *Rhamnus* is the most markedly variegated of all these, *R. alaternus* 'Argenteovariegata' being a really outstanding shrub with elegantly white-touched leaves. Ascending to some eight feet (2.4 m), it has two disadvantages: it is sometimes spoiled by cold weather, and it needs a stake because its roots are inclined to be infirm. It is not particular about soil and will thrive in sun or shade.

Among ground covers, we cannot pass by *Pachysandra terminalis* 'Variegata', which is a fairly compact plant and by no means as vigorous in spreading its roots as the normal green kind, which is a ground cover for large spaces. Both prefer the shade and grow to about nine inches (22 cm), the variety being prettily outlined in cream.

I think one of the most valuable of cream-striped plants is the form of *Iris foetidissima*, the Gladwin Iris or Gladdon, known as 'Variegata'. Just very occasionally it may flower (but the flowers are dingy and likely to be overlooked), with the result that seed pods are formed, revealing at year's end their orange red seeds. But they are not as free or conspicuous as those of *I. foetidissima* 'Citrina'. The Latin name refers to the smell, scarcely offensive, of its leaves when crushed.

We are left with the ivies, and a redoubtable lot they are, too. Contrary to my usual procedure, we will take one of the smallest first. It is *Hedera helix* 'Little Diamond', a non-climbing, dwarf, spreading bush, flat-growing and distinctly and heavily marked with white. It looks particularly well next to some of the bergenias whose winter colouring verges on beetroot, such as *Bergenia ligulata*. Among climbing variants there are many. Although it is not so heavily marked with cream or white as some, I give high marks to *H. helix* 'Marginata Major'. It is vigorous, mixed grey with the cream and very seldom reverts to green. Other more distinctly marked are the silvery 'Glacier' and creamy 'Adam'. One would go far on a winter's day to find anything exceeding their beauty. With very large leaves (a little tender) is *H. canariensis* 'Gloire de Marengo'. Occasionally whole leaves are white, but normally they are

Hedera helix 'Little Diamond'

particoloured with grey and green. It is frequently grown in our rooms, but I have not known it to suffer in Surrey gardens. 'Danny' is another good ground-covering variant of compact, almost bushy growth a few inches high.

ENVOI

Christmas is gone, the New Year is upon us, and we speculate on what the winter weather will bring. Except in periods when the land is locked in frost, we may expect flowers to be with us.

> They will come again, the leaf and the flower . . . ,
>
> . . .
>
> And wandering scents to the memory bring.

So wrote Lawrence Binyon in the last century, in his "The Burning of the Leaves," adding:

> Nothing is certain, only the certain spring.

Edmund Spenser wrote similarly, some four hundred years earlier, in "The Garden of Adonis":

> Daily they grow, and daily forth are sent
> Into the world, it to replenish more;
> Yet is the stock not lessened, nor spent,
> But still remains in everlasting store.

OPPOSITE: *Chamaecyparis lawsoniana* 'Winston Churchill' with *Cornus alba* 'Sibirica' in the Cambridge University Botanic Garden. The conifer is a favorite of the author's, and the Cambridge Botanic Garden is where he began his long career in gardening.

In Spenser's Britain, flowers appeared almost entirely in spring and summer; in autumn and winter, they were nearly absent. Thanks to dauntless travellers and collectors, this has been much altered, and we now have flowers throughout the year. Are we gardeners not blessed beyond compare? And every year sees new selections of plants coming our way. In this book, the array of plants I have conjured up is from happy memories over seven decades and yet is but a choice of garden joys that happen to have delighted me in one way or another.

I do not expect that the plants of my choosing will appeal unreservedly to all gardeners. Fortunately there are enough plants in cultivation for us all to make our individual and separate collections, and at times the almost unfathomable array may bewilder us if we look through the current volume of the Royal Horticultural Society's *The Plant Finder*. The Society has been doing its best to help gardeners by recommending plants for its Award of Garden Merit. I was on the A.G.M. Committee in its early days, and this book has been written with its work in mind.

INDEX

*The hardiness zones given in square brackets indicate the coldest climate zones
in which the plant is known to thrive. Page references in italics indicate illustrations.*

PHOTO CREDITS

My thanks to the photographers for their help in illustrating this book. The drawings and watercolors are all my own.

PLANT HARDINESS ZONES IN THE UNITED STATES

This hardiness map was developed by the Agricultural Research Service of the U.S. Department of Agriculture. The hardiness zones are based on the average annual minimum temperature for each zone. All plants are designated with a number spread, the lower number indicating the most northerly area where they will reliably survive the winter, and the higher number the most southerly area where they will perform consistently. Many factors, such as altitude, degree of exposure to wind, proximity to bodies of water, snow cover, soil types and the like, can create variations of as much as two zones in winter hardiness, while cool nights, shade and amount of water received can extend the southern limits.

See Index for zone listings.

HARDINESS ZONE
TEMPERATURE RANGES

°F	ZONE	°C
below −50	1	below −45
−50 to −40	2	−45 to −40
−40 to −30	3	−40 to −34
−30 to −20	4	−34 to −29
−20 to −10	5	−29 to −23
−10 to 0	6	−23 to −17
0 to 10	7	−17 to −12
10 to 20	8	−12 to −7
20 to 30	9	−7 to −1
30 to 40	10	−1 to 5

The roman text typeface for *The Garden through the Year* is Centaur, designed by Bruce Rogers

in 1914 for the Metropolitan Museum of New York; he used it in the celebrated

1929 *Oxford Lectern Bible*. Arrighi, the italic text type, was designed by Frederic Warde

in 1925 to accompany the Monotype Corporation's cut of Centaur.

The display type is Titling Forum, designed by F. W. Goudy around 1912.